Albert S. Bolles

The Financial History of the United States

from 1774 to 1789 - embracing the period of the American Revolution

Albert S. Bolles

The Financial History of the United States
from 1774 to 1789 - embracing the period of the American Revolution

ISBN/EAN: 9783337234737

Printed in Europe, USA, Canada, Australia, Japan

Cover: Foto ©Suzi / pixelio.de

More available books at **www.hansebooks.com**

THE

FINANCIAL HISTORY

OF THE

UNITED STATES,

FROM 1774 TO 1789:

Embracing the Period of the American Revolution.

BY

ALBERT S. BOLLES,

LECTURER IN POLITICAL ECONOMY IN THE BOSTON
UNIVERSITY.

NEW YORK:

D. APPLETON AND COMPANY,

549 AND 551 BROADWAY.

1879.

Electrotyped and Printed by Rand, Avery, & Co., Boston.

TO THE

Hon. GALUSHA A. GROW,

WHOSE HIGH POLITICAL IDEALS, AND RARE SUCCESS

AS A LEGISLATOR, ARE WIDELY AND

DESERVEDLY KNOWN,

This Volume is Dedicated

AS A MARK OF THE AUTHOR'S FRIENDSHIP

AND ADMIRATION.

PREFACE.

THE present work has been written with the belief that it would serve a useful purpose. The early period of the financial history of the United States is treated only in the slightest manner by Dr. Von Hock in his "Die Finanzen und die Finanzgeschichte der Vereinigten Staaten von Amerika;" while the brief efforts of Breck, Schuckers, Bronson, and occasionally a magazine-writer, are but little more than passing glimpses of a great theme. Even Phillips, in his work upon Continental Paper Money, which is valuable in many respects, looks at the subject from an antiquarian point of view, rather than as a student of finance.

It is the intention of the author to trace the narrative, in another volume, from 1789, when the Federal Constitution was adopted, to the outbreak of the Civil War in 1860, and, in a final one, from the latter period to the resumption of specie payments. Each volume, therefore, will cover a clearly-defined historical period, though, of course, every period of history is necessarily linked to what has gone before as well as to the time succeeding.

To have written merely an abstract of the financial legislation passed during the period included within this volume, interspersed with comments, would have been an easy but not a satisfactory task. To possesss any interest or value, a financial history must trace the causes and consequences of the legislation described. To do this, however, was difficult, as the materials too frequently were very scanty and of poor quality. The author has sought to obtain information from every source relating to the subject within his knowledge; and if, in some cases, the reader shall find the causes and consequences of financial experiments not as fully set forth as he desires, let him first consider whether any thing more could be found relating to them, before finding fault with the author.

The idea of unity of proportion has been kept in mind in the preparation of the work, which will explain why a few chapters, especially the one upon the Legal Tender Laws of the Revolution, were not extended beyond their present limits.

To Mr. C. A. Cutter, Librarian of the Boston Athenæum, the author feels deeply grateful for the exceedingly liberal use of books belonging to that association. This, he realizes, is a feeble acknowledgment to make for such valuable assistance: doubtless a far greater satisfaction may be derived from knowing, that, if the work possesses any value, its readers are indebted to him for putting the author within convenient reach of much of the material found within these pages. To Mr. Robbins Little, Superintendent of the Astor Library, and to Mr. Frederick Saunders, Librarian of the same, the author would also express his heartiest thanks for the generous use of the books of that noble institution. Nor would he forget to acknowledge favors of a similar character on the part of the officers of the New-York Historical Library.

CONTENTS.

BOOK FIRST.

*FROM SEPTEMBER, 1774, TO THE FINANCIAL ADMINISTRA-
TION OF ROBERT MORRIS.*

BOOK SECOND.

*FROM MORRIS'S FINANCIAL ADMINISTRATION TO THE CLOSE
OF THE CONFEDERATION.*

BOOK I.

FROM SEPTEMBER, 1774, TO THE FINANCIAL ADMINISTRATION
OF ROBERT MORRIS.

FINANCIAL HISTORY

OF

THE UNITED STATES.

CHAPTER I.

CONGRESS AND THE COLONIES.

THOUGH but little more than a century has passed since the first Continental Congress met, in September, 1774, the financial history of the United States during the subsequent period is thickly strewn with financial experiments amply rewarding investigation. In surveying the field, many transactions evincing sound wisdom and rare integrity will appear interwoven with other deeds, variously colored by accident, dishonesty, or ignorance. If no other country can boast of making such progress during the first century of its existence as the United States, no other has committed so many and such serious mistakes. In the history of American finance, men have appeared on nearly every occasion comprehending the exigency, and whose advice, if followed, would have averted many a disaster. But measures springing from incapacity or dishonesty often teach lessons not less impressive than measures displaying the highest wisdom. It will not prove a profitless task, therefore, to garner some of the fruits lying within the field of inquiry, whether they were ripened under the watchful eye of Morris, Hamilton, or Gallatin, or whether they were the product of less skilful and less honest husbandmen.

The object of the first Continental Congress was to obtain a redress of grievances, not separation from Great Britain. The first important enactment regulated the manner of voting, and provided that each Colony should have a single vote in Congress.[1] The larger Colonies contended for the exercise of more power, and yielded solely because the occasion required immediate unanimity on the part of Congress. This rule, thus early established, continued until the adoption of the Federal Constitution, in 1789, although every Colony was represented in Congress by two or more delegates, as the body rarely numbered less than fifty members during all the more important sessions.

The only act beside this, requiring mention, prohibited the importation of goods from Great Britain and Ireland after the first of September, 1774, which provided further, that, after the month of September the year following, the exportation of all merchandise, &c., to Great Britain, Ireland, and the West Indies, ought to cease, unless the grievances of America were redressed before that time.[2] The graver consequences of this act were not foreseen; but they appeared early, giving rise to warm debate, and personal and sectional bitterness.

The next May, delegates assembled from all the Colonies except Georgia, whose representatives appeared before the close of the year.[3] They were chosen, in most

[1] Sept. 6.   [2] Oct. 20.   [3] Sept. 13.

cases, by conventions of the people; in a few, by the popular branch of the Colonial Assembly. In still fewer instances the choice of the Assembly was ratified by a convention; in some, the process was reversed. The authority confided to these delegates usually was very limited; and as Congress was endowed with no power beside that conferred upon members, until the Articles of Confederation were ratified in 1781,[1] many an error sprang from this cause. More than one delegate did not legislate as wisely as he knew, because of the limitations set around him by the Colony he represented. In order to get a clear idea of the power of Congress, let us ascertain what authority was confided by the several Colonies to their representatives composing this body.

The Assembly of Rhode Island believed that satisfactory terms could be made with Great Britain; consequently, the instructions to her delegates were framed with this end in view. They were authorized to join with the commissioners, or delegates from the other Colonies, in consulting upon proper measures to obtain a repeal of the several acts of the British Parliament for levying taxes upon his Majesty's subjects in America, without their consent, and to establish the rights and liberties of the Colonies upon a just and solid foundation, agreeable to the instructions given them by the General Assembly. Connecticut endowed her delegates with more general authority. They were to join, consult, and advise with the delegates of the other Colonies in proper measures for advancing the best good of all. The New-Hampshire delegates were clothed with authority to

---

[1] March 1.

consult and agree to all measures which Congress should deem necessary to obtain a redress of American grievances. The delegates from Massachusetts were empowered to act in union with the delegates of other Colonies in ordering such measures as should appear to them the best calculated for the recovery and establishment of American rights and liberties, and for restoring harmony between Great Britain and the Colonies. New Jersey, Pennsylvania, and Virginia appointed delegates without saying a word concerning their authority. New Jersey and Delaware required their delegates to report the proceedings of Congress to their respective Assemblies. Maryland and North Carolina went further; the former Colony giving her delegates authority to consent and agree to all measures which Congress should deem necessary and effectual to obtain a redress of American grievances. She, moreover, bound herself to execute all resolutions adopted by Congress. The delegates from North Carolina were invested with the authority necessary to make their acts done in behalf of that Province obligatory upon any inhabitant thereof. The instructions given to the South-Carolina delegates related only to a redress of grievances; while the representatives from Georgia were empowered to join with the several delegates from the other Colonies in all matters which should appear fit for the preservation and defence of their rights and liberties, and for the restoration of harmony, upon constitutional principles, between Great Britain and America.

Such was the constitution of this unique body, whose nearest resemblance was the confederacy of the Netherlands during the latter part of the sixteenth century,

when waging her ever-memorable war with Spain. It
will be seen that Congress had no clearly-defined powers;
the members, with only two or three exceptions, were
confined to a narrow sphere of legislation; and until the
adoption of the Confederation, in March, 1781, the States
regarded themselves as masters of the situation, and never
hesitated to instruct their delegates whenever the occasion seemed to require a fresh exercise of state tutelage
or discipline. With the unfolding of unexpected events,
Congress did indeed exercise a larger measure of power
than had been granted to any of the members; yet they
always moved with great circumspection, clearly knowing
that their continuance as a body depended wholly upon
the will of the people. Thus the power of Congress was
not inherent, but directly conferred, and could be easily
abridged or withdrawn. Prior to the execution of the
Articles of Confederation, says Madison,[1] " The power of
Congress was measured by the exigencies of the war,
and derived its sanction from the acquiescence of the
States." When independence was declared, the States
enlarged somewhat the power of their delegates; yet at
all times they were unable to exercise a commanding
authority, such as the occasion imperatively demanded
for fighting successfully the battle of independence, and
for stimulating the development and growth of an infant
nation.[2]

Financially the Colonies were badly off; for they had
just liquidated the debts contracted in the French war,

----

[1] Writings, vol. iv. p. 126.

[2] See Hamilton's Letter to Duane, Sept. 3, 1780, Hist. of Repub.,
vol. ii. p. 86.

and in their treasury were only a few thousand pounds.[1] Before them was the prospect of stagnation or interruption of trade, and possibly warfare with Great Britain. Neither Congress nor the Colonial Governments possessed credit. Without alliance with other nations, with less than twelve million dollars[2] in specie in all the Colonies, and perhaps not half that sum, — such was the financial condition of the country at the opening of the second Continental Congress.

[1] J. Adams's Works, vol. vii. p. 296.

[2] Pelatiah Webster, Political Essays, p. 6, note c. Hamilton estimated the "current cash in this country" previous to the war, specie and paper, at thirty million dollars, of which sum eight millions were specie (Works, vol. i. p. 228). Noah Webster affirmed that "ten millions of dollars in specie were supposed to be the medium in America before the war" (Coll. of Essays, p. 133).

CHAPTER II.

ORGANIZATION OF THE TREASURY DEPARTMENT.

If the organization of a department of government be always a difficult task, especially true was this of the various departments of the American Confederation, whose beginning was enveloped in war with a powerful foe possessing a well-disciplined army and a never-failing exchequer. America was poor: the specie coming thither quickly found its way to Great Britain by the operation of a policy long pursued and deemed wise by the mother-country. The members of Congress were ignorant of legislative proceedings, save in the small and partially-stifled Provincial Assemblies. The colonists had never administered the affairs of state. How unreasonable, therefore, to suppose them capable of organizing a treasury, war, navy, and other departments, immediately, and of putting all the affairs of government in smooth running order! The several departments of the British Government were not the thought of the day: they were the growth of centuries. The departments of the Government of the United States were created more rapidly, though not without trial and heavy cost, before reaching their greatest efficiency.

The treasury department was organized earlier than any other department of the government. By the genius of Hamilton, during the first administration of Washington its province was pretty clearly defined, and its mode of conducting business practically established; yet no one can understand how it came to be thus organized, until he has learned how the finances were administered during the Revolution.

As independence was not at first debated in Congress, and every one was seeking to find a peaceful solution of the difficulties with Great Britain, the early financial measures of that body were of a temporary character. Committees were appointed to do specific things, to raise money, to pay accounts, and the like, but not to do any thing requiring much investigation, or outlay of money. The method of devising measures through committees, thus early adopted, has been continued to this day.

The first financial committee were appointed on the 3d of June, 1775, to prepare an estimate of the money required to pay the expenses of Congress. This committee reported, four days afterward, in favor of issuing bills of credit; and their report was subsequently adopted. On the 19th of July another committee were appointed, to prepare an estimate of the expenses incurred by the resolutions of Congress. Having failed to report as soon as Congress desired, on the 6th of November a third committee were chosen for the purpose, who, in addition, were required to ascertain what money remained in the treasury unapplied, and to form an estimate of the public debts already incurred, and which were likely to become due by the 1st of June the following year. This committee lived until the 17th of February, 1776, when a standing committee of five for superintending the treasury were appointed. The powers granted to them were more specific and extensive than the powers delegated to either of the previous committees: they were required to examine the accounts of the treasurers who had been appointed to receive funds from the Colonies, and occasionally to report to Congress the condition of the treasury; to consider the ways and means for supplying the army in Canada with gold and silver; to employ and instruct proper persons for liquidating the public accounts, including those of the paymasters and commissaries in the Continental service, committees of safety, and all others who had been or should be intrusted with the public money, and to report the condition of such accounts to Congress; to superintend the emission of bills of credit; and, lastly, to obtain from the different assemblies and conventions of the United Colonies the number of inhabitants in each Colony.

From time to time the powers of the committee were enlarged, and the work of administering the finances was systematized. They were authorized to employ clerks for keeping and liquidating the public accounts, and to provide books and a suitable office for their business. Power was also given them to call upon the various committees of Congress, assemblies, conventions, councils or committees of safety, Continental officers, and private persons who had been or should be intrusted with public money, for their accounts and vouchers, and for such other materials and information as the committee deemed needful " in stating, checking, and auditing the public accounts." [1]

[1] Feb. 23.

As the resolution conferring this power was deemed too indefinite, more explicit resolutions were soon after adopted.[1] A treasury office of accounts was instituted, to be kept wherever the sessions of Congress should be held, which was put under the direction and superintendence of the standing Committee of the Treasury. An auditor-general, also, together with a proper force of assistants, was authorized for keeping the public accounts. In respect to the presentation of accounts at this time, a portion of them went to the Committee on Claims; but all accounts and claims of articles the price of which had been previously fixed by contract, or otherwise ascertained by Congress, were liquidated and settled at the treasury office, and reported to Congress for allowance, and then passed, and entered at the place of liquidation. All contracts, securities, and obligations belonging to the United Colonies were lodged and kept in the treasury office of accounts; and any one receiving public money was charged with the same in the books of the treasury office: and every warrant drawn therefor, previous to its payment, was entered there, while entry was also made upon the warrant itself by one of the committee of the treasury, the auditor-general, or one of his assistants or clerks. An exception, however, was made in those cases where orders or warrants were issued by committees appointed by Congress to draw on the treasurers for particular purposes. These orders were paid directly, and then charged to the committee who drew them, and afterwards settled by Congress. Other resolves were also passed at this time; yet, as they were but little more

<hr>

[1] April 1.

than an affirmation of previous instructions already described, they need not be repeated.

This committee were known by several names, though the most common were the Board of Treasury and the Treasury Office of Accounts. During the year 1776 five more members were added, making ten in all.[1]

In respect to auditing and paying accounts, perfection in these matters could not be expected in the beginning. The first auditing board was composed of the delegates from Pennsylvania, concerning whom it was resolved to place ten thousand dollars in their hands for the purpose of paying the expenses incurred in raising and arming rifle companies, expresses, and other small charges of which Congress had not been able to procure exact accounts.[2]

As soon as Congress re-assembled in 1775,[3] the Pennsylvania delegates reported, that, on account of various difficulties, they had not executed the duties assigned to them, and desired that some members from other Colonies where debts had been contracted might be added; whereupon five other persons were chosen.

Shortly afterward the committee made a report.[4] They had drawn on the treasury for nearly twelve thousand dollars to settle the accounts mentioned; and, as only ten thousand dollars had been previously placed at their command, Congress voted an appropriation sufficient to pay the balance. The committee having discovered other outstanding accounts which they were not authorized to

---

[1] Five persons were at first chosen; June 18 two more were added; Sept. 23, two additional members were chosen, and a week later Hopkinson was added.

[2] Aug. 1, 1775. [3] Sept. 14. [4] Sept. 25.

liquidate, but which it was the duty of Congress to settle, the discovery led to the appointment of a committee of accounts or claims, consisting of one member from each Colony, to whom all accounts "against the Continent" were to be referred, and who were to examine and report upon the same "in order for payment." The appointment of this committee gave rise to a lively discussion, which John Adams has reported in his diary. When Sherman of Connecticut made a motion for the appointment of such a committee, Harrison of Virginia supposed it was a reflection upon the one which had just reported concerning the public accounts, and he exclaimed, "Is this the way of giving thanks?" Samuel Adams, who seconded Sherman's motion, replied that he meant no reflection upon the committee, and "was sorry that the worthy gentleman from Virginia conceived that any was intended; he was sure there was no foundation for it."   Another member, Paine, thought that justice and honor required a careful examination of all accounts, and how the public moneys were expended, "that the minister would find out our weakness, and would foment divisions among our people; he was sorry that gentlemen could not hear methods proposed to settle and pay accounts, in a manner that would give satisfaction to the people, without seeming to resent them."   As this explanation satisfied Harrison, he rapidly cooled, the motion for the appointment of the committee prevailed, and, the members having been chosen, the former committee were directed to deliver to the new one all the books, accounts, and papers in their possession.[1]

---

[1] J. Adams's Works, vol. ii. p. 450.

Their mode of adjusting accounts was to examine them, and determine what was due, and report thereon to Congress without recommendation; whereupon that body would order payment. The committee then drew orders, in conformity with the direction of Congress, upon the Continental treasurers who had been appointed a few months previously; these were signed by the president of Congress, after which they were ready for presentation to the treasurers, who paid them without further delay.

When the powers of the Board of Treasury were more minutely defined in April, the following year,[1] it was provided that all accounts and claims against the United Colonies for services or supplies, the prices of which had not been ascertained by Congress, should be presented to the Committee of Claims, liquidated by them, and reported to Congress, and, having been allowed by that body, should be "passed at the treasury office." Thus the duty of examining the accounts of Congress was divided between the Committee of Claims and the Board of Treasury, and so continued for about four months, when all unsettled claims and accounts were referred to the Board of Treasury, and the Claims Committee were discharged.[2] From this time forth, the Board of Treasury were required to provide funds for sustaining the government, and to examine and liquidate all public accounts.

From time to time, commissioners were appointed to settle particular accounts, like those growing out of the Canadian expedition, or the claims between the Confederation and New York and Virginia, the accounts of the Northern department, army accounts, and others which had grown large, and could not be easily ascertained.

<hr>

[1] April 1, 1776.   [2] July 30.

As thus organized, the Board of Treasury continued nearly two years, though the system was very cumbrous and inefficient. It was impossible for the delegates of Congress to transact the business of the treasury department properly, and also to perform their duties in the sphere of legislation. Morris clearly saw the inefficiency of the system. Writing to the Committee of Secret Correspondence, near the close of 1776, he very plainly says, "If the Congress mean to succeed in this contest, they must pay good executive men to do their business as it ought to be, and not lavish millions away by their own mismanagement. I say mismanagement, because no man living can attend the daily deliberations of Congress, and do executive parts of business at the same time. I do aver there will be more money lost, totally lost, in horses, wagons, cattle, &c., for want of sufficient number of proper persons to look after them, than would have paid all the salaries Payne [a delegate who has usually found an antitype in every assembly of similar character since] ever did or ever will grumble at."[1] Yet nothing more was done for nearly two years, at the end of which time the board reported several important changes in the mode of administering the finances.

The report was debated several weeks, when it was resolved[2] to provide a house at Philadelphia for the several offices of the treasury, which were to be the following: a comptroller, annually appointed by Congress, who was authorized to employ two clerks; an auditor and two clerks, the three to be chosen in like manner; a treasurer and one clerk, similarly chosen; and two chambers

---

[1] Am. Archives, fifth series, vol. iii. p. 1241.   [2] Sept. 26.

of accounts,[1] each chamber consisting of three commissioners and two clerks, who were to be appointed by Congress. The auditor, treasurer, and comptroller were not to be appointed by the votes of less than nine States, and they were to be responsible for the conduct of their clerks, — a provision worthy of the serious consideration of legislators in these days, when so much incapacity, and too often dishonesty, abound in almost every department of the public service.

The duties of each officer are next stated. The auditor was to receive all accounts against the " United States " for money lent, expended, or advanced, goods sold or purchased, services performed, or work done, with the vouchers; and he was to refer them to one of the chambers of accounts after indorsing them in a specified manner; then the commissioners were to deliver them to their clerks to be stated, and to number and arrange the vouchers, examine the castings, and make copies; and, after completing their work, they were to make a proper indorsement thereon; after which process it was the duty of the commissioners to examine the authenticity of the vouchers, reject all which did not appear to be genuine, compare them with the articles to which they related, and determine whether they supported the charges. They were to reduce such articles as were overcharged, reject improper charges, and then indorse the accounts in the manner prescribed by the resolution, and transmit them, with the vouchers, to the auditor, " and cause an entry to be made of the balances passed." Having received the vouchers and accounts from the commissioners, the

---

[1] This idea was probably copied from the old French system of finance.

auditor, or rather his clerk, was to examine them. The articles were to be compared with the vouchers; and, if a person appealed from the judgment of the commissioners, he, as well as they, was to be called before the auditor to be heard, from whose decision no appeal lay, except to Congress. Having examined the accounts in this manner, they were to be indorsed, and a duplicate of the indorsement was to be filed in the chamber of accounts, while the accounts, with their vouchers, were to be sent to the comptroller.

The duties of the comptroller are next described, which were numerous and important. He was to keep the treasury books, and seal and file all accounts and vouchers, and direct the manner of stating and keeping them. He was to draw bills, under seal, upon the treasurer, for sums due by the United States on accounts that had been audited, which, however, were to be countersigned by the auditor previous to payment. He was also to draw bills, in a similar way, for such sums as Congress from time to time should order. When moneys were due the United States on accounts which had been properly audited, he was to notify the debtor, and, after hearing him (if he desired to be heard), fix a day for payment as the circumstances of the case might require, not exceeding ninety days, of which time he was to give notice in writing to the auditor.

The treasurer was to receive and keep the moneys of the United States, and to issue them on bills drawn by the comptroller, as previously described, and file duplicates thereof with the auditor day by day as he should make payment. On the receipt of moneys, he was required to give a receipt therefor, and transmit the same to the comptroller. He was also required to "draw out" and settle his accounts quarterly, "giving the same in to the auditor for examination by one of the chambers of accounts, to be from thence transmitted, through the auditor, to the comptroller," who was required to compare them with the treasury books, ascertain the balance, and return a copy thereof to Congress.

The resolution further provided that the comptroller should receive from the treasurer all receipts signed by himself, and, after entering them, charge the treasurer, and credit the proper accounts; this done, the comptroller was to indorse them, and deliver them to the party who made payment; and every quarter of the year he was to cause a list of the balances on the treasury-books to be made out by his clerks, and lay the same before Congress. To this provision another was added relating to the collection of money due to the United States, which clearly displayed the weakness of the government. In all cases of delinquency the comptroller was to give the debtor a reasonable time to appear; and, in case he did not, the auditor, on proof that proper notice had been sent, made out a requisition, the form of which was prescribed in the act, which was sent by the comptroller to whom? To the debtor? No, but to the executive authority of the State wherein the debtor resided. Congress dared go no further than to recommend the States to enact laws for the seizure of property and persons of debtors to the United States neglecting to discharge their public obligations.

This act indicates great progress in the mode of collecting and disbursing the public revenues. Several of its more important features are still preserved, and it would be quite difficult to improve them. If to any one, either at that time or afterward, Congress seemed slow in organizing the treasury department, the vastness as well as the suddenness of the Revolution, — for, after all, the event was unexpected, notwithstanding the long, unconscious course of preparation, — and the feebleness of the country's resources, must be remembered as among the chief causes of dilatory action by that memorable body.

More than a month elapsed before filling the several offices of the treasury.[1] Jonathan Trumbull, jun., was elected comptroller; John Gibson, auditor; and Michael Hillegas, who had held the office of treasurer from the beginning, was continued in the same position. Since the resignation of Mr. Clymer, Hillegas had acted as sole treasurer, and, from his continuance in that office, had probably administered it in a successful manner. Commissioners of the chambers of accounts were also chosen. To the comptroller and treasurer was given a salary of four thousand dollars; the auditor received thirty-five hundred dollars; and the commissioners, each three thousand dollars.[2] Subsequently a secretary to the Board of Treasury was appointed, with a salary of two thousand dollars per annum.[3]

Marked as were the improvements in the treasury de-

---

[1] Nov. 3.   [2] Oct. 29.

[3] Feb. 11, 1779. But a secretary was not appointed until May 29 of that year, when Robert Troup was chosen.

partment, within twelve months another re-organization occurred.[1] A very considerable portion of the former organization was retained. The principal new feature was the abolition of the comptroller's office, and the addition of a board consisting of three commissioners who were not members of Congress, besides two other persons belonging to that body. These five members were elected by Congress, the former three annually, and the latter two for the term of six months; nor could a State be represented at any time by more than one member in the board. The other officers of the treasury were retained, with the addition of six auditors for settling the accounts of the army.

"The Commissioners, or Board of Treasury," as the new body is called in the ordinance, were to have the general superintendence of the finances of the United States, and of the officers intrusted with the receipt and expenditure or application of the public money; to inspect the treasury; to lay before Congress estimates of the public expenses and necessary supplies; to execute the will of Congress respecting the emission of bills of credit and of exchange, loan-office certificates or other securities, and establishing lotteries; deposit the public funds in proper places; look after the keeping of accounts and the punishment of public debtors; instruct all officers in any way connected with the finances needing instruction, and to suspend any of them for negligence or misdemeanor until the pleasure of Congress was known; register and preserve all contracts and securities; grant, under the seal of office,

[1] July 30.

"a quietus" to accountants on final settlement; and various other duties which do not need specifying. The duties of the auditor-general, treasurer, and the chambers of accounts, were more minutely defined. The auditors of the army were sorely needed to adjust the numerous accounts growing out of the neglect, or rather impossibility, of the Board of Treasury to settle them. These auditors were to report to the auditor-general, and were directed to adjust all other accounts, besides those specifically mentioned, ordered by the Treasury Board. The officers under the old system, except those belonging to the comptroller's office, were continued until the 9th of November, when a new election was made, though many of the former officers were elected to various positions in the new organization.

As thus organized, the Board of Treasury continued in power until the appointment of Robert Morris as superintendent of finance, in February,[1] 1781, and, indeed, for several months thereafter, when the organization was finally abolished.[2] As the appointment of

---

[1] Feb. 20.

[2] Hamilton, writing in September, 1780, about the imperfection of the present system, says, "A single man, in each department of the administration, would be greatly preferable. It would give us a chance of more knowledge, more activity, more responsibility, and, of course, more zeal and attention. Boards partake of a part of the inconveniences of larger assemblies; — their decisions are slower, their energy less, their responsibility more diffused. They will not have the same abilities and knowledge as an administration by single men. Men of the first pretensions will not so readily engage in them, because they will be less conspicuous, of less importance, have less opportunity of distinguishing themselves. The members of boards will take less

Morris marks a new era in the finances of the Revolution, we shall wait until reaching his administration before describing the machinery employed to administer the finances during that period. We have traced the history of organizing the treasury department through the embryonic, or rather chaotic, period of the government; we have seen order gradually arise out of confusion, which was the more remarkable because Congress, in the earlier days, was expecting to make peace with Great Britain. When this delusion faded away, and Congress undertook seriously the work of organizing permanently the several departments of government, ought not the members to be praised rather than blamed, considering the grave difficulties besetting their path, for creating a practical financial system as rapidly as they did?

pains to inform themselves, and arrive at eminence, because they have fewer motives to do it. All these reasons conspire to give a preference to the plan of vesting the great executive departments of the State in the hands of individuals. As these men will be, of course, at all times under the direction of Congress, we shall blend the advantages of a monarchy and republic in one constitution. A question has been made, whether single men could be found to undertake these offices. I think they could; because there would be then every thing to excite the ambition of candidates. But in order to this, Congress, by their manner of appointing them, and the line of duty marked out, must show that they are in earnest in making these offices, offices of little trust and importance. I fear a little vanity has stood in the way of these arrangements, as though they would lessen the importance of Congress, and leave them nothing to do" — *Hist. of Repub.*, vol. ii. pp. 92, 93.

CHAPTER III.

THE FIRST ISSUE OF CONTINENTAL MONEY.

AT the opening of the second session, Congress began to wrestle with the grave question of finance. An issue of paper money or bills of credit — a practice in which all the Colonies had indulged — was regarded as the best expedient; yet several weeks elapsed before taking final action thereon. In the mean time, the matter was referred to the several Colonial Assemblies for their opinion.[1] Previous to this reference, the Provincial Assembly of New York had appointed a committee to consider the propriety of emitting a Continental paper currency; and on the 26th of May, 1775, the Assembly addressed a letter to the Congressional delegates representing that Colony, on the subject. To the scheme of issuing a universal paper currency, says the address, "it may naturally be objected, that it will be imprudent in one Colony to interpose its credit for the others. On the other hand, it is clearly impossible to raise any sum adequate to the service, by tax; and the necessary intercourse of expenditures throughout the Colonies will be obstructed by separate emissions on the respective credits of the several Colonies, which cannot, in their nature, gain uni-

---

[1] See Letter of Lieut.-Gov. Colden to the Earl of Dartmouth, Documents relating to Col. Hist. of New York, vol. viii. p. 579.

versal circulation. We have this important subject under serious deliberation, and are still at a loss for the best expedient most effectually to answer the purpose. We have therefore appointed a committee of our body to give it their closest attention," whose report was to be communicated to the delegates without delay. If Congress is considering the subject, concludes the letter, "we earnestly request that its determination may be so postponed as to furnish an opportunity of acquainting you with our more mature sentiments on this most important point."[1]

The delegates from New York were not blind to the importance of the question and to the need of a better knowledge concerning it. This is shown by their reply to the letter of the Assembly, in which they express the wish of a speedy determination, "as it may throw some light upon the subject we may otherwise want." Dark, indeed, was the subject in the beginning; yet it grew darker as the days and years went by.

Not long afterward, the report of the committee, prepared by Gouverneur Morris, was sent to Philadelphia, where Congress was in session. It displays a pretty thorough comprehension of the situation, and evinces a high order of financial ability, which the author on more than one occasion subsequently exhibited. Concluding an issue of paper money by Congress to be necessary, the report discusses the several modes of issuing it, which were the following: first, "that every Colony should strike for itself the sum apportioned by the Continental Congress; secondly, that the Continental Congress should strike the

---

[1] Am. Archives, fourth series, vol. ii. p. 845.

whole sum necessary, and each Colony become bound to sink its proportionable part; or, thirdly, that the Continental Congress should strike the whole sum, and apportionate the several shares to the different Colonies," every Colony becoming bound to discharge its own particular part, and all the Colonies to discharge the portion which any particular Colony should be unable to pay. The committee recommended the adoption of the latter plan, sagely remarking that there were only two obstacles in the way of emitting paper money: the first was, "to give it an immediate and ready currency;" and the second, "to provide ways and means for sinking it." They had no doubt about its ready reception throughout the Continent; and, on the second point, the committee observed, that "whenever a paper currency has been emitted, and obtained a general credit, it will be a new bond of union to the associated Colonies, and every inhabitant thereof will be bound in interest to endeavor that ways and means be fallen upon for sinking of it."[1]

Before any plan had been perfected, the need of money to purchase powder for the Continental army, which was already organized, had become so great, that Congress resolved to borrow six thousand pounds for the defence of America, pledging the faith of the Colonies for repayment.[2] The Pennsylvania delegation were appointed a committee to execute the resolution. Phillips says,[3] "The desire of borrowing so small a sum, which even if obtained would have been of very slight assistance, shows

[1] Am. Archives, fourth series, vol. ii. p. 1202.

[2] June 3, Secret Jour. of Cong.   [3] Cont. Paper Money, p. 23.

conclusively the reluctance of Congress to use its paper credit." May not the reason have been, that Congress needed only a small sum as a temporary expedient while perfecting a plan for the issue of paper money? As only six thousand pounds were borrowed, is not the inference very strong that Congress expected to issue paper money at an early day, otherwise a much larger sum would have been absolutely necessary? Congress afterward ordered sixteen thousand dollars in Continental bills to be paid for the specie thus obtained.[1]

What opposition was made to issuing paper money we have only scanty information. The records of Congress are silent concerning the discussion of all questions; and we can glean but little from the votes of Congress and the hints of members. Had not secrecy upon their proceedings been enjoined, which was most faithfully kept, doubtless the letters and diaries of some of the members would have thrown much light upon the deliberations of that body: in consequence of this injunction, however, not much knowledge can be gleaned, even from these sources.

Two kinds of paper money had been tried in the Colonies, with a marked difference in their operation. The improved method had been practised most successfully in Pennsylvania, and consisted in emitting a certain amount of paper for a given time, say ten years, at the expiration of which period it was all redeemed. The paper was put into circulation in the form of loans to individuals, secured by mortgages on their land. One-tenth of each loan was repaid annually, with interest. Thus, at the

---

[1] Aug. 1.

end of ten years, the whole was returned to the loan offices, and redeemed; the government in the mean time having gained the interest, and the community having had the benefit of the circulation. It was made a legal tender for the payment of debts, and it generally maintained its original value, with slight fluctuations caused by the rise of gold and silver when a larger quantity of these metals than usual was wanted for exportation.[1] This form of paper currency delighted Pownall, an English writer upon the "Administration of the Colonies;"[2] for he declares that "paper money thus lent upon interest will create gold and silver in principal, while the interest becomes a reserve that pays the charges of government. This currency is the true Pactolian stream, which converts all into gold that is washed by it."[3] The other kind of paper money was emitted by a Colony, upon the pledge of certain taxes, which were considered sufficient to redeem it within a specified time. This was the older and more general method employed among the Colonies.

The bill passed by Congress, authorizing the first issue of bills of credit, certainly encountered the opposition of Franklin; for he wrote to Samuel Cooper that he took all the pains he could in Congress to prevent their depreciation, by proposing that the bills should bear interest. This amendment, however, was rejected, and they were struck in a different manner.[4] It is quite probable that

---

[1] Sparks's Franklin, vol. i. p. 303. This plan evidently grew out of the bank experiment of South Carolina, devised in 1712.

[2] 4th ed., p. 186.

[3] Bills of credit had been issued as loans in New Hampshire, based upon real-estate security. — BELKNAP, *Hist. of New Hampshire*, vol. i. p. 378.

[4] Sparks's Franklin, vol. viii. p. 328.

other delegates shared his views, or favored the adoption of the Pennsylvania plan, which had proved so successful; for, as the need of money was very great, had there been no opposition to the report of the committee, it would have been speedily adopted. Both Congress and the Colonies needed funds, yet congressional action was delayed.

Paper money had been tried in all the Colonies, and nowhere had the experiment worked satisfactorily, save in Pennsylvania. Of all the numerous issues, none had been redeemed in conformity with the promise of the government; and hardship, extravagance, and corruption, even in those primitive days, had grown out of the employment of paper money.[1] We may readily believe that

[1] Ramsay says that the issue of paper money "was in some degree owing to a previous confidence, which had been begotten by honesty and fidelity, in discharging the engagements of government. From New York to Georgia there never had been in matters relating to money, an instance of a breach of faith. In the scarcity of gold and silver, many emergencies had imposed a necessity of emitting bills of credit. These had been uniformly and honestly redeemed." (*Hist. of Am. Rev.*, vol. ii. p. 132, ed. 1789.) The truth is, hardly a case had occurred in which the Colonies redeemed their bills in fulfilment of the promise written thereon. John Adams wrote to Count de Vergennes in 1780, "In the late Province of the Massachusetts Bay, from the years 1745 to 1750. we had full experience of the operation of paper money. The Province engaged in expensive expeditions against Louisburg and Canada, which occasioned a too plentiful emission of paper money, in consequence of which it depreciated to seven and a half for one. In 1750, the British Parliament granted a sum of money to the Province to reimburse it for what it had expended more than its proportion in the general expense of the empire. This sum was brought over to Boston in silver and gold, and the Legislature determined to redeem all their paper with it at the depreciated value. There was a similar alarm at first, and before the

more than one delegate knew of the evils springing from
the use of credit as money. John Adams had "seen
paper annihilated at a blow, in Massachusetts, in 1750 : "
was not this event enough to make him sceptical respecting the virtues of paper money? That he was no friend
of it, is evident from his reply to the letter of John
Taylor, recommending the latter to read Count Destutt
Tracy's work upon "Political Economy," which had
just been translated by Jefferson. Adams says, "His
chapter 'Of Money' contains the sentiments that I have
entertained all my lifetime." After quoting a passage
declaring that to diminish the quantity of metals in
coins is to steal, the quotation continues: "A theft of
greater magnitude and still more ruinous, is the making
of paper money; it is greater, because in this money
there is absolutely no real value; it is more ruinous,
because, by its gradual depreciation during all the time
of its existence, it produces the effect which would be
produced by an infinity of successive deteriorations of the
coins. All these iniquities are founded on the false idea,
that money is but a sign."[1] If John Adams entertained
these sentiments all his lifetime, as he affirms he did, he

matter was understood, but after the people had time to think upon it,
all were satisfied to receive silver at fifty shillings an ounce, although
the face of the bills promised an ounce of silver for every six shillings
and eightpence." (*Works*, vol. vii. p. 200.) Paper money passed at
seven for one of specie in South Carolina in consequence of the wars of
1739 and of 1756, and, "for many years anterior to the commencement
of the late unhappy distractions, payments were made in specie in
the proportion, it is imagined, of eight or nine for one of the paper
currency" (*Observations of English Commissioners*, Nov. 25, [1780,
ALMON's *Rememb.*, 1781, part 1, pp. 214, 215).

[1] *Works*, vol. x. p. 376.

could not have favored the issue of paper money by the Continental Congress.

However divergent were the views of the delegates upon the question of issuing paper money, or the mode of issuing it, Congress decided, near the end of June,[1] to issue bills of credit, not exceeding two million Spanish milled dollars,[2] pledging the faith of the twelve Confed-

[1] June 22.

[2] The standard Spanish pillar dollar contained, of fine silver, 385.72, and of alloy 31.75 grains.

Various explanations of the dollar-mark, and when it was introduced, have been put forth; but the following explanation, which first appeared in the Historical Magazine, is the most satisfactory of any we have seen.

"The dollar-mark ($) appears to have derived its origin from the ancient Romans through the modern Italians, and specially through those great traders and money-dealers of mediæval Europe, the Lombards.

"Amongst the ciphers and abbreviations of the Romans, we find (Ursato de notis Romanorum Patav. 1672) some with horizontal lines, as S, ȊIS (sestertius, sestertium); and some, though but few, with sloping and not quite upright lines, such as are now used in the dollar-mark. Amongst this smaller number we find the form ꞩ (semis, weight, or coin), which is probably the origin of the modern $.

"This last, which is now employed as the dollar-mark, came into use in the middle ages, to express the current value of the old *Spanish* dollar, which was good for *eight reals*. Of this value the dollar-mark is not merely an arbitrary token, but a significant representative.

"The Spanish dollar, being equivalent to eight reals, used to be called accordingly, in French, 'piéce de *huit*;' in German, stück von *achten*; in Italian, pezzo d'*otto*; in English, a piece of *eight*. This will account for *one* component part of the dollar-mark, namely, the figure of 8. In Spanish, also, the dollar was called pieza de à *ocho*.

"But the two sloping lines of the dollar-mark (‖) have also their explanation. Among the old Spanish dollars those are decidedly best which bear on their reverse *two pillars*, or columns, and which have

erate Colonies for their redemption. This was the plan recommended by the committee of the New-York Assembly, and it received the support of the delegates representing that Colony in Congress.

The next day some minor matters respecting the bills were settled, and a committee, consisting of John Adams, John Rutledge, James Duane, Benjamin Franklin, and James Wilson, were appointed to engrave the plates, procure paper, and arrange for printing the notes. Frank-

therefore been termed *pillared dollars*. These two pillars, a little sloped by the pen, do duty as the two parallel lines, which, combined with the figure of 8, compose the dollar-mark.

"It has been supposed, indeed, that the two lines in question are the double l of the word castellano, which sometimes stood in old Spanish for a dollar; or that they are perhaps taken from the word vellon, which is still used in the phrase, 'reals vellon.' But the explanation first given seems preferable to either of these, which are a little far-fetched, and will not bear examination."

When the dollar-mark was first used is a question not so easy to answer. "The reply, however, lies within certain limits, to determine which we must go a little way into the *history* of the Spanish dollar.

"'*Dollar*' is not, after all, a Spanish term. The word is German and Dutch (thaler, daalder, and, in old Dutch, daelder). The Spanish name is *peso ;* and it was not till, under Charles V., the Spanish peso, bearing his name as King of *Spain*, began to be struck in *Holland* and *Germany*, that the peso began to be called a dollar (thaler, or daelder). Then, also, the mark $ appears to have first attached itself, for distinction, to the Spanish peso, or thaler. The Spaniards had no need of a mark which merely indicates that their peso was worth eight good reals; for they all knew it. But the old thalers of Holland and Germany, coined long before the time of Charles V., had *various values ;* and therefore it was very natural, when a new Spanish coin appeared in the midst of them, and acquired the name of thaler, that the Lombards and others who dealt in money should designate the new variety by a distinguishing mark, which indicated that this was a dollar of eight reals." — Vol. i. p. 245.

lin was more familiar with this work than any other member, as he had printed paper money for the Colony of New Jersey, and devised the first copper-plate press for printing the bills.

The Continental bills were of several denominations, from one to twenty dollars, and in form as follows: —

Continental Currency.

No.   Dollars.

This bill entitles the bearer to receive   Spanish milled dollars, or the value thereof in Gold or Silver, according to the resolutions of the Congress, held at Philadelphia, on the 10th day of May, A. D., 1775.

In thus issuing paper money, it has been affirmed that Congress committed two capital errors: first, in issuing any bills whatever; and, secondly, in not taxing the Colonies immediately to redeem them. It is easy for us to discover errors strewn over the past; but, to judge fairly of the wisdom or ignorance displayed by Congress, we must transport ourselves back to those troubled times, and survey as accurately as possible the situation of the actors of that period.

In the first place, when this issue was ordered, it was not believed that the sum would be very much, if at all, increased. Never in the history of issuing paper money has any one supposed that a large amount would be forthcoming. This is one of the dangers of embarking upon this always deceptive sea. One issue authorized, others are sure to follow; but the Continental Congress of 1775, like the Congress of 1863, never intended, in the beginning, to flood the country with paper money. No one dreamed of the long and fearful contest before the country. When, therefore, the first issue appeared, it was thought the trouble with great Britain would be soon adjusted; that the total amount of paper issues would be small, and consequently could be easily discharged.

Nor did Congress suppose that paper money would float without taxing the Colonies for its redemption. Accordingly, Congress apportioned to each Colony its share of the sum required, on the basis of population. True, this was an injustice; but what else could Congress do? It was impossible to form an accurate idea of the wealth of the Colonies; and, though the estimate of the inhabitants was a crude one, yet, so far as we can discover, it was the most satisfactory basis which could be adopted.

Bronson and other writers declare that Congress ought to have assessed and collected taxes, leaving no authority to the States upon the subject. But Ramsay, Bancroft, and many other historians, assert that Congress had no power to tax the Colonies. This answer is true in one sense, though not in another. Congress had no authority to tax the Colonies: on the other hand, there was no legal prohibition. Congress had just as much power to tax, as to issue bills of credit. Whether Congress should tax them, or not, was a question of expediency. The course to be pursued depended on the temper of the people. Congress was obliged to look to them for the sanction and enforcement of all legislation. Surely it were not wise to enact a law which the people would not obey, however correct it might be in principle; because, if not observed, Congress was powerless to enforce obedience. Of what use was it to tax the Colonies if they would not pay? Congress could not enforce the collection of it: there lay the root of the whole difficulty.

If the Colonies had been directly taxed, probably they would have refused to pay, and then denounced Congress for daring to exercise so much power.[1] Lieut.-Gov. Colden wrote to the Earl of Dartmouth, during the debate on this subject, "The Congress are well aware that an attempt to raise money by an immediate assessment upon the people would give disgust that might ruin all their measures, and therefore they prefer to do it by issuing paper money."[2] The people had rebelled because Parliament assumed the right to tax the Colonies without their consent; and would they allow Congress to do what they had denied to Parliament? This was to contradict the very idea of resistance. Whatever might have been the opinion of Congress in respect to direct taxation, the inexpediency of resorting to such a measure was manifest; and any enactment involving the right would have been disobeyed, and treated with contempt. Having recommended the Colonies to pay their respective quotas of the sum required to redeem

---

[1] Noah Webster says, "The advantages the Colonies had derived from bills of credit, under the British Government, suggested to Congress, in 1775, the idea of issuing bills for the purpose of carrying on the war. And this was perhaps their only expedient. Money could not be raised by taxation; it could not be borrowed." — *Sketches of the late Revolution, written in the years 1787, '88, and '89, Coll. of Essays*, p. 191.

[2] June 7, 1775, Documents relating to the Col. Hist. of New York, vol. viii. p. 579.

the bills, Congress went to the verge of safety. To have attempted to go further might have caused the speedy and inglorious end of that body.

Congress, it has been said, ought never to have issued bills of credit, but provided funds in some other way. Whether a loan could have been obtained when Continental bills were first issued, it is impossible definitely to ascertain; but surely the credit of Congress must have been very poor, as the organization was only a few days old, while many regarded the future with uncertainty and alarm. What if the Colonies were unsuccessful in their demands of Great Britain, and were prohibited from redeeming the obligations incurred by Congress? Would any one trust the government under such circumstances?[1]

Nevertheless, Dr. Franklin urged Congress to resort to loans, instead of issuing any more paper money, when the question of a second issue arose, showing, that, in his opinion, money might at that time have been obtained in that manner. Whether the country would have loaned funds to any extent or not, no one will question the wisdom of such a policy, had it been practicable.

From all that can be learned about public sentiment during this period, it is probable that Congress issued

---

[1] Many believed the issue of paper money to be a necessity, and justified the act on that ground. John Adams wrote to Mrs. Warren, "A paper currency, fluctuating in its value, will ever produce appearances in the political, commercial, and even the moral world, that are very shocking at first sight; but, upon examination, they will not be found to proceed from a total want of principle, but, for the most part, from necessity" (Dec. 15, 1778, ADAMS's *Works*, vol. ix. p. 475). Hamilton entertained the same opinion (*Works*, vol. i. pp. 118, 119).

these bills in obedience to the popular demand, just as that body many a time since has enacted measures, not because they were right, but for the sake of pleasing the people. It must be remembered, however, that, in those days, Congress was obliged to follow public sentiment closely in order to exist: now Congress can fall back upon the Constitution in defence of the measures adopted. The people, as we have observed, had tried paper money in all the Colonies, and knew its virtues, as well as its defects; and they believed it was the best mode of raising funds to carry on the government. These were sorely needed to purchase supplies for the army: the Colonies "had stretched their own public faith as far as it would go;"[1] yet they had faith in a currency issued by Congress upon pledge of payment by all the Colonies, and circulating in all of them. The paper currencies then existing were local, and many and grievous were the complaints arising from their use. These, it was believed, would not occur if bills of credit were issued by Congress. Such was the way the people reasoned; and nothing except paper money would satisfy them.[2] "Their representations," says Phillips, "seem

[1] From letter of New-York Provincial Congress to delegates representing that Colony in Continental Congress, Am. Archives, fourth series, vol. ii. p. 1281.

[2] When Congress determined to strike the first bills, the whole country acquiesced. In an address to that body by the inhabitants of Philadelphia, early in 1780, it was said, "That whereas, at the commencement of the present war, the country being then destitute of the proper forms and powers of government, there appeared no other method, sufficiently expeditious and practicable, for raising the current supplies, than by striking money by this honorable house, in such portions and at such

at last to have wrought on Congress a knowledge that
their constituency, whether for well or ill, desired a
Continental paper currency which should be equally current in all the Colonies."[1]   On the 17th of June, Duane,[2]
a delegate from New York, wrote to his constituents,
"Your great complaint of the want of money will, I
hope, be soon removed. For your present satisfaction,
we have obtained leave of the Congress to inform you
that the general committee of the whole body have reported a resolution to emit, in Continental paper currency, a sum not exceeding the value of two millions
of Spanish dollars, for the redemption of which all the
Colonies are to be pledged." Within a week the recommendation of the committee was adopted.

It is not fair to impute all the blame for enacting this
measure to the people, because it is very probable that
many of the delegates were sincere advocates of it.
During one of the debates on this subject, a member
rose, and said, "Do you think, gentlemen, that I will
consent to load my constituents with taxes, when we can
send to our printer, and get a wagon-load of money, one
quire of which will pay for the whole?"[3] The conclusion
that may be fairly drawn is, the people wanted paper
money, and Congress could not have done otherwise than
it did, in satisfying this desire. It was necessary for
Congress to obey the people, in order to exist.

periods as to them should seem meet and proper. The necessity gave
countenance to the proceeding, and, convinced thereof, the whole
country unanimously acquiesced." — ALMON's *Rememb.*, 1780, p. 301.

[1] Cont. Paper Money, p. 24.

[2] Am. Archives. fourth series. vol. ii. p. 1016.

[3] Webster, Political Essays, p. 7, note d.

A month elapsed before any measures were taken for printing the bills. Finally, on the 21st of July, a committee were appointed for this purpose. Finding the amount authorized insufficient to supply the demands made upon Congress, four days later that body issued an additional million. Franklin opposed this measure, for he declared, in a letter to a friend, "After the first emission I proposed that we should stop, strike no more, but borrow on interest those we had issued. This was not then approved of, and more bills were issued."[1]

As the signing of so large a number of bills consumed more time than the committee appointed for that purpose could give to the business, another committee were raised, composed of persons residing in Philadelphia, two of whom were required to number and sign each bill, and deliver them to Michael Hilligas and George Clymer, joint treasurers of the Colonies.[2] The notes are fine specimens of the progress to which the art of engraving had attained in the country at that period.

Congress supposed that each Colony would provide ways and means for sinking its proportion of the bills, in the manner most effectual, and best adapted to the condition, circumstances, and equal mode of levying taxes therein.[3] An assessment also was prepared, based upon the supposed population of the Colonies, including the negroes and mulattoes, which was to be revised as soon as the correct list of each Colony could be obtained. As Georgia had not yet linked her fortunes with those of the other Colonies, the sums assigned to each Colony were the following: —

---

[1] Sparks's Franklin, vol. viii. p. 328.   [2] July 25.   [3] July 29.

New Hampshire . . . $124,069½	Delaware 37,219½
Massachusetts Bay . . 434,244	Maryland 310,174½
Rhode Island . . . 71,959½	Virginia 496,278
Connecticut 248,139	North Carolina . . . 248,139
New York 248,139	South Carolina . . . 248,139
New Jersey 161,290½	
Pennsylvania . . . 372,208½	$3,000,000

Each Colony was to pay its respective quota in four
equal payments annually, commencing with the last day
of November, 1779.[1] One of the links in the system
was for the several Colonies to levy and collect taxes,
which were to be applied in sinking the bills. When
these were received by the collectors, they were to send
them to the Continental treasurers; and in case they
could not secure their quota, either directly in the way
of receiving the bills for taxes, or by exchange of Colonial notes for them, the deficiency was to be made up in
silver or gold. The treasurers appointed by the Colonies,
before sending their bills to Philadelphia, were to " take
care to cut, by a circular punch of an inch in diameter,
a hole in each bill, and to cross the same, thereby to
render them unpassable, though the sum or value is to

---

[1] The Colonies promptly responded to the recommendation of Congress. The Provincial Congress for the Colony of New York, on the
24th of May, " Resolved, That this Congress will, before they rise, provide the best ways and means in their power, as representatives of the
people, for the discharge of such money, as is now lent, or shall be
subscribed or otherwise advanced or supplied, on the public faith, to
defray the charges that are or shall be incurred in the present exigences
of the Colony, or that shall hereafter be expended or incurred by
recommendation of the Continental or this Provincial Congress." The
other Colonies passed similar resolutions.

remain fairly legible." As fast as the bills were received, they were to be destroyed by a committee appointed for that purpose; and the silver and gold sent to make up deficiencies in quotas were to be retained until demanded in redemption of Continental bills. The act further provided, that, whenever the treasurers had gold or silver in their possession for the redemption of Continental bills, they should "advertise the same, signifying that they were ready to give silver or gold for such bills to all persons requiring it in exchange."

It may seem singular that a people who had been trying to establish these two great principles, no taxation without representation, and representation based on population, should have committed the palpable injustice of recommending a tax founded on population, and not on property. Let no one, though, forget how chaotic was the condition of the country at that time, or the infancy of the central government, which was only half formed, and without clearly defined powers. The Colonial governments, too, were in the same condition; nor had any estimate ever been made of the wealth of the Colonies. It is true none had ever been formed of the inhabitants; but, amid the confusion of the time, the rule adopted was likely to give rise to less dissatisfaction than the adoption of any other.

CHAPTER IV.

OPERATIONS OF THE BOARD OF TREASURY.

1775-1777.

WHEN the first issue of paper money was ordered by Congress, many confidently believed the debt thus created would be promptly redeemed without loss to any one. But events not foreseen in the beginning, nor even imagined, prevented the fulfilment of this hope. Eminent as was the ability of many of the political leaders of the American Revolution, no one among them was endowed with the Promethean genius to forecast the future. The Colonies were rapidly drifting towards revolution, without knowing it or the cost of the movement. Only a few days after the first emission of bills of credit, the battle of Breed's Hill was fought; and gradually the hope of a cheap and peaceful solution of the grievance with Great Britain faded away.

Small as was the amount of bills authorized, two months after their authorization not enough had been signed to answer the urgent calls upon the treasury.[1] The signers neglected or refused to attend to their duties; and the bills did not come into general circulation before the middle of August, and even then in no great quantity. Indeed, so negligent were the signers of their duty, that

---

[1] Am. Archives, fourth series, vol. iii. p. 11.

Congress, on the 10th of November, directed the delegates to call upon those who had been appointed to sign the bills, and request them to complete their task without further delay. Of course, such slight aid could not go far towards supplying the needs of Congress and the Colonies. Consequently, on the 25th of July another million was authorized, and, before the year closed, it was resolved to issue three millions more of paper money. This measure was strenuously opposed by Dr. Franklin,[1] who advocated borrowing the bills already issued upon interest. This plan he had favored when the preceding issue was under consideration; but his protest on both occasions proved unavailing, and so the third issue came forth printed from the same plates, and under similar superintendence, as the former issues.

Congress was not unmindful of the necessity of providing a way for redeeming these obligations. Accordingly, each Colony was once more directed "to provide ways and means for sinking its proportion of bills in the most effective manner, and best adapted to the condition and equal mode of levying taxes in each Colony."[2] Congress also directed that each Colony should pay its proportion of the bills, determined by the number of its inhabitants, in four equal amounts, beginning the last day of November, 1783, a year after the redemption of the issues ordered at the last session of Congress, and ending three years later. The other features of the previous resolve, relating to the redemption, exchange, and destruction of bills, were re-enacted. The year, therefore, closed

---

[1] Letter to Samuel Cooper, Sparks's Franklin, vol. viii. p. 328.

[2] Dec. 26.

with six millions of paper money either afloat or soon to be put in circulation.

Early the next year,[1] ten thousand dollars were struck for the purpose of exchanging ragged and torn bills. Every day, however, the pressure grew stronger for another issue of paper money. The Colonies and Continental armies were without funds, and the only resource seemed to be that of the printing-press: consequently, on the 17th of February, 1776, a fourth issue of four millions was ordered. To give the bills more currency, and to assist the people with small change in place of silver, which had been withdrawn from circulation, a little more than one-half of the issue was struck in fractional bills of one-sixth, one-third, one-half, and two-thirds of a dollar.[2]

Before the fifth issue appeared, Continental bills had begun to depreciate; and every one must have seen the inevitable consequence of increasing the quantity.[3] But no other expedient could be devised. The States (for independence was now declared) were not accustomed to taxation: the General Government was weak, and without credit; nevertheless, every eye was turned toward it for aid.

The singular spectacle was presented of the retention

---

[1] Jan. 5.   [2] Feb. 21.

[3] Numerous false reports were circulated in those days, for the purpose of impairing the credit and power of the Confederation. The following is a fair illustration: "A report prevails here that the Congress is separated and that Dr. Franklin and six more are gone to France or some other place to secure their dollars, for they have got most of the cash of the country into their hands, you may guess for what purpose." — *Letter from New York, Nov. 5, 1776, addressed to a gentleman in Bristol, Eng.*

of nearly all the power by the States, and of a refusal on their part to exercise it, preferring to trust a weak and inefficient General Government rather than to rely upon stronger local organizations. The depreciation of Continental money ought to have taught Congress the plainest lessons concerning the inevitable effect of authorizing new issues; yet the lesson was imperfectly heeded, and the quantity was increased five millions more.[1]

Fifteen millions were now authorized. The depreciation was too patent to be ignored. Money was needed by the States and by the army, and the calls upon Congress were incessant. Seeing the evils attending the issue of paper money, Congress determined upon other measures for relief.

A loan was proposed. In those days this was not a common practice among nations,[2] and serious opposition arose to the measure.[3] But the principal dispute in Congress related to the rate of interest. Congress proposed to fix it at four per cent, — a rate too low to tempt the lenders of money to subscribe. This rate, however, was established; and five millions of Continental dollars were to be immediately borrowed, the United States pledging their faith to the lenders for the repayment of the same with interest.[4] The following was the form of certificate issued : —

[1] July 22.

[2] Carthage was the most advanced of all the states of antiquity in respect to finance, and perhaps was the first nation to make a foreign state loan (see MOMMSEN's *Hist. of Rome*, vol. ii. p. 29, Am. ed.). For history of early state loans in Greece, see BOECKH's *Public Economy of the Athenians*, pp. 760-763.

[3] Webster, Political Essays, p. 18.   [4] Oct. 3.

The United States of America acknowledge the receipt of
        dollars from   , which they promise to pay to
the said   , or bearer, on the   day of   ,
with interest annually, at the rate of four per cent per annum,
agreeable to a resolution of the United States, passed the third
day of October, 1776. Witness the hand of the Treasurer, this
      day of   , A. D.

This certificate was countersigned by a loan-office commissioner, Congress having authorized the appointment
of one by every State, who was responsible to the appointing power for the rightful discharge of his duties.
No certificate was to be given for less than three hundred dollars, and the money thus borrowed was to be
repaid at the expiration of three years. The commissioners were paid a commission of one-eighth of one per
cent upon all loans made for the benefit of the government.[1] The resolutions were published by order of Congress, and the States were directed to send to the
Committee of the Treasury the names of the commissioners as soon as they were appointed.

This scheme for raising money did not succeed (nor
were those disappointed who opposed it), because so low
a rate of interest was offered. It was the hope of many
that a considerable sum of money would be raised in
this way; but lenders could not see the wisdom of letting
the government have their money at four per cent upon
the uncertain pledge of the government, when they
could get six per cent from private borrowers with

---

[1] Sept. 20, 1778, the rate of compensation was changed, and the
commissioners were allowed two per cent on the amount of interest
paid for transacting the business.

ample security. Is it not plain, then, why the government failed in such a competition for money?

Now and then patriotism rose above profits, or even security, and some person would repair to a loan-office, and subscribe to the national loan; but either because those patriots were so few in number, or because they subscribed for such small amounts, the government was not materially aided with funds flowing from this source.

In the early part of February, 1777, John Adams[1] wrote to his friend Warren of Boston, that four per cent interest "was not an equitable allowance;" by which he meant that it was "not so much as the use of the money is honestly worth in the ordinary course of business, upon an average for a year; and I have accordingly exerted all the little faculties I had in endeavoring to raise the interest to six per cent." Continuing his letter, he declared that he trembled for the consequences of this determination of Congress. "If the loan officers should not procure us money, we must emit more, which will depreciate all which is already abroad, and so raise the price of provisions and all the necessaries of life, that the additional expense to the Continent for supplying their army and navy will be vastly more than the two per cent in dispute, besides all the injustice, chicanery, extortion, oppression, and discontent which is always occasioned everywhere by a depreciating medium of trade. I am much afraid of another mischief. I fear that for want of wisdom to raise the interest in season, we shall be necessitated,

---

[1] Works, vol. ix. p. 452.

within a few months, to give eight or ten per cent, and not obtain the money we want after all." He then very quaintly adds, "I have been so often a witness of the miseries of this after-wisdom that I am wearied to death of it." Before the letter was sent, the decision of Congress was wisely reconsidered; and Adams had the pleasure of writing a postscript, dated a month later, that, after many days of deliberation, the rate of interest had been raised to six per cent.

As not enough money flowed into the treasury from this source to meet the demands upon the government, another experiment was attempted, which was a familiar method of raising money at that period, though long ago condemned by law and public opinion.[1] This new scheme

---

[1] The lottery had been in existence in England two hundred years; for in 1569 one was formed (perhaps the first) in which forty thousand chances were sold at ten shillings each, the prizes consisting of articles of plate, and the profits were employed in repairing certain harbors. In 1694 a loan of a million pounds was raised by the sale of lottery-tickets at ten pounds per ticket, the prizes in which were funded at the rate of fourteen per cent for sixteen years. Half a century later, in 1746, a loan of three million pounds was raised on four-per-cent annuities and a lottery of fifty thousand tickets of ten pounds each; and, in the following year, a million pounds was issued by the sale of a hundred thousand tickets, the prizes in which were funded in perpetual annuities at the rate of four per cent per annum. Thirty years afterward, in August, 1776, Great Britain sought to raise six hundred thousand pounds by lottery to carry on the war with America. The last lottery of the kind which occurred there was in 1780, when every subscriber of a thousand pounds toward a loan of twelve million pounds at four per cent received a bonus of four lottery-tickets, the intrinsic value of each of which was ten pounds. In France, lotteries had been often tried by the government in order to raise money for public purposes; and in 1779 one was formed to raise a fund of thirty-

was a lottery, which had been often tried in the Colonies, as well as in the Old World, both for public and private purposes. Many a church still stands in New England built with funds raised in this manner.

The Board of Treasury reported a plan on the 1st of November, and subsequently all the details were added. It was resolved that the lottery should consist of one hundred thousand tickets: each ticket was divided into four billets of ten, twenty, thirty, and forty dollars respectively, which were to be drawn in four classes. Phillips says it was estimated that one million five thousand dollars would be drawn into the Continental Treasury in this way, though he has omitted to give any authority for the statement. The tickets were to be sold for ready money, which Breck construed to mean specie; and some of "the fortunate adventurers," as the resolution terms them, were to receive, at their option, "a treasury bank-note," or certificate payable in five years with interest at four per cent; while others were to receive their money from the loan-office commissioner of the States where the drawers resided.[1]

While Congress was discussing this scheme, the need of money was so great, that the Board of Treasury were directed to prepare materials for a new emission of five millions, one-tenth of which was to be issued immediately

six million livres, which sum was to be employed in continuing the war against Great Britain. With such well-known examples, there was no ground for hesitation on the part of Congress in respect to the propriety or expediency of the measure. The condemnation of lotteries on moral grounds is the result of a later and deeper investigation of moral principles.

[1] Nov. 1, 18, 19.

in small bills of two-thirds, one-third, one-sixth, and one-ninth of a dollar; nor was the issuing of the balance long delayed.[1]   Phillips[2] affirms that no vestiges of these notes remain, and that persons throughout the country who have made investigation about them can obtain no information concerning them.   They have never appeared in any list of the various issues of paper money; and Phillips is probably correct in saying, that, for some reason unknown, they were never sent into circulation.   As the amount was very small (only five hundred thousand dollars), perhaps the Board of Treasury did not regard the relief which would thus be furnished of enough account to justify them in getting the materials, and making the issue.   From no source could Congress obtain funds, though never were they more greatly needed.

On the 14th of January it was resolved to borrow two million dollars more from the loan-offices; and the commissioners were directed to receive bills of credit emitted by the States, and use them in paying the government.   How much had been subscribed to the previous loan cannot be ascertained: in some measure, however, it had been successful, else the experiment upon similar conditions would not have been repeated.

Happily, the loan-office and lottery experiments did not exhaust the fertile mind of Congress.   The Legislatures of the several States were asked to raise by taxation in the course of the year, and remit to the treasury, so much as they thought proper, considering the present condition of their inhabitants.[3]   These sums were to be

---

[1] Nov. 2, Dec. 28, 1776.   [2] Cont. Paper Money, p. 57.   [3] Jan. 14.

placed to their credit, and reckoned in the settlement of expenses for which the States were severally holden. Probably it was the injustice of assigning a sum to be raised by each State in proportion to its inhabitants which led to this new method of getting money from them. The plan was free from the criticism pronounced upon the mode first adopted for paying Continental notes, of basing the quotas upon the erroneous principle of population rather than property. The weakness of this last measure, however, was apparent; for only the most sanguine could hope for a favorable response from the States. But what more could Congress do? Without authority to coerce the States into the payment of money, having no stronger prerogative than to recommend and request, Congress could not enforce compliance with any requisition for a single dollar.

The Continental treasurer, also, was directed to borrow money on loan-office certificates countersigned by the auditor-general.[1] In conducting this business he was to proceed in the same way as the loan-office commissioners: indeed, the loan-office system was simply extended so as to include the Continental treasurer among the number of those authorized to borrow money for the use of the government.

Thus, within a very short time, four schemes had been launched for raising money to carry on the government, — the issue of Continental notes to be discharged by the States, loans to the government by individuals through loan-offices, a lottery, and advances of money by the several States. This variety of methods was owing to

---

[1] Jan. 15.

the great difficulty of raising funds in the ordinary manner for public uses. Neither method had succeeded so well as that of Hippias, who, to obtain money, sold those portions of the houses of Athens, which in the upper stories, or by doors opening outward, projected into the public streets. The doubtful existence of the government, and its weakness, the poverty of the States, and their ignorance, and unwillingness to submit to taxation, were the leading obstacles in the way of obtaining funds. Unwilling to be taxed by Great Britain for the benefit of the parent government, they had come to regard taxation with strong dislike, even when it was a measure absolutely necessary to rescue themselves from still greater taxation, and evils far worse, if failing to secure independence.

Unable to obtain all the funds needed, from these several fountains, five million dollars upon the credit of the United States, of the same denomination and on the same conditions as the last emission, were ordered,[1] and as much more three months afterward.[2] As counterfeiting the issues of Congress had become an extremely common practice, special pains were taken to print the bills in such a manner as to defy the art of the counterfeiter. The following form was employed: —

No.   Dollars.
This bill entitles the bearer to receive   Spanish milled dollars, or the value thereof in gold or silver, according to a resolution of Congress, passed at Philadelphia, May 20, 1777.

[1] Feb. 26.   [2] May 20.

They were also ornamented, and bore escutcheons and secret marks, devised by the Board of Treasury. Several resolutions were added relating to the manner of signing, striking, numbering, and issuing the bills; but these particulars need not be given.[1]

Although the States retained exclusive authority to raise money from their members by taxation, they obtained only small sums in this way, and with great difficulty and cost, while they were continually calling upon Congress for assistance. Choosing to retain the power, the States ought to have accepted the responsibility and burden; but, instead of doing this, they put too much faith in a weak, incapable, central government, and not enough in their own local ones. The States furnished some aid to the General Government; but this was fully reciprocated.

The accounts of the States with Congress are so inextricably mixed, that it is difficult to tell how much support was rendered on the one side and the other during the early part of the war. Georgia appears to have been more prompt in furnishing assistance than any other State. So marked, indeed, had been her course, that commissioners were appointed to go there and find out how much was due from the United States; while Congress remitted four hundred thousand dollars on account of assistance thus rendered, and three hundred thousand dollars more for the pay and subsistence of the Continental troops conducting operations in that quarter. As this amount did not then happen to be in the Continental treasury, the printing-press was started, by direction of Congress, to add another million dollars to the amount already existing.[2]

[1] May 22.   [2] Aug. 15.

As summer waned, the cause of the Union grew desperate. Early in September, President McKinley of Wilmington was captured, and also all the papers and money in the loan-office there, amounting to twenty-five thousand dollars. Philadelphia was no longer tenable, and the contents of the loan-office in that city were removed to East Town. On the 18th of the same month Congress adjourned to Lancaster, and on the 30th to Yorktown. The demands made upon Congress at this time were more numerous than ever. A mutiny had occurred among some of the troops, owing to the distress caused by paper money, and from want of the necessaries of life. Though the flame was quickly subdued, the fires of discontent still smouldered, nor could they be entirely extinguished.

The 7th of November marked a fresh issue of paper money, to the extent of one million dollars; and, soon after, another emission of the same amount appeared: thus the year closed with five emissions of paper money, aggregating thirteen million dollars.

CHAPTER V.

ADMINISTRATION OF THE BOARD OF TREASURY.

1778.

As the year 1777 was drawing to a close, articles of confederation were formed, and passed by Congress for ratification by the States, from which the central government was to derive larger as well as more certain powers.[1] Notwithstanding the necessity of this measure, like many of the needs of the time, the work of ratification was sadly delayed.

Congress saw clearly enough how the issue of so much paper money without providing for its redemption would depreciate its value: indeed, this unwelcome truth could not be put out of sight. It was a matter of public concern and alarm. Congress, therefore, appealed once more to the States for assistance. They were earnestly recommended to raise during the year five million dollars by taxes levied on the inhabitants of the various States in the following proportions :[2] —

New Hampshire	$200,000		Virginia	$800,000
Rhode Island	100,000		Delaware	60,000
New York	200,000		New Jersey	270,000
Pennsylvania	620,000		Connecticut	600,000
Maryland	520,000		Massachusetts Bay	820,000
North Carolina	250,000		Georgia	60,000
South Carolina	500,000			

[1] Nov. 15, 1777.   [2] Nov. 22, 1777.

These sums were not regarded by Congress as the true proportions which the Colonies should advance, but only approximate estimates; nor was it necessary to be very exact in distributing the amount, since the funds coming from this source were to be considered a loan bearing six per cent interest. At the same time, the States were recommended to refrain from issuing any more bills of credit, and, where the Continental circulation was sufficient for the wants of business (and doubtless it was everywhere), to withdraw their own local issues, " and, for the future, to provide for the exigencies of war and the support of Government by taxes levied within the year, or such other expedient as may produce a competent supply."

No one will question the wisdom of this recommendation; but it was nothing more, and proved ineffectual. Had Congress been clothed with power to enforce the measure, how suddenly the financial prospect would have changed! The loan-office system also was extended. The States were recommended to open offices in every town and district, under the inspection of proper persons clothed with authority to issue certificates for loans as small as two hundred dollars.

Soon another recommendation appeared concerning the property of those who had abandoned their allegiance to the States, and passed over to the enemy. The property of all such persons, it was recommended, should be confiscated, and the proceeds invested in loan-office certificates, which were to be appropriated as the States should direct.[1] The recommendation was heeded, and all the

---

[1] Nov. 27, 1777.

States,[1] during some period of the war, passed acts to confiscate and sell the property of loyalists, applying the avails in redeeming certificates and bills of credit, or paying other expenses incurred through the conflict with Great Britain. The debtors, also, of British creditors, were enabled to discharge their debts by paying into the State treasuries or loan-offices paper money in fulfilment of their obligations. Under some of these laws, many individuals were attainted by name; others were banished forever from the country, and, if found within the State, were declared felons without benefit of clergy. In some States the estates and rights of married women, of widows and minors, and of persons who had died within the territories possessed by the British, were forfeited. In New York the Courts were enjoined to prefer bills of indictment against persons, alive or dead, who had adhered to the king, or joined his fleets or armies, and who were the owners or claimants of property. In some States confiscated property was applied to other than war purposes; in others, as rewards to persons for military service. In one instance the property which had been mortgaged to a British creditor was released, by special act of the Legislature, from the encumbrances, and given to the representatives of the mortgagee, who had fallen in battle.[2]

[1] Charles Carroll of Carrollton, and several others, opposed the enactment of confiscation laws by the Legislature of Maryland. There was a warm debate on the subject, but the law was passed. — *Md. Gazette.* See ALMON's *Rememb.*, 1780, part ii. p. 172.

[2] See correspondence between Hammond, British minister, and Jefferson, Secretary of State, Am. State Papers, vol. i. p. 102, Boston, 1815; also elaborate account in Secret Journal of Congress, October, 1786, vol. iv. pp. 185–287.

The right to confiscate the property of loyalists was not questioned at the time the States seized it; but when the war closed, and the terms of peace were under discussion, the commissioners on the part of Great Britain proposed a restitution of all the property confiscated. The answer made by the American commissioners was, that they had no power from the various States to restore it; and, if they had, it would be just for them to insist upon compensation for the desolation wrought by the British forces on the towns, private houses, and property of American citizens, contrary to the rules of war, an account of which had been taken by order of Congress. This rejoinder was so complete, that it was agreed no actual stipulation should be made for the restitution of the confiscated property. The States, as they pleased, were to restore or keep the property thus taken as a satisfaction for the loss incurred by the ravages of the British armies; though the American commissioners promised that Congress should recommend the States to restore it.

The States, however, did not consider favorably the recommendation of Congress. New York could discover no reason for restoring property which had been confiscated or forfeited, as no compensation had been offered on the part of Great Britain for the damages sustained by the States and their citizens from British military ravages. The other States saw the matter in the same light. An English writer [1] in 1783, the year peace was made, in commenting upon this part of the settlement, remarks, "The amount of the sum claimed by the United

---

[1] The Case and Claims of American Loyalists, p. 135.

States for the damages done by the British forces far surpassed that now claimed by the loyalists. And, as Great Britain must have paid for those damages, or have continued the war, had she not given up the property confiscated, it is evident that she had disposed of it for more than an adequate consideration, and is a considerable gainer by the bargain." This was a not altogether cheerless view to those whom the writer was addressing, and doubtless he made his countrymen believe, that, in the peace which Great Britain had just made, she had not lost every thing. The States having failed to recompense the loyalists for the losses they had sustained, the British Government finally paid them £3,292,452.[1]

Early in the year, Congress resolved to borrow ten million dollars on the credit of the United States, the loan bearing interest at six per cent, and loan-office certificates were to be struck for that amount. Four months later this action was rescinded. Not long afterward came the news of the French alliance. The amount of paper money then in circulation was $55,500,000.

While the British occupied Philadelphia, there was published in " The Pennsylvania Gazette "[2] a statement of the debt of the government, in which appeared the following items: —

1777, December 31. — To amount of several emissions of Continental paper dollars, as appears by the resolves of Congress, and certificates from the committees appointed for superintending the press, etc., amounting in the whole to 115,000,000 dollars.

---

[1] Sabine's American Loyalists, vol. i. p. 112.

[2] Almon's Rememb. for the Year 1778 and Beginning of 1779, p. 193.

To amount of twenty millions of paper dollars, borrowed on the credit of Congress in the several United States, as appears by certificates from the loan offices erected for that purpose, 20,000,000 dollars.

The interest on this loan being fixed at six per cent per annum, till repaid by Congress, these two sums consolidated make a clear apparent Continental debt of one hundred and thirty-five millions of dollars, which at 7s. 6d. per dollar, amounts to 50,625,000 pounds.   135,000,000 dollars.

This statement was a fearful exaggeration of the truth, and, of course, was prepared and made public for the purpose of depressing the spirits of the people by showing the impossibility of ever liquidating such a vast load of indebtedness. The errors in the statement were too patent to delude any one. The Continental paper in circulation was not so large by fifty millions as the amount therein given, while the indebtedness of the States was heavier than represented. Even the English periodicals saw fallacies in the statement too large and numerous to be passed without comment.

When the French alliance was formed, Congress was not slow in applying to France for aid; yet there were a few members opposed to this step, among whom was Henry Laurens of South Carolina. To him the foundation for drawing bills did not seem substantial; the practice was dangerous; and the measure, except for things absolutely needed in carrying on the war, was not necessary. The drawing of bills of exchange he declared to be essentially emissions of paper money upon the very worst terms, aggravated by six per cent interest per annum. It was putting the debt already existing out of sight for a little time; but he affirmed that it would infallibly return with accumulated force. To borrow money from a foreign power was to mortgage our soil; while the boasted generosity of the King of France in feeding us lightly, and demanding no security, was liable to the suspicion of being insidious.[1] "When the loan-office certificates," he continues, "are put on a beneficial plan, if money shall not be furnished in sums equal to the public exigency, it will be a proof that past emissions are not excessive. The demand for money, at this time, is not confined to the capital towns and cities within a small

---

[1] The fears of Laurens, that possibly America, by leaning too heavily on France, might not gain her independence, were not altogether without foundation; for among other secret papers found in the cabinet of Louis XVI., which afterwards saw the light of print, was one written by Turgot, entitled "Reflections upon the manner in which France and Spain ought to regard the consequences of the quarrel between Great Britain and her Colonies," in which he declared the event the "most desirable for the interests of the two crowns, would be the reduction of the colonies again under the yoke of England." His reasons for this view are very striking, and reveal at once the worth of his friendship for the Colonies. "If the colonies should not be reduced till after the ruin of all their resources, England would lose the advantages which she has hitherto drawn from them, not only for the augmentation of her commerce in time of peace, but in the use of their forces in time of war. If, on the contrary, the colonies should be subdued without the destruction of their wealth and their population, they would preserve also their courage and their desire of independence; and England would be compelled to employ part of her forces, in preventing a new revolt." To accomplish this end, the Colonies were to be aided by France in making resistance, until all our resources were destroyed, and then we were to be left severely alone by France. This assistance was not to be granted directly, but indirectly through the merchants, and thus save France from becoming embroiled in war with Great Britain. See R. G. Harper's Works, pp. 103, 104. Baltimore, 1819.

circle of trading merchants, but spread over a surface of 1,600 miles in length, and 300 broad; nor is it now the practice to give credit for one and more years for seven-eighths of the whole traffic. Every man is now a money-holder, and every article is paid for in cash; it is hence obvious that an immense sum is necessary for a complete circulation. No man would be so void of understanding as to keep Continental bills idle and at a risk, in his desk, when he might, upon the same security, improve them at six per cent per annum." [1]

Having shown the causes of the sudden rise of prices, Laurens closes by affirming that borrowing from a foreign power would not increase the value of paper money: such a step, probably, would be the source of extending the depreciation to several years beyond the term when, if in debt only at home, it might be redeemed. "Such, and many other arguments," he affirms he used upon the occasion; but, when the vote was taken, only four persons were found to agree with him: so, on the 19th of May, bills of exchange were ordered to be drawn upon the commissioners of the United States at Paris, to pay interest due on the loan certificates.

Congress, so Laurens affirms, was at first opposed to borrowing ten million dollars, and subsequently defeated a proposition to borrow half that amount; and not until the 9th of September was the motion carried to draw bills on the commissioners, who were then in Paris, at the rate of five livres of France for a Spanish dollar, for the payment of interest upon all money loaned to the government through the loan-office before the first of

---

[1] Gibbes' Doc. Hist. of Am. Rev., 1776–1782, p. 88.

March. It was expected, with this certainty of paying interest promptly, that twenty million dollars would be raised by the first of March, and that no more emissions of paper money would be necessary.

The precise terms of the agreement by which France agreed to pay interest upon loans made in the United States have never been ascertained. Laurens says, "The Commissioners gave Congress assurances of money received and promised sufficient, by subsidies, to pay the interest of twenty millions, if we should be obliged to borrow that sum." He afterward had reason for apprehending that the commissioners were sure of receiving only enough to pay interest upon five millions.[1] That France guaranteed the payment of interest upon all the money that could be borrowed in America, believing the sum would not be large, or for a stipulated amount, is pretty certain; for in a letter written by Morris to Franklin, in November, 1781, he says that "it was a point understood in Congress very early, that His most Christian Majesty would pay the interest of certain.moneys to be borrowed by Congress in America. Your Excellency knows better than any other man what passed on that subject. Those circumstances which rendered an express stipulation improper then, have introduced much delicacy into it now; and, therefore, I do not expect that the Court will recur to a formal acknowl-

---

[1] Franklin wrote, May 26, 1779, "When the commissioners of Congress made the proposition of paying the interest at Paris of the money borrowed in America, they understood the loan to be of five millions of dollars." — *Dip. Cor.*, vol. iii. p. 86.

edgment of what was then, perhaps, rather a personal, than national, obligation."[1]

As the army was suffering at this time for want of supplies, the Executive Council of Pennsylvania laid an embargo for thirty days on the importation of provisions, Congress[2] having previously recommended such action. If the Confederate Government was slow and timid in assuming authority, it did not hesitate to recommend the severest measures to the States for their adoption.

The financial condition of the country continued to grow worse. Congress did not fully comprehend the gravity of the situation, and relying too confidently for aid upon France, now that an alliance was formed, fell into a deplorable lethargy. Says William Hosmer, a

---

[1] Dip. Cor. vol. xii. p. 35. The commissioners in France wrote, April 9, 1777, "having convinced the ministry of the great importance of keeping up the credit, and fixing the value of our currency, which might be done, by paying in specie the interest of what we borrow, or in bills upon France, for the amount, . . . we are now assured, that" quarterly payments of five hundred thousand livres will be continued "for the purpose of paying the interest of the five million dollars, you are supposed to have borrowed, which we believe will be punctually complied with" (*Dip. Cor.* vol. i. p. 274). The commissioners do not make any subsequent reference to the promise of the French Government in their allusions to the subject. See letters dated May 25, 1777, Ibid., p. 204 ; Sept. 8, 1777, Ibid., p. 321; Oct. 6, 1777, Ibid., p. 331; Nov. 30, 1777, Ibid., p. 342; Aug. 28, 1778, Ibid., p. 429. Nov. 7, 1778, the commissioners write, "when it was proposed to pay the interest here, we had no idea of so much being borrowed" (Ibid., p. 401). They were informed in the last-mentioned letter by the auditor-general that the amount of interest then annually due upon the loan-office certificates amounted to two million livres and a half.

[2] June 8.

delegate from Connecticut, in a letter to Gov. Trumbull[1] of that State, "I wish I could with truth assure Your Excellency that, in my view, our affairs are in a happy train, and that Congress has adopted wise and effectual measures to restore our wounded public credit, and to establish the United States, their liberty, union and happiness upon a solid and permanent foundation. I dare not do it while my heart is overwhelmed with the most melancholy presages. The idleness and captiousness of some gentlemen, maugre the wishes and endeavors of an honest and industrious majority, in my apprehension, threaten the worst consequences." Perhaps Congress thought, that by appointing, as they did,[2] three days in the week for the consideration of financial questions, nothing more could be done to relieve the country. A permanent committee, consisting of Robert Morris, Gerry, R. H. Lee, Witherspoon, and G. Morris, were finally appointed "to consider the state of the money and the finances of the United States," and report thereon from time to time.[3]

Within a month this committee made a report, the contents of which can only be conjectured from the disposition made of it. Such parts as related to a confederal fund, and the mode of issuing and accounting for loan-office certificates, were referred to a committee consisting of Duer, Gerry, and Adams.[4] Four days later, another financial report was made; but whether it emanated from this newly-created committee, or the earlier

[1] Stuart's Life of Trumbull, p. 413, note.

[2] Aug. 12, 13.   [3] Aug. 27.   [4] Sept. 15.

one, the records of Congress do not show. Evidently the report contained some startling facts and opinions; for only sixty copies were printed, and the printer was required, under special oath, to keep its contents secret, and print no extras.

Doubtless many plans were suggested for supplying the national exchequer with money; but among the most interesting observations preserved are those of Silas Deane, who for a considerable period served as commissioner to France. His memorial to Congress on the subject is lost; but a letter addressed to the same body from Paris, two weeks later, is supposed to contain essentially the same ideas. In this communication he declares that "to emit more bills will be rather dangerous; for money, or whatever passes for such, whenever it exceeds the amount of the commerce of a State, must lose its value; and the present circumscribed state of the American commerce is perhaps within the amount of your emissions already made. Your bills, therefore, must be borrowed of individuals by the public at interest, or those already emitted paid off by taxes and new emissions. Some colonies may now be content with a tax, but it is most probably quite out of the power of some, and a measure rather impolitic in a majority of the colonies or States, *durante bello.* The relying on future taxes is holding up to the people a succession of distresses and burthens which are not to cease even with the war itself, whereas could they have a prospect of paying the expenses of the war at the close of it, and enjoying the remainder of their fortunes clear of encumbrance, it must greatly encourage and animate both the public and private spirit in pushing it on with vigor." [1]

The difficulty of raising funds for prosecuting the war is strikingly illustrated by the adoption of a measure, near the close of 1778, for furnishing the troops with provisions. This was nothing milder than a recommendation to the States to authorize commissioners to seize all goods required for the use of the armies, giving therefor certificates expressing the quantity and quality of the commodities seized, with the prices affixed, which were similar to those established by the several States a few months previously.[2] A circular letter, setting forth

[1] Letter to Com. of Secret Corres., Dip. Cor., vol. i. p. 77. See also his "Plan for sinking fifty-three millions of dollars of the Continental Currency," &c. Ibid., p. 160. It would be quite impossible to give all the peculiar ideas entertained about paper money by the leading actors of the revolutionary period; but the following views of Thomas Paine, who was a very clear thinker and writer, are worthy of a place here. In the years 1778-79 he wrote several papers signed "Common Sense," addressed chiefly to Englishmen, in one of which he notes how "the people of England seem to mistake their poverty for their riches; that is, they reckon their national debt as a part of their national wealth." After showing the error in this mode of reckoning, he observes, "The very reverse of this was the case with America; she began the war without any debt upon her, and in order to carry it on, she neither raised money by taxes, nor borrowed it upon interest, but created it; and her situation, at this time, continues so much the reverse of yours, that the taxing would make her rich, whereas it would make you poor. When we shall have sunk the sum which we have created, we shall then be out of debt, be just as rich as when we began, and all the while we are doing it, shall feel no difference, because the value will rise according as the quantity increases." — ALMON's *Rememb. for the Year* 1778, *and Beginning of* 1779, pp. 323, 324.

[2] Oct. 2.

the necessity of adopting so stringent a measure, was prepared by Congress, and transmitted to the States. To what extent this edict was executed we are unable to ascertain. There is strong reason, however, for concluding that many things were taken for the use of the army.

Though paper money was taken, with more or less reluctance, in return for most things, some services were rendered only upon promise of receiving specie. It was needed chiefly by the generals in procuring intelligence concerning the movements of the enemy, as no amount of paper money constituted a sufficient inducement to men to perform this dangerous service. Specie was also proposed as a bounty to men if they would enlist in the armies; yet this measure did not meet with general approval, as many thought the effect of it would be to hasten the depreciation of paper money, which was "already of little value." Specie also had been employed in the expedition against Canada. Six thousand three hundred and sixty-four pounds Pennsylvania currency, in gold and silver,[1] was obtained for the use of this expedition, which was transported as far as Ticonderoga, and remained there for many months; while debts were pouring into Congress from every quarter, to be discharged. During the entire year of 1778, while a vast amount of paper money was expended, the specie paid out was exceedingly small. In the Appendix to the Journal of Congress[2] for that year the following figures are found: —

---

[1] Secret Journal of Cong., Oct. 10, 1775.   [2] Dec. 29.

Currency	.	.	.	.	.	.	$62,154,842 63
Specie .	.	.	.	.	.	.	78,666 60
Livres .	.	.	.	.	.	.	28,525 00

This handful of solid coin, which in gold would weigh only seven hundred pounds, and might be put into a wheel-barrow, was the foundation, says Breck,[1] of the campaigns of that year.

The war, therefore, had been prosecuted thus far almost wholly with paper money. When it was proposed to capture Canada, Congress recognized the necessity of providing specie for the use of the expedition, and it was forthcoming, yet failed to see that specie was just as necessary in the campaigns at home. Though patriotism was a living force, which gave a wonderful impetus to the Revolution, — indeed, was at the bottom of it, — nevertheless, many were quite as desirous of receiving a real money equivalent for what they sold as others were to whom the principle of patriotism was a stranger. Those living south of the St. Lawrence were of the same flesh and blood as those beyond the stream, and were actuated by the same principles in making exchanges; and Congress ought more firmly to have grasped this fact. Difficult as was the effort to procure specie, it was equally difficult to extract value from a paper currency based upon nothing. The mistake of Congress was in not applying the same principles in dealing with Americans which the members proposed to apply in treating with the inhabitants of Canada.[2]

---

[1] Hist. Sketch of Cont. Paper Money, p. 13.

[2] The Canadian campaign proved a failure; and the complete annihilation of the credit of the United States in that country is illustrated by

During the year 1778 fourteen issues of paper money were authorized, aggregating $63,500,000. Two issues in December were for ten million dollars each; another issue of the same amount was ordered in September, and twenty million dollars during the months of May, June, and July. The effect of these measures was well understood, but Congress felt compelled to resort to them to raise money. Not that other measures were disregarded, as we have already seen.

the following incident, extracted from the report of the commissioners in Canada to the president of Congress: "Your army is badly paid; and so exhausted is your credit that even a cart cannot be procured without ready money or force. We will give you an instance of the lowness of your credit. Three barrels of gunpowder were ordered from Chamblay to Montreal; this powder was brought from Chamblay to a ferry, about three miles off, where it would have remained had we not luckily passed by, and, seeing the distress of the officer, undertaken to pay ready and hard money for the hire of a cart to convey it to Longueil." — *Report* dated May 27, 1776: CARROLL's *Visit to Canada in* 1776, p. 29.

CHAPTER VI.

ADMINISTRATION OF THE BOARD OF TREASURY.

1779.

ONE of the earliest financial measures of the year was a fresh attempt, on the part of Congress, to provide a fund for the liquidation of all bills of credit issued by the government, besides any additional issues that might be put forth. To this end, Congress requested the several States to raise their respective quotas of fifteen million dollars for the year 1779, and six million dollars annually for eighteen years thereafter, as a fund for sinking the emissions and loans which had now grown so numerous and heavy. As though Congress had despaired of obtaining financial aid in any other manner, it was provided "that any of the bills emitted by order of Congress, prior to the year 1780, and no others, be received in payment of the said quotas," thus restricting the use of State issues, and impairing their value; while the value of Continental money, instead of improving, was unfavorably affected by the measure. Congress had recommended the States to withdraw their bills, in payment of taxes, and in other ways; but, whether the States complied with the recommendation or not, they could not force the General Government to receive them contrary to the will of Congress. The resolutions also prescribed how the bills received within the time limited should be applied. Except those issued for the year 1779, the bills were to be applied, first, in payment of the interest, and, secondly, of the principal, of loans made by the United States prior to the year 1780; and the residue, together with those received on the quotas of the year 1779, were to be destroyed.[1]

Congress also ordered the Board of Treasury to prepare a circular letter to the States to accompany the foregoing resolves. This may be thought a very impotent enforcement of the determination of Congress; but what else could be done? It must ever be kept in mind that many of the delegates were very jealous concerning the exercise of any authority over the States by the General Government, while their constituents at home shared this feeling still more strongly. So long as such fears existed, which were often openly expressed, is it not just to suppose that Congress went to the furthest boundary of prudence in making demands upon the States?

The circular letter[2] accompanying the resolutions declared that, "from necessity" was attempted the expedient of emitting paper money on the faith of the United States, for the expenses of the war, — an expedient which had often been successfully practised in the separate States while they were subjected to British rule. The implacable vengeance with which the States had been pursued had compelled them to the most strenuous and unremitting efforts. Large issues of money, consequently, were indispensably necessary, and the paper currency had mul-

---

[1] Jan. 2, 5, 14.   [2] Jan. 13.

tiplied beyond what was competent for the purpose of a
circulating medium. "This alone could not fail to discredit it in some degree: the arts of an unprincipled
enemy have increased the mischief. In despair of sub-
duing the free spirits of America by the force of arms
or intrigues of negotiation, as their last effort they have
had recourse to fraud. Their emissaries have been employed in a variety of artifices to debase our money, and
to raise the price of commodities. The fears and apprehensions of the people have been alarmed by misrepre-
sentations, while our enemies of the highest rank have
not hesitated to counterfeit the bills of credit and dis-
perse them through the United States."

These embarrassments to a free circulation of paper
money loudly called for a remedy; and Congress, from
a regard to good faith, to private justice, and to public
safety, felt bound to apply it. To raise the value of
paper money, and to redeem it, would not be difficult;
nor would the effort to check and defeat the pernicious
circulation of counterfeits be impracticable. Without
public inconvenience or private distress, the whole of
the debt incurred in paper emissions might be cancelled
by taxes, and within a period so limited as to leave the
possessor of the bills satisfied with his security; and if,
by a continuance of the war, the public service should
demand further emissions, they, too, might be cancelled
within the same period, " it being evident that our ability
to sustain a tax must increase in proportion to the quantity of money in circulation."

The danger from counterfeits could only be avoided
by calling in and exchanging the emissions with which

the counterfeiter had chiefly busied himself. To publish the marks of detection, and still leave the true bills current, would not be prudent, as it would afford an opportunity of correcting defects, and cheating more securely.

"To defend the emission intended for the exchange from counterfeit, the strongest guards will be devised, and it is expected that the marks of authenticity will be so obvious, and the difficulty of successful imitation so great, as to discourage the attempt or elude its effects."

Congress evidently had a premonition of the immense amount of paper money to be put afloat during the year; for the Committee of the Treasury were authorized to contract with proper persons to act as signers of the bills for the year, whose remuneration was not to exceed four dollars per thousand for each signer.[1] Just before this action, Congress had ordered another issue,[2] which was to be exchanged for the counterfeits withdrawn from circulation, and, during the first four months of the year, $65,000,880 were issued. Congress also sought to procure a domestic loan for twenty million dollars more.[3]

The effect of these enormous emissions was to impair irretrievably the value of all the issues; yet Congress, unmindful of the extremely critical condition of the finances, and without attempting to devise proper remedies, was engaged in a profitless and discreditable controversy with Silas Deane concerning his conduct as one of the commissioners of the United States to the French court.

[1] Jan. 4, 13.   [2] Jan. 2.   [3] Feb. 3.

It may not be without interest to the reader to stop for a moment and look at a picture of the condition of the country, drawn by a Frenchman, Baron de Bonstellin,[1] who had followed the fortunes of Lafayette, and was at this time serving as lieutenant-colonel in the army: "This country is in a state of languor and despair, or rather anarchy, for every one does as he pleases, from whence proceed the greatest horrors and calamities imaginable. Among other things the dearness of provisions, and of every other necessary of life exceeds all example. Nothing is to be seen but Congress paper, which is so depreciated, that a piastre in money is worth twelve or fifteen in paper. Few ships come here, on account of the little value of Congress paper, and that there is nothing but tobacco to be had in return, which bears a very low price in France at this time. It was with the utmost difficulty that they could procure a little flour for d'Estaing's fleet, and it requires every exertion they can make to supply their own army which, after all, is wretchedly provided. Upon the whole, this country suffers more from its internal management, than from the war itself, and if peace is not soon made, and good order re-established, it will experience such revolutions as are shocking to think of. The Congress likewise are perplexed how to act, having lost all authority over the people. Every one proceeds with caution; distress and misery are daily increasing."

Paper money had depreciated so much by the last of May, that the president of the Council of Pennsylvania, and other gentlemen, presented a memorial to Congress,

---

[1] Newspaper Cuttings, vol. v. p. 215, N. Y. Hist. Lib.

setting forth their hardships, and asking for co-operation and relief.[1] Their object was to avert an impending popular movement. A public meeting had been called, for the purpose of considering the subject of depreciation, and it was feared, that, if the people grew excited, they might become violent. The petition was referred to the Treasury Board, and their report, which was an address to the States, declared that the present situation of public affairs demanded the most serious attention, especially that the condition of the currency required the immediate, strenuous, and united efforts of all true friends to their country for preventing an extension of the mischiefs which had already flowed from that source.

Having declared that Congress was "obliged to emit paper money,"[2] the policy was defended by affirming the people knew this expedient had "been before generally and successfully practised on this Continent." Congress was sensible of the inconveniences — a very mild term in which to express the consequences of using paper money — which would attend too frequent emissions, and had endeavored to avoid them. For this purpose, loan-offices were established as early as October, 1775; and, from that time to the present, Congress had repeatedly and earnestly solicited the people to loan their money on the faith of the United States. Nevertheless, the sums received in this way had proved unequal to the public exigencies. In consequence of the activity of the enemy, both on sea and land, taxation at home, and borrowing abroad, had been alike impracticable. Hence the necessity of continuing emissions of paper money.

----

[1] Phillips, p. 118.   [2] May 26.

But depreciation was not imputed to these causes alone. "We have too much reason to believe it has been in part owing to the artifices of men who have hastened to enrich themselves by monopolizing the necessaries of life, and to the misconduct of inferior officers employed in the public service." Vain, indeed, were the efforts of Congress to form plans of economy, to stop emissions of paper money, if the people did not zealously co-operate in promoting this design, and use the utmost industry to prevent the waste of money in every branch of service. A compliance with the recommendations for supplying money, it was properly added, might enable Congress to give speedy answers to the public, that no more emissions should take place, and thereby close that source of depreciation.

At the same time, Congress "judged it indispensably necessary" to call for forty-five million dollars in addition to the fifteen millions asked at the beginning of the year, which the States were requested to pay into the Continental treasury as soon as possible, and, at the farthest, before the end of the year. Probably this was not a very acceptable reply to many a grumbler; but what better answer could Congress make? Every conceivable way had been tried to raise money beside resorting to paper emissions.

The delegates from Rhode Island were opposed to raising so large a sum from the States; but they were almost alone in their opposition, as the representatives from only one other State shared similar views. William Ellery,[1] one of the Rhode-Island delegates, wrote to Gov.

---

[1] May 25, 1779, Staples's Hist. of R. I. in the Cont. Cong., p. 235.

Greene, that the great majority on this occasion, and the declarations made by members during the course of the debate, led him to believe that great exertions would be made by the States to collect their quotas. He then adds, " The more that is collected by taxation, the less it will be necessary to loan, in order to put a stop to further emissions, which is the wish of all. A stoppage of the press once effected, our liberties are established, and an end is put to the war. Our enemy's whole dependence now rests upon our being crushed with whole reams of depreciated paper money. Once remove that ground of hope and they will offer us honorable terms of peace."

The people of Philadelphia, alarmed at the condition of the money, and desirous of aiding the government, adopted a plan at a town-meeting[1] for stopping the paper issues of Pennsylvania, and for raising a revenue by subscription. It was known as "The Citizen's Plan;"[2] and, in the address directed to the President and Supreme Executive Council of the State, they were requested to confer with Congress on the subject, and to urge that body to recommend the general adoption of the plan. The Executive Council were also requested to transmit the scheme to the several States, under the sanction of their recommendation; while the citizens themselves resolved to send the plan to citizens of each State at the earliest opportunity. The people were divided upon the efficiency of this measure; and President Reed[3] of Pennsylvania wrote that an interesting struggle was

[1] Penn. Packet, July 27, 1779.   [2] Penn. Archives, vol. vii. p. 621.
[3] Ibid., p. 572.

going on concerning the Continental money, as to whether it would die without hope of resuscitation, or whether, by a vigorous political effort, it would emerge from the trial, having the confidence and value imposed in it during the earlier days. When received by Congress, the plan was referred to the Board of Treasury.

Shortly after the address of Congress, which has been briefly sketched, two committees were appointed, — one to make thorough inquiry "into the establishments and contingent expenses of the respective boards and departments," and to report what retrenchment and reformation seemed expedient: the other to conduct a more special investigation, with reference to the expense of the medical commissary-general and quartermaster-general's departments.[1] These had grown enormous, and it was generally believed that this state of things had arisen from " allowing commissions to the numerous persons employed in purchasing for the army." Truly there was urgent need of investigation. Extravagance had crept into every department, nor was corruption unknown even in those early days.

These committees suggested improvements in the manner of keeping the paymaster-general's office, also that the governors of the States should be requested to make an inquiry into the conduct of those employed to transact the business of the General Government, for the purpose of removing suspected persons, and of securing various other needed reforms.[2] Not the least among the reforms at this time executed was the removal of Dr.

---

[1] May 28.   [2] May 29, July 9.

Morgan, director-general of the hospitals and physician-in-chief to the armies.[1]

Congress might have discovered a way of saving much by altering the mode of enlistments in the army. The policy of enlisting men for a short time had been continued from the beginning, notwithstanding the contrary advice of Washington and others, who clearly saw the great expense and other evils growing out of the prevailing system. "Had my advice," says Washington,[2] writing in August, 1779, "respecting this matter been pursued in the years '75 and '76, our money would have been upon a very different establishment in point of credit to what it is at this day, and we should have saved millions of pounds in bounty money, and the consequent evils of expiring armies and new levies." Yet the old system was continued, notwithstanding the obvious economy and efficiency of permanent enlistments.

The next effort of Congress in the way of raising money outside of the old expedient of issuing more bills of credit was a loan of twenty million dollars which Congress vainly hoped would be raised by the loan-offices.[3] The States were recommended to appoint per-

---

[1] Independent Chronicle, Sept. 9, 1779.

[2] Letter to Reed, Reed's Life of Reed, vol. ii. p. 124.

[3] June 11. Ellery and Collins, delegates from Rhode Island, wrote to Gov. Greene of that State, June 4, 1779, "Congress has ordered a loan of twenty millions continental dollars, but has not yet agreed upon the terms of borrowing. As it may be very difficult to collect our quota of the continental tax in season, would it not be advisable to hire a part of it at a moderate interest, to be paid when the tax should be collected. It is thought that those who hold considerable sums, would be willing to lend on this occasion. Every effort will be made by

sons of character and influence in every county, town, and district, to receive subscriptions. None were to be taken for less than five hundred dollars, and, if any person subscribed ten thousand dollars or more, he might pay one-half of the subscription within fourteen days from the time of subscribing, and the remainder before the first of October; and, by way of an inducement to make so large a subscription, the whole amount was to draw interest from the time of the first payment, provided the balance was punctually paid. Each lender was to elect, either to receive the principal at the expiration of three years from the date of the loan, or to continue it on interest "until the whole amount of Continental bills circulating shall not exceed the sum in circulation at the time of the loan." One of the greatest difficulties in this scheme was to regulate the payment of interest, since the Continental money was depreciating, and payment of six or seven per cent might turn out to be an exceedingly small compensation for the use of the money. It is true that Congress, until this time, had stoutly maintained the worth of Continental paper money; but the bill which finally passed on the 29th of June clearly recognized the fact of depreciation. Considerable discussion arose in determining the rate of interest, and the subject was repeatedly taken up and postponed before reaching a conclusion. In the end, it was decided that interest

Congress to put our finances on such a footing as to stop any further emission of money; and it is hoped that every friend to his country will lend his aid to give efficiency to this measure." — STAPLES. *Hist. of R.I. in the Cont. Cong.*, p. 241.

should be paid annually at the loan-offices where the money was subscribed; and then follows the resolution which puzzled Congress so long: "When the interest on monies which have been or may be placed in the several loan offices on or after the first day of March, 1778, shall become due and be paid, the same, until some more accurate standard of value can be devised, shall be increased in proportion to the increase of the sum of Continental paper money which may be in circulation after the date of such loans respectively."[1] Such was the result of the deliberations of Congress in dealing for the first time with the question of a depreciated money. Doubtless, the members did this tremblingly; for they must have seen what a blow they were to give to paper money, the force of which the public would soon inevitably feel.

On the 16th of August the Board of Treasury reported a table of the first year's interest to be paid on moneys which had been placed in the several Continental loan-offices between March and September, 1778, calculated for each day on which the money had been lent, in pursuance of the resolve regulating the interest payable on the public loan, whereupon the board was directed to take proper measures for carrying out the resolution.

While Congress was trying to borrow money through the agency of the loan-offices, that body still contrived to push out paper money into the fearfully swollen stream. Between the first of May and first of September, $35,000,480 had been issued; yet there seemed to be no other resource. Efforts to borrow money had succeeded

---

[1] June 18, 23, 25, 29.

poorly, taxes were reluctantly paid, foreign loans were negotiated with extreme difficulty, and, whatever could be done in that way, Franklin, Adams, Jay, and other agents had accomplished. On the 26th of August the Board of Treasury were directed to lay before Congress, by the 10th of September, an account of the money received at the loan-offices to that date, and also the amount of paper emissions then afloat. Concluding that an absolute limit ought to be fixed to the emission of bills of credit, Congress resolved that on no account should more than $200,000,000 be emitted, nor any more, indeed, provided a sufficient supply of money for the public exigencies could be obtained in any other way.[1] Two days later the same declaration was repeated.

Not long afterward, Congress issued another address to their constituents.[2] The debt was described as consisting of $159,948,880 already emitted and circulating; money borrowed before the first of March, 1778, amounting to $7,545,196, bearing interest payable in France; money borrowed since that time, the interest of which was payable in America, $26,188,909. Other sums due abroad, but not exactly known, the balance not having been transmitted, were estimated at $4,000,000. Not more than $3,027,560 had been brought into the treasury in the way of taxes; so that all the funds supplied to Congress by the people of America did not exceed $36,761,665. "Judge then," says the address, "of the necessity of emissions and loans, from whom and from whence that necessity arose."

The swelling of prices incident to the issue of so much

<hr>

[1] Sept. 1.   [2] Sept. 13.

money was considered, and also the necessity of providing troops and supplies to continue the war, after which Congress proceeded to discuss the causes of the depreciation of paper money: "The depreciation of bills of credit is always either natural or artificial, or both. The latter is our case. The moment the sum in circulation exceeded what was necessary as a medium in commerce, it began and continued to depreciate in proportion as the amount of the surplus increased; and that proportion would hold good until the sum emitted should become so great as nearly to equal the value of the capital or stock, on the credit of which the bills were issued. Supposing, therefore, that $30,000,000 was necessary for a circulating medium, and that $160,000,000 had issued, the natural depreciation is but little more than as five to one: but the actual depreciation exceeds that proportion, and that excess is artificial. The natural depreciation is to be removed only by lessening the quantity of money in circulation. It will regain its primitive value whenever it shall be reduced to the sum necessary for a medium of commerce. This is only to be effected by loans and taxes."

The artificial depreciation was regarded as a more serious matter. It had grown out of distrust entertained by the mass of the people, either in the ability or inclination of the United States to redeem their bills. The ability of the United States to redeem them depended, first, upon the success of the present Revolution, and, secondly, on the sufficiency of the natural wealth, value, and resources of the country.

Having shown the certainty of success in the Revolution, the reasoning in the address on the second point was as follows: "Let us suppose for the sake of argument, that at the conclusion of the war, the emissions should amount to $200,000,000; that exclusive of supplies from taxes, which will not be inconsiderable, the loans should amount to $100,000,000, then the whole national debt of the United States would be $300,000,000. There are at present 3,000,000 of inhabitants in the thirteen States; three hundred million of dollars, divided among three million of people, would give to each person one hundred dollars; and is there an individual in America unable, in the course of eighteen or twenty years, to pay it again? Suppose the whole debt assessed, as it ought to be, on the inhabitants in proportion to their respective estates, what would then be the share of the poorer people? Perhaps not ten dollars. Besides, as this debt will not be payable immediately, but probably twenty years allotted for it, the number of inhabitants by that time in America will be far more than double their present amount." Thus a great part of the debt would be payable, not merely by the present number of inhabitants, but by a large addition attracted thither from the Old World. "Let it be remembered that paper money is the only kind of money which cannot '*make unto itself wings and fly away.*' It remains with us, it will not forsake us, it is always ready and at hand for the purpose of commerce or taxes, and every industrious man can find it."

Thus far the address proceeded very glibly; but the second portion, relating to the inclination of the people to pay the debt, it was not so easy to write in hopeful and inspiring language. Three questions were considered: —

Whether, and in what manner, the faith of the United States had been pledged for the redemption of their bills;

Whether they had put themselves in a political capacity to redeem them ; and

Whether, admitting the two former propositions, there was any reason to apprehend a wanton violation of the public faith?

The first two questions Congress found no difficulty in answering ; for, assuredly, if ever a government had pledged its faith, Congress again and again had pledged the public faith in respect to the payment of the bills of credit issued by their authority. Concerning the second question, Congress declared that, " there does at present exist a perfect solemn confederation, and therefore that the States now are and always will be in political capacity to redeem their bills, pay their debts and settle their accounts."

In regard to the apprehension of a wanton violation of the public faith, Congress, with a lofty indignation, declared it was with great regret and reluctance that "we can prevail upon ourselves to take the least notice of a question which involves in it a doubt so injurious to the honor and dignity of America." In the same high-toned language Congress proceeds: "We should pay an ill compliment to the understanding and honor of every true American, were we to adduce many arguments to show the baseness or bad policy of violating our national faith, or omitting to pursue the measures necessary to preserve it. A bankrupt faithless republic would be a novelty in the political world, and appear among respectable nations like a common prostitute among chaste and respectable matrons. The pride of America revolts from the idea: her citizens know for what purposes these emissions were made, and have repeatedly pledged their faith for the redemption of them; they are to be found in every man's possession, and every man is interested in their being redeemed, they must therefore entertain a high opinion of American credulity, who suppose the people capable of believing, on due reflection, that all America will, against the faith, the honor and the interest of all America be ever prevailed upon to countenance, support, or permit so ruinous, so disgraceful a measure."

Such are the main points of this remarkable address, which ought to have stirred the heart of every patriot to renewed exertions in aiding the weak and throttled government. Congress had been frank, and had told the people the worst, — an example worthy of imitation in all governments and great institutions. Nothing was concealed: the enormous indebtedness, the weakness of the government, the necessity of the States coming to the rescue, were set forth in the pure color of truth. Congress now determined to make stricter requisitions upon the States. This could be done, because the success of the Revolution was assured, and the people had relinquished all hope of reconciliation with Great Britain. Besides, the members of Congress had recovered from their fright, and now realized the absolute necessity of getting relief from the States, or else of seizing whatever was needed in order to sustain the armies, and carry on the war. Therefore, in October,[1] it was re-

---

[1] Oct. 6, 7.

solved to call upon the States for fifteen million dollars in addition to previous sums, which they were to raise in such a manner as they deemed most expedient, and which were to be paid into the Continental treasury, or to the order of Congress, in monthly instalments, between the first days of February and of October following. They were also charged with interest at six per cent upon all deficiencies in the several quotas previously requested. To encourage persons to make loans of ten thousand dollars or more, the time for making them was extended; and, when one-half of such a loan was paid, the whole was to bear interest, if the balance were forthcoming within two months from the time of the first payment.

At the same time this action was taken, a letter was sent to the States,[1] telling them the paper money that Congress was at liberty to emit would probably be expended by the beginning of December, after which time supplies must be furnished by the States. The prospect was dark enough; yet Congress cherished the hope, that, by means of taxes and other salutary measures, the prices of things would be reduced, the quotas asked, in part at least, be paid, and, after paying other expenses, a balance be left to apply on the public debt.

Before the close of November two hundred million dollars of paper money had been issued, the final issue slightly exceeding five million dollars.[2] During the year, $140,052,480 had been thrown into circulation, — nearly three-fourths of the entire amount issued during the war. No wonder why such a vast mass so soon sunk out of sight.

---

[1] Oct. 9.   [2] Oct. 14, Nov. 17, 29.

The fountain of paper money having become completely dry, and the army being in a very reduced condition, Congress requested the States to furnish supplies of corn, wheat, and flour.[1] Virginia was requested to furnish twenty thousand barrels of Indian corn, and transport it to certain places indicated by the commissary-general; while the Legislatures of Maryland and other States were requested to furnish other specific supplies.[2] A few days later,[3] all the States were asked to contribute supplies; and each one was at liberty to furnish such things as best suited its convenience. Supplies thus furnished were credited as though money had been advanced. Clothing also was seized; and, having been appraised, Congress ordered payment for the amount. Thus the year ended with an exhaustion of the paper-money scheme; and the systems of seizure and State supplies of provisions and other necessaries begun. Severe, indeed, were these expedients; yet had not Dionysius, Lacheres, Tachus, and other Greek leaders, seized and appropriated the wealth of the heathen temples for the benefit of the State two thousand years before? and had not even the many-gifted Pericles advised the Athenians to remove a portion of the gold which covered the statue of Minerva for the same patriotic purpose?

[1] Oct. 18.   [2] Dec. 11.   [3] Dec. 14.

CHAPTER VII.

ADMINISTRATION OF THE BOARD OF TREASURY.

1780.

CONGRESS ceased to issue paper money when it became so worthless that nothing could be obtained for it in exchange. Without question, the disastrous consequences attending the issue of paper money were seen by every member of that body; for they were so fearful as to startle every one who cared any thing for his country. Not from lack of wisdom, but from necessity, did Congress continue to sow unhealthy seed long after it was known what manner of fruit would inevitably grow. Money must be had from some source, and from this one something could be obtained, though at much cost. During these troubled years Congress had not been idle: numerous experiments had been devised and tried, as we have seen; and Congress was ever ready to adopt any new scheme which gave promise of relief. It must be borne in mind how weak Congress was in authority over the States; not much more could be done than to recommend measures to them for their adoption. Congress could not appoint tax-gatherers, and send them forth with arbitrary instructions to collect taxes, notwithstanding the urgency of the measure. Such an exercise of power on the part of Congress would have been regarded everywhere as an usurpation, and would not have been tolerated for a moment. All that Congress could do had been done, namely, to recommend taxation to the States, to ask for loans, and apportion them among the States as perfectly as the knowledge of the members would permit. Congress had tried to borrow money at home and abroad, to raise it by lottery, and, lastly, it was found necessary to ask the States to furnish specific supplies to the army to prevent the troops from starving or disbanding. This mode of obtaining supplies was an extremely arbitrary one, and involved the government in a fresh set of evils. But the plan found many eminent advocates. Not the least among the defects of the scheme arose from the distance between the army and some of the States furnishing supplies, the transportation of which cost more than they were worth at the points where they were sent for consumption. Other consequences of a still graver character will be described in another part of this narrative.[1]

[1] "The present mode of supplying the army by state purchases," Hamilton wrote in September, 1780, "is not one of the least considerable defects of our system. It is too precarious a dependence, because the states will never be sufficiently impressed with our necessities. Each will make its own case a primary object, the supply of the army a secondary one. The variety of channels through which the business is transacted, will multiply the number of persons employed, and the opportunities of embezzling public money. From the popular spirit on which most of the governments turn, the state agents will be men of less character and ability; nor will there be so rigid a responsibility among them as there might easily be among those in the employ of the continent; of course not so much diligence, care, or economy. Very little of the money raised in the several states will go into the continental treasury, on pretence that it is all exhausted in providing the

While the army was in winter-quarters at Morristown, Hamilton gave the first proofs of his great genius for finance, which were so strikingly displayed a few years later, when acting as the chief executive of the treasury department. He addressed a lengthy letter to Robert Morris, in which the causes of the depreciation of paper money were discussed, the impossibility of obtaining by taxation all the means needed to maintain the government, and, consequently, the necessity of getting pecuniary assistance from other nations. He next proceeded to consider how the means thus acquired should be employed. Two plans, he affirmed, had been suggested; the first was that of purchasing the paper issued by the government, a plan which he opposed because it would cause a rapid artificial appreciation of the paper; while the other plan, of converting the loan into merchandise, and importing it on public account, though less objectionable than the other, was, after all, very defective. The plan proposed by himself was to establish a national bank, the details of which were carefully sketched. He also affirmed that Congress ought immediately to appoint a minister of finance, and closed by saying that he should be very happy to hear that Congress had said, " Thou art the man." [1]

quotas of supplies, and the public will be without funds for the other demands of government. The expense will be ultimately much greater, and the advantage much smaller. We actually feel the insufficiency of this plan, and have reason to dread, under it, a ruinous extremity of want." (*Hist. of Repub.*, vol. ii. p. 94.) Hamilton's fears were well grounded; for the army was less adequately supplied than ever, while the system imposed so much discretionary authority upon officials, that corruption among them became still more prevalent.

[1] Works, vol. i. p. 116.

The letter evinces a complete grasp of the situation, and of the measures necessary to extricate the country from financial peril. The financial legislation of Congress, though showing considerable fertility of plan, was generally tentative and narrow, resting, for the most part, upon no broad and enduring principles, and devised chiefly for the present exigency. Among so many blunderers it is refreshing to see a mind emerge like that of Hamilton, displaying a profound mastery of the situation.

The plan of calling upon the States for specific supplies, adopted toward the close of 1779, was resumed in February [1] the year following. A more minute request was made to the States for certain quantities of beef, rum, salt, hay, flour, corn, pork, &c. For the articles thus furnished, the States were to be credited at prices fixed by Congress, and the taxes which they had been directed to pay were reduced to five millions in consequence of this new order, though this latter portion of the resolution was soon after repealed. It was also determined that the accounts between the General Government and the States should "be kept and finally settled in Spanish milled dollars and the balance finally be paid in specie."

Massachusetts, through her delegate Gerry, [2] found fault with this apportionment, deeming the burden imposed upon her too large by any just principle of assessment. She had willingly contributed freely of her resources, and at last, becoming jealous of an attempt on the part of the other members of the Confederacy to load her with an unreasonable weight, she resolved to obtain

---

[1] Feb. 25.   [2] See Austin's Life of Gerry, vol. i. p. 319.

some relief. The discussion that followed was bitter and protracted, and led to the resignation of Gerry; but finally the opposition of Massachusetts died away, on account, doubtless, of the feeble compliance by the States, and Massachusetts among the rest, of the resolves of Congress. Had Massachusetts been compelled to execute the measure, she probably would have sought to abate the apportionment before making any more contributions.

Although this scheme was elaborated with considerable skill, it was soon found to be impracticable; and Congress evolved another measure, fraught with the gravest consequences.[1] This was nothing less than a redemption of all the Continental money by new issues, based upon the credit of the States, at a discount of forty dollars of the old emission for one of the new. Silver and gold, also, were to be receivable at the same rate, and, so fast as the bills were presented for the discharge of past contracts, they were to be destroyed. The new issue was not to exceed one-twentieth part of the nominal value of those destroyed: in other words, was not to exceed ten million dollars. They were redeemable within six years, and bore interest at the rate of five per cent per annum, which was to be paid at the time of redeeming the bills, or, "at the election of the holder, annually, at the respective Continental loan offices, in sterling bills of exchange, drawn by the United States on their Ministers in Europe, at 4s. 6d. sterling per dollar." It was further provided, that, in case any State was incapable, by the events of war, from redeeming those emitted upon its credit, the

---

[1] March 18.

United States were to pay them; which undertaking was to be indorsed thereon. The face of this new emission read as follows: —

The possessor of this bill shall be paid   Spanish milled dollars by the 31st day of December, 1786, with interest, in like money, at the rate of five per cent. per annum by the State of   according to an Act of the Legislature of the said State of the   day of   , 1780.

Accompanied with the following indorsement: —

The United States insure the payment of the within bill, and will draw bills of exchange for the interest annually if demanded, according to a resolution of Congress on the 18th day of March, 1780.

The new bills were struck, under the direction of the Board of Treasury, in due proportion for each State, determined by their monthly quotas, and were lodged in the several Continental loan-offices; but they were to be issued only in proportion of one to twenty of other bills returned and destroyed. Six-tenths of the quantity issued were to be used by the States; the balance was to be sent to the Board of Treasury for general use. The States were also directed to raise a sum sufficient to sink or redeem one-sixth part of the whole amount every year. Congress, hopeful of every new-born plan, notwithstanding the fearful shock given to the public from the issue of so much paper money, had at least one member who was sanguine concerning the measure, if the States could only be induced to do their duty: this was Ellsworth of Connecticut. In his letter to Gov. Trumbull,[1] he de-

---

[1] Hamilton, Hist. of Repub., vol. ii. p. 76.

clares: "This is precisely the point of time for the several Legislatures to act decidedly, and in a manner that the world will forever call wise. It is now in their power by a single operation to give a sure establishment for public credit; to realize the public debt at its just value; and without adding to the burdens of the people, to supply the Treasury." "This measure," justly remarks a writer, "from which so much was expected, was entirely in a wrong direction. It was, however, in the spirit of the new articles of confederation, and substituted the credit of the States with a mere illusory ultimate pledge for that of the Union."

An Act of so grave a character, as may easily be imagined, could not be passed without creating much excitement among the people. By many it was heartily approved; while others condemned it in unsparing terms. It met with approval in Connecticut, as did also the plan previously adopted by Congress, asking the States for specific supplies. The merchants of Hartford issued an address declaring, that notwithstanding the losses they had sustained by sea, the depreciation of Continental currency, and the receiving of payment of many debts at a nominal sum, they were willing and determined to sell their merchandise to the public at the rates affixed by Congress, and to receive the new emissions therefor, "having a firm reliance that the bills will be punctually and justly redeemed. And we do assure ourselves that our brethren, the farmers and tradesmen, will be as ready as we are to furnish, in the same manner we do, their produce and manufactures, as we believe a spirit of harmony and friendship is like to prevail between the trade and landed interest, and that all orders of men in this State are resolved immediately to contribute all in their power to furnish supplies for the armies of the United States, and to continue these supplies to the end of the war." As further proof of their good intentions, the merchants besought the Assembly to direct the "purchasing commissary" to purchase such things as they had at their disposal, in order to show their willingness to comply with the action of Congress and of the State.[1]

Two months after the Act was passed, at a public meeting in Philadelphia, a German said,[2] "I am near seventy years of age, I have a large family of children to provide for, a great part of my property has been sold long since for Continental money, which I have kept by me in confidence it would have been redeemed at the value I received it; but I am disappointed and ruined. My loss is very heavy, and it greatly afflicts me; yet the insolent triumph of my disappointed neighbors wounds me still more deeply, but I will never forsake the cause of liberty and turn Tory; if I die of a broken heart, I will die a friend of my country." This was an exhibition of patriotism rivalling that displayed by Greece and

---

[1] Penn. Packet, May 6, 1780. Gerry wrote to John Adams, May 5, 1780: "The resolutions of congress for calling in and cancelling the two hundred millions of dollars emitted by them, have in general been well received. The depreciation is stopped, and specie, which before the passing of the resolves, was sold for upwards of seventy for one, is now current at sixty, and has been lately at fifty-five. The advantage of this plan will be great to the landholder, inasmuch as the national debt, including certificates and foreign demands, does not now much exceed five millions sterling." — J. ADAMS's *Works*, vol. vii. p. 188.

[2] Penn. Packet, May 9, 1780.

Rome in the height of their glory, and which was a mighty force in sustaining the anxious leaders of the infant republic. This German, whose name is lost to us, expressed the sentiments of many others who were injured or ruined by the forty-for-one Act, but who, nevertheless, retained their devotion to their country.

In August, Gen. Armstrong,[1] a very intelligent observer, wrote to a friend, " How the scheme of business and finance contained in the resolution of the 18th of March last will operate for our relief is yet uncertain but doubted by too many ; for altho' it is considered by many good judges to be at once just and wise respecting the public at large, yet various individuals suppose themselves injured or disappointed by fixing the money at forty to one, and therefore decry the measure." In a subsequent chapter the effects of the Act will be more minutely traced.

Two days after the Act was passed, the States were recommended to revise their laws, making Continental bills of credit a tender in discharge of debts and contracts, and " to amend the same in such manner as they shall judge most conducive to justice in the present state of paper currency."

It was not long before the States were asked to pay into the Continental treasury ten million dollars, for the purpose of bringing the army into the field, and of furnishing it with supplies.[2] This sum was to be credited to the States on their quotas then due to the govern-

---

[1] He wrote from Philadelphia, Aug. 3, Hist. Mag. vol. viii. p. 16, 1864.

[2] May 19.

ment. At the same time, the Board of Treasury were directed to draw bills on Dr. Franklin for twenty-five thousand dollars, and upon Mr. Jay for a similar sum, which were to be sold in Massachusetts, Rhode Island, Connecticut, Pennsylvania, Maryland, and Virginia. If more supplies were needed from the States than those specified in a previous resolve, they were to be taken by a committee appointed for that purpose, upon the advice of the commander-in-chief of the army, and with the consent of the legislative or executive power of the States. The committee also were to give assurance, that, for the things thus "purchased or otherwise procured on the credit of the United States," their true value was to be paid, "with interest at six per cent as fast as money can be raised for that purpose."[1] Certificates given in this way multiplied rapidly; yet, as they were receivable for taxes, all was not lost in receiving them.

The condition of the army in respect to subsistence and payment was more critical now than at any former period of the war.[2] The officers and men had not been

---

[1] June 1.

[2] Charles Petit, acting quartermaster-general, wrote from Philadelphia, July 13, 1780: "The Continental Treasury is wretchedly poor, and affords so little, or at least so little comes from it to me, that I have no money at command on the most pressing emergencies" (GREENE'S *Life of Greene*, vol. ii. p. 313). Hamilton wrote in December, from Morristown, "I find our prospects are infinitely worse than they have been at any period of the war, and unless some expedient can be instantly adopted, a dissolution of the army for want of subsistence is unavoidable. A part of it has been, again, several days without bread, and for the rest, we have not, either on the spot or within reach, a supply sufficient for four days. Nor does this deficiency proceed from accidental circumstances, as has been the case on former occasions, but

paid for several months, and, even when they were, the money received was only such in name. All the efforts to induce the States to forward supplies proved nearly fruitless, and several officers were compelled to resign their commissions. Washington feared the loss of many officers of rare experience and value, and he exerted himself to the utmost to persuade Congress to grant relief. When all hope seemed to have fled, the citizens of Philadelphia formed an association to procure a supply of articles for the suffering soldiers.

When the spirit of the Roman Government, near the close of the first Punic war, grew faint, as the resources of the nation began to fail, the citizens awoke, and by a purely voluntary act gave the government money enough to build and equip a new fleet, with which a decisive victory was won : so now, when the prospect was cheerless, as the means to continue the war seemed to be nearly spent, the ladies of Philadelphia inspired a new hope by making a generous contribution for the relief of the suffering soldiers; which movement, doubtless it was, that roused the other sex to put forth a still greater effort in the same direction. When their plan was perfected, Congress was informed by letter[1] of the creation of a bank for the purpose of assisting the government, and of the desire on the part of the directors to confer with a committee, appointed by Congress, upon the subject. Gladly complying with the request, the committee

from the absolute emptiness of our magazines everywhere, and the total want of money or credit to replenish them. We have never experienced a like extremity at any period of the war." — *Hist. of Repub.*, vol. i. p. 566.

[1] June 21.

reported to Congress the next day the end sought to be accomplished: it was to supply three million rations and three hundred hogsheads of rum to the army, with the expectation of receiving a re-imbursement from foreign loans. As the bank expected to make nothing out of the enterprise, but was a purely patriotic effort, Congress pledged the faith of the United States to the subscribers of the bank for their indemnity; and the Board of Treasury were directed to deposit therein bills of exchange to the amount of a hundred and fifty thousand pounds, to secure the bank in this undertaking.[1] If occasional assistance were needed, Congress promised to advance as much as could be spared from other sources. The amount contributed in this way in gold and silver was two hundred and sixty thousand pounds.[2]

A financial picture drawn at that time by Gen. Cornell,[3] in Philadelphia, is not less true than startling: "The situation of our finances is such as to make every thinking man shudder. The new money ordered into circulation by the resolution of the 18th of March meets with so many obstructions I almost despair of the credit it will have in the States that comply with the resolution. If that should fail, good God, what will be our fate, without money or credit at home or abroad? We have not one farthing of money in the Treasury, and I know of no quarter from which we have a right to expect any. Yet we go on contented, pleasing ourselves with the

[1] June 22.

[2] Niles's Princ. and Acts of the Rev., p. 236. Robert Morris subscribed ten thousand pounds.

[3] Letter to Gen. Greene, Aug. 13, 1780, Greene's Life of Greene, vol. ii. p. 323.

sanguine hopes of reducing New York. I have seen many new scenes before I came to this place. But what I have experienced since, exceeds any thing I have ever seen before. I never before saw a set of men that could quietly submit to every kind of difficulty that tended to the ruin of their country, without endeavoring to make one effort to remove the obstruction. I believe they wish their country well, but suffer their time almost wholly to be taken up in business of no consequence."

By the last of August,[1] paper money had become so unpopular, that the quartermaster and commissary-general were directed to issue all certificates thereafter for specie, "or other current money equivalent," which were to bear interest at six per cent, from the time stipulated for their payment, until paid. Such action was taken in conformity with Pickering's suggestion.[2] But this measure of giving certificates, as already shown, was fraught with the gravest dangers: it could not be justified, save upon the extreme ground of necessity. The State agents were required[3] to transmit to the commander-in-chief, as well as to the commissary-general, monthly returns of the provisions coming into their hands, and the States were recommended to compel a prompt obedience of the order; yet the agents were exceedingly remiss in complying, and the States did nothing in the way of compelling them to make returns. Congress soon learned some of the difficulties growing out of the use of these certificates; for it was affirmed, in a letter sent to the States not long afterward, that "they continue to obstruct every

<hr>

[1] Aug. 23, 26.   [2] Pickering's Life of Pick. vol. i. p. 255.
[3] Oct. 24.

plan which hath been devised for restoring public credit and supporting the war." [1]

On the 5th of September, another loan of a million dollars in specie value was offered to the public. From this time henceforth, all moneys loaned were received at a specie valuation.

The final measure of the year, of a financial nature, was a recommendation to the States to levy a tax equal in value to six million silver dollars, to be paid, partly in specific articles at prices fixed in the Act itself, and the balance in gold and silver, or bills of credit of the new emission.[2] Previous to this time, New Hampshire, Massachusetts, Connecticut, and other States, had been requested to furnish supplies for the army.[3]

Congress, amid a mountain of trials, succeeded in pulling the country through another year of war. It is wonderful how much the army endured; yet soldiers and officers neither fainted nor faltered, though desertions were not infrequent. Perhaps more suffering was experienced from lack of funds than from any other cause; still it is impossible to describe the evil consequences of a constantly depreciating money which unsettled values, and embarrassed all exchange.

Throughout the year, Congress was constantly adjusting salaries and accounts to prevent losses by the depreciation of paper money.[4] The adjustment of interest on public loans was the most serious question with which Congress wrestled. How could lenders be compensated,

---

[1] Jan. 15, 1781.　　[2] Nov. 4.　　[3] Sept. 15, 19, 21.

[4] See especially the action of Congress, Dec. 31, 1779, Jan. 1, 15, 27, of the following year.

without loss either to themselves or to the government? It was finally determined to pay them in hard money, giving each creditor as much as his paper money was worth at the time the government received it.[1] But how was the scale of depreciation to be ascertained? All was uncertainty, and no fixed rule prevailed anywhere. " A progressive rule of depreciation " was finally evolved, though there is good reason for doubting whether, in the application of it, much clamor did not arise.

While Congress was so seriously pressed for funds, the country was literally overrun with cash. The English and French armies had brought thither large sums ; a considerable quantity also had come from Havana. Says a writer, whose statement there is no reason for questioning, " hard money was never more plenty or more easily collected than at that time."[2]

Congress had done much in the way of methodizing business. By degrees, order was evolving from chaos: accounts were more regularly kept, even if there were funds enough to discharge only a small portion of them. Especially in the regulation of the affairs of the army, Congress passed a large number of resolves, the chief purpose of which was to introduce a more systematic and economical mode of administering the various departments.

[1] June 28.   [2] Webster, Political Essays, p. 75, note.

CHAPTER VIII.

ADMINISTRATION OF THE BOARD OF TREASURY.

1781.

THE first financial act of the new year related to the payment of loan-office certificates to the "fortunate adventurers," as they were called, in the third class of the lottery,[1] whose inception has been noted in a previous chapter.

More than four years had passed since the adoption of the lottery scheme; but, like most of the financial experiments of Congress, only scanty fruit had appeared. After many delays, the several drawings occurred, though the tickets of neither class were all sold. In payment of the first class of billets, treasury bank-notes were issued, which was the introduction of a new financial measure. The following was the form of note given: —

Number   Dollars   Number.
Dollars.

The United States of America acknowledge themselves to be indebted to   in   dollars, for a prize of that value, drawn in the United States' lottery, which they promise to pay to the said   or bearer, on the   day of   with interest annually, at the rate of four per cent agreeable to a resolution of the United States passed the 18th day of November, 1776.

UNITED STATES LOTTERY.

<hr>

[1] Jan. 2.

They were signed by the treasurer or his son, and countersigned by one of the managers of the lottery; while other regulations were added in respect to numbering and distributing the notes.[1] Afterward the rate of interest was raised to six per cent[2] upon all certificates issued for prizes; and the "fortunate adventurers" in the second class, who had drawn more than five thousand dollars each, were required to wait five years before receiving their money.[3] Like most of the business of Congress, the accounts of the lottery became confused; and it was finally resolved to receive the tickets as vouchers for the prizes drawn, and to "certify the same as debts of the United States at and after the rate of one dollar in specie for every forty dollars for such prizes,"[4] — an end doubtless disappointing to the ticket-holder, but not in the least to the reader who has traced the perpetually failing plans of Congress.

On the middle of January, Congress issued an address[5] to the States, which was chiefly a review of the events of the year, and an appeal to put forth greater exertions in the future. The States were asked to send $879,342 in specie, — one-half without the least delay, and the remainder by the 1st of April, — to pay the armies, and to provide for carrying on the war. To what small figures did the estimates of Congress shrink as soon as specie was restored !

Having repudiated their promises once on a grand scale, Congress came very near repeating the act not long afterward. Paper money having ceased to circulate,

---

[1] May 14, 1777.   [2] May 2, 1778.   [3] Oct. 30, 1779.
[4] Dec. 21, 1782.   [5] Jan. 15.

Congress sought to establish specie prices.   But the legislation of that body was not altogether consistent; and soon a grave question arose.   On the 11th of July, 1780, Congress resolved to pay the officers and men in the navy "in specie, or other money equivalent," and four days afterward the resolve was extended to the pay of the army.   Notwithstanding the obvious meaning of these acts, which were not open to misconstruction, Congress, toward the close of that year, resolved that the salaries of certain civil officers, which had been made payable also "in specie or other current money equivalent," should be paid in bills of credit of the new emission.[2]

Naturally, such a deliberate infringement of law would create the suspicion that other officials also, beside those holding civil positions, might be treated in like manner. Pickering, who was then quartermaster-general, accordingly wrote to the president of Congress upon the subject; but receiving no satisfactory answer, if any whatever, repaired to Philadelphia, and wrote another letter, in which he said it did appear to him "indispensably necessary to come to a decision."   "Trusting to the plain obvious meaning" of the resolves of Congress, he had "ventured to assure the persons concerned, that the moneys promised to be paid in specie or other current money equivalent would really be so paid, and that no bills of credit should ever be tendered to them as such equivalent, unless they were current among the people at the rate of specie."

[1] "Public credit is so totally lost," writes Greene to Hamilton, the 10th of January of this year, "that private people will not give their aid, though they see themselves involved in one common ruin." — HAM. *Hist. of Repub.* vol. ii. p. 164.

[2] Sept. 13, 25, and Nov. 15, 1780.

By these assurances he had been able to organize the department, and to issue some certificates in lieu of money. But, as doubts disquieted the minds of many, he requested of Congress an explanation of the words in question. Even were Congress to declare in the most candid and explicit terms, that the salaries of persons in his department, and the specie contracts they had made, should be paid in gold and silver, or other money equivalent, still he affirmed that he should be embarrassed; for the tender laws hung over his head, which threatened severe penalties if he attempted to act honestly by rating the current paper money at its just, instead of its legal value. Yet there was not a single member of any public body in America who would accept a paper dollar of the new emission as an equivalent to a silver dollar. But a public officer must tender it as such. "Hard condition to an honest man engaged in the service of his country! Why such a man, in his public office, should be obliged to do what, in his own private affairs, he would be ashamed of, I know not. Credit, or the reputation of integrity and good faith, is alike essential to the public as to an individual."

In such plain terms did Pickering[1] show the ill effects of tampering with the public faith. His letter attracted general attention. The majority of Congress were willing to settle the question fairly; but a timidity was exhibited against going to the bottom of the matter.

Thus declared Pickering to his wife, six days after writing the foregoing letter,[2] adding, "'Tis time to have

---

[1] March 3, 1781, Pickering's Life of Pick., vol. i. p. 277.

[2] March 9, Ibid., p. 281.

done with patchwork. We have been nearly ruined by it already." Pickering's appeal was not in vain; for in a short time Congress settled the question in favor of honesty as well as expediency.

Congress now earnestly applied itself to remodelling the various departments of government. It could not have escaped their attention how cumbrous was the machinery of the Board of Treasury, while other departments were in still greater need of re-organization. The Treasury Board was a great improvement over any previous organization for administering the affairs of the treasury department; but the members were exceedingly slow, as every one having any thing to do with them had learned by experience.

So Congress resolved upon another plan, the leading features of which had been previously sketched by Hamilton in his letter to Morris.[1] It was resolved[2] to replace the Board of the Treasury with a superintendent of finance, whose duty should be to examine into the public indebtedness and revenues; to digest and report plans for improving and regulating the finances, and to establish order and economy in the expenditure of the public money; to direct the execution of all plans that should be adopted by Congress respecting revenues and expenditure; to superintend and control the settlement of all public accounts; to direct and control all persons employed in procuring supplies for the public service and in the expenditure of public money; to obtain accounts of all the issues of specific supplies furnished by the States; to compel the payment of all moneys

---

[1] Ante, p. 92.   [2] Feb. 7.

due to the United States, and to prosecute all delinquences respecting the public revenues and expenditures; and to report to Congress the officers necessary to assist him in the various branches of his department. To fill this office Congress wisely selected Robert Morris,[1] who had developed greater financial capacity than any other man of his time.

Thus Congress, after a series of costly experiments, determined to place the financial department of the government into the hands of a single man, — a step which Hamilton and other leading spirits of the Revolution had long and earnestly contended was absolutely necessary for the successful administration of the finances. France had passed through a somewhat similar experience nearly two centuries before, and the same remedy was devised, — putting the finances under the control of one man, the honest and devoted Sully. The French minister, entering upon his extremely difficult task with a zeal as rare as it is worthy of all praise, succeeded in uprooting the numerous thieves, who for a long period had been enriching themselves and their friends at the expense of the State, and who fancied they were so deeply rooted, that even Sully would fail in digging them out, and retired from his post with the heavy cloud of a huge national debt hanging over his head when he assumed office all cleared off, and with a large balance to the credit of the government remaining in the treasury. It remained to be seen whether Morris would be as successful in his new sphere as had been his great exampler.

<hr>

[1] Feb. 20.

As Morris did not accept the office at once, the Board of Treasury continued to administer the finances of the government. Bills of exchange were struck[1] for the payment of interest to all the holders of loan-office certificates entitled thereto, although somewhat different provision was made in respect to the certificates issued from the loan-offices in South Carolina and Georgia;[2] while warrants were issued upon loan-offices in seven of the most Northern States to pay in bills of the new emission the soldiers in those sections of the country.[3] The commissioners of all the loan-offices were directed[4] to exchange with the treasurers of their respective States bills of credit of the old emission coming into their hands "by the sale of bills of exchange, or on loan for bills of credit of the new emissions, issued in the same State," for the purpose of retiring the paper money belonging to the old emission as early as possible. It was also resolved[5] that all debts due from the United States, which had been liquidated in specie value, and all debts payable in the same manner, should be thus paid, or in other money equal thereto, according to the current exchange. The States were also recommended to amend their laws making the bills of credit emitted under the authority of Congress a legal tender, so as to prevent their use in this manner, except at their current value compared with gold and silver.

It was during this period, prior to Morris's acceptance, that the Articles of Confederation between the several States were executed. This was an important event, for by them additional power was conferred upon the General

---

[1] Feb. 23.   [2] March 29.   [3] Feb. 28.   [4] April 14.   [5] March 16.

Government. Let us glance at the financial features of these articles. All charges of war, and other expenses incurred for the common defence or general welfare, were to be defrayed out of a common treasury, and no treaty of commerce could be made restraining the legislative power of the States from imposing such imposts on foreigners as their own people were obliged to pay to other countries, or from prohibiting the exportation or importation of any commodities whatever. The regulation of the coinage, weights and measures, were to be given to Congress, besides power to borrow money or emit bills of credit; and all bills of credit emitted, moneys borrowed, and debts contracted by authority of Congress, before the assembling of the States under the new Confederation, were to be deemed a charge against the United States, for payment whereof they and the public faith were pledged.[1]

Thus, after many delays, the States yielded some of their powers in order to strengthen the General Government; yet it was still too weak to be very effective. Months had passed between the proposal to form a stronger confederacy and the consummation of that object, and in the mean time Congress had tried several times to obtain smaller grants of power to collect a revenue from the States, but in vain.

On the 13th of March,[2] Morris wrote a letter to Congress, informing that body how fully he realized the high honor conferred upon him, but also that he was concerned with other persons " in certain commercial establishments " which he was bound in honor and by contracts

---

[1] Ratified March 1.   [2] Dip. Cor., vol. xi. p. 348.

to support. "If, therefore," he continues, "it be the idea of Congress, that the office of superintendent of finance is incompatible with commercial concerns and connections, the point is settled; for I cannot on any consideration consent to violate engagements or depart from those principles of honor, which it is my pride to be governed by. If, on the contrary, Congress have elected me to this office under the expectation, that my mercantile connections and engagements were to continue, an express declaration of their sentiments should appear on the minutes, that no doubt may arise or reflections be cast on this score hereafter." How clearly do these words show the delicate sense of honesty which animated Morris! Well would it be if all public servants were endowed with as fine a sense of public and private duty. Morris thought, too, and rightly, that all persons who were to co-operate with him should be appointed by himself, Congress determining the number of secretaries, clerks, and other officers, and fixing their salaries. "I conceive," he adds, "that it will be impossible to execute the duties of this office with effect, unless the absolute power of dismissing from office or employment of all persons whatever, that are concerned in the official expenditure of public moneys, be committed to the superintendent of finance. For unless this power can be exercised without control, I have but little hopes of efficacy in the business of reformation, which is probably the most essential part of the duty." He also observed, that, in the Act describing the duties of the superintendent of finance, the execution of many things was required without providing adequate powers, and for which, therefore, he ought not to be held responsible. These matters, however, he left for future discussion.

Congress readily assented[1] to Morris's requests concerning his business engagements, and gave him power to appoint and remove delinquent officials in his office; but that part of his communication describing the execution of many things for which adequate powers were not provided, and for which, consequently, he could not be expected to be held responsible, was referred to a committee, who subsequently saw Morris, and drew from him a second letter, containing several interesting features. It appears that the committee, who probably reflected the opinion of Congress, especially of Samuel Adams,[2] who was afraid of delegating even the smallest shadow of power to anybody, wanted more definite information concerning the persons included under the control of the removing power of Morris, and desired him to make a list of them. This he affirmed[3] he was unable to do, but declared that such power was absolutely necessary, "to enable him to remedy and prevent public abuses; and the extent should be measured by the necessity and the use." He then described the business of finance, and, as the reader is probably desirous of knowing what were the views entertained by Morris upon this grave matter, we shall let him state them in his comprehensive yet concise way. "It is to raise the public revenues, by such modes as may be most easy and most equal to the people; and to expend them in the most frugal, fair, and honest manner. In our case the

---

[1] March 20.   [2] Wells's Life of S. Adams, vol. iii. p. 130.
[3] Dip. Cor., vol. xi. p. 353.

first part must ever be the business of congress, and the legislatures of the respective states; because the powers of taxation cannot be delegated. The second I take to be the most essential part of the duty of the superintendent of finance. He must ever have it in view to reduce the expenditures as nearly as possible to what in justice and in reason they ought to be; and to do this, he must be vested with power to dismiss from employment those officers he shall find unnecessary, unequal to their stations, inattentive to their duty, or dishonest in the exercise of it." He then defines more precisely the persons who should be subject to the removal of the superintendent of finance, and then enlarges upon the necessity of a frequent adjustment of accounts, if the era of public economy was to be introduced. "The financier ought, therefore, to have the power of removing any of the officers whose business is to examine and settle the public accounts, that so he may be enabled to obtain a proper and early settlement, and prevent the dangerous effects of inattention or corruption on one hand; and of delay, insolence, and tyranny to individuals concerned in such accounts, on the other." Thus Morris reasoned concerning the necessity of putting this extraordinary yet necessary power of removal in his hands. It may be thought singular that a body possessed of so little power as Congress, and so fearful of delegating it to individuals rather than to committees, should have consented to bestow so much authority upon Morris. But he knew, and so did Congress, though less perfectly, how weak and inefficient had been the administration of the Board of Treasury,

and how essential it was for him to have the power he
desired, in order to uproot deeply penetrating abuses,
and to carry out the great work of reform, which was
what he conceived to be the chief reason for his appointment. Congress, therefore, granted [1] the authority to him
for which he so earnestly pleaded, not, as he himself said,
" for the sake of the power," but for the sole purpose of
correcting abuses connected with the administration of
the Treasury Department.

[1] March 21, April 21, 27.

CHAPTER IX.

HOW PAPER MONEY WAS RECEIVED.

HAVING traced the history of the administration of the Board of Treasury from the beginning, to the appointment of Robert Morris as superintendent of finance, let us now consider how the financial measures devised and adopted during this period were received by the country, and how they affected the morality and prosperity of the people.

We are prone to believe, that, in the earlier and more trying days of the republic, greater ability and virtue abounded than are displayed in our own degenerate times. Not a few imagine, that, in the fierce conflict to acquire independence, every one was a patriot, and willing to do or suffer almost any thing to achieve success. Had this been the case, victory would have been more easily won ; but in truth the land was full of loyalists, — persons whose hearts beat warm for England, and who in various ways checked the progress of the Revolution. Others there were, and not a small number, who just as eagerly sought to accumulate fortunes by fraudulent practices upon the government or upon individuals, as any one did during the late civil conflict.[1] They did not hesitate

[1] See Letter of Col. Pickering, Nov. 22, 1779, Pickering's Life of Pick., vol. i. p. 245.

to take advantage of a fluctuating money to speculate in it, just as others speculated in gold at a time when the business was generally condemned as unpatriotic and selfish. In Pennsylvania, under the eye of the government, the discrediting of Continental money became an established business, and even Continental officers trafficked in specie.[1] So fast did the practice grow, the Council of Pennsylvania took the matter into consideration, and discovering in it a dangerous tendency to lessen, if not entirely to destroy, the credit of the Continental money, a committee were appointed to inform the Board of Treasury about the matter, and to consider what remedy would effectually suppress the practice.[2]

The impossibility of getting gold and silver for carrying on the war was one of the reasons, doubtless, why the British Government determined to settle the controversy in America by the sword. Yet an English general, in the early part of 1776, reported [3] to his government, " the congress paper is in the highest credit,"[4] though, before the year closed, paper money in the northern section of the country was struck with a mortal blight. The writer of an intercepted letter to Sir Gray Cooper declared that Congress paper depreciated beyond the rate of one hun-

---

[1] Am. Archives, fifth series, vol. iii. p. 185.   [2] Ibid.

[3] Almon's Rememb., 1776, part i. p. 363.

[4] " The bills of Congress being thrown into circulation on a favorable foundation of public confidence," says Ramsay, " were readily received. The enthusiasm of the people contributed to the same effect. That the endangered liberties of America ought to be defended, and that the credit of their paper was essentially necessary to a proper defence, were opinions engraven on the hearts of a great majority of the citizens." — Ramsay's *Hist. of Am. Rev.*, vol. ii. p. 132, ed. 1789.

dred soon after the King's troops entered Jersey, and, in many places in that Province remote from the army, was not current at any rate. In many cases, merchants converted their paper money into commodities, and instructed their agents to do likewise. None escaped the alarm. Philemon Dickinson [1] wrote to his brother, "receive no more continental money on your bonds and mortgages. The British troops having conquered the Jersies and your being in camp are sufficient reasons. Be sure you remember this. It will end better for you."

Gen. Putnam, who was now in command at Philadelphia, Congress having shortly before adjourned to Baltimore,[2] issued an order expressing his great astonishment because several of the inhabitants refused to take Continental money in payment of goods. "In future," he directed, "should any of the inhabitants be so lost to public virtue and the welfare of their country, as to presume to refuse the currency of the American states in payment for any commodities they may have for sale, the goods shall be forfeited, and the person or persons so refusing, committed to close confinement." [3]

Putnam enforced this order, and closed or pillaged stores, fined and imprisoned their owners; yet it was impossible to restrain the fears of the people respecting the unsoundness of the currency. Robert Morris [4] wrote to Deane, who, in company with other commissioners, was trying to solicit aid from France: "I must add to this gloomy picture one circumstance, more distressing than

---

[1] Am. Archives, fifth series, vol. iii. p. 1255.   [2] Dec. 12, 1776.

[3] Am. Archives, fifth series, vol. iii. p. 1214.

[4] Dec. 21, 1776, Dip. Cor., vol. i. p. 238.

all the rest, because it threatens instant total ruin to the American cause, unless some radical cure is applied, and that speedily ; I mean the depreciation of the continental currency. The enormous pay of our army, the immense expenses at which they are supplied with provisions, clothing, and other necessaries, and, in short, the extravagance that has prevailed in most departments of the public service, have called forth prodigious emissions of paper money, both continental and colonial. Our internal enemies, who, alas, are numerous and rich, have always been undermining its value by various artifices, and now that our distresses are wrought to a pitch by the successes and near approach of the enemy, they speak plainer, and many peremptorily refuse to take it at any rate. Those that do receive it, do it with fear and trembling, and you may judge of its value, even amongst those, when I tell you that £250 continental money, or 666⅔ dollars is given for a bill of exchange of £100 sterling, sixteen dollars for a half johannes, two paper dollars for one of silver, three dollars for a pair of shoes, twelve dollars for a hat, and so on; a common laborer asks two dollars a day for his work, and idles half his time.

" All this amounts to real depreciation of the money. The war must be carried on at an expense proportional to this value, which must inevitably call for immense emissions, and, of course, still further depreciations must ensue."

Two days later he writes to the president of Congress: [1] " It is very mortifying to me when I am obliged to tell you disagreeable things; but I am compelled to inform

[1] Am. Archives, fifth series, vol. iii. p. 1372.

congress that the continental currency keeps losing in credit. Many people refuse openly and avowedly to receive it; and several citizens that retired into the country must have starved if their own private credit had not procured them the common necessaries of life, when nothing could be got for your money. Some effectual remedy should be speedily applied to this evil or the game will be up. Mr. Commissary Wharton has told the general that the mills refused to grind for him, either from disaffection or dislike to the money. Be that as it may, the consequences are terrible for I do suppose the army will not consent to starve."

The situation grew more and more critical, until Gen. Washington was vested with power[1] to take whatever provisions were needed for his army if the inhabitants were unwilling to sell them at a reasonable price, and to arrest and confine all who refused to receive the Continental money. At the same time the Council of Safety of Pennsylvania were requested to apply speedy and vigorous measures in punishing those who declined to receive paper money, and to call for aid on the general commanding, if needful, to carry out their determination.

On the last day of the year, the Council of Safety of Pennsylvania[2] declared, as a consequence of the disaffection concerning the issues of paper money and of the dangerous schemes devised for the purpose of destroying the public credit, that any person who should refuse to take Continental currency in payment of any debt or contract whatsoever, or for any goods or commodity

---

[1] Dec. 27, 1776. [2] 1776, Penn. Archives, vol. v. p. 147.

offered for sale, or should ask a greater price for any commodity in such Continental currency than in any other kind of money or specie, should for the first offence be considered as a dangerous member of society, and forfeit the debt, or goods purchased, to the person who contracted for the same, and should, moreover, be subject to a penalty of five pounds for all contracts under that sum, and, for the second offence, should be subject, not only to the above mentioned penalties, but also to banishment from the State to such place as the council should direct.

In consequence of the reverses suffered by the national arms, the credit of the Union rapidly weakened. Even quondam associators refused to receive the money. Commodities could not be bought, except with specie, or bills of credit issued during the colonial period, which, it was believed, might perhaps be redeemed. " The tavern keepers took down their signs and refused to entertain the passing stranger. The continental money was freely offered at *two* for *one;* the contest seemed hastening to an inglorious end; the war could not be carried on. The soldiers, deprived of all other sources of money save those which the congress offered to them, were unable to procure the commonest necessaries of life. The most stringent measures were indispensable to hold together the structure which eighteen months had raised and Independence had cemented." [1]

The year 1777 was marked with the enterprise and capture of Burgoyne. His intention was to march down from Canada, and effect a juncture with Sir Henry Clin-

---

[1] Phillips, Cont. Paper Money, p. 64.

ton, who was stationed at New York, thus cutting the Union in twain. The effect of this movement, when known, was to hasten the depreciation of the Continental money. James Lang,[1] writing from Lancaster in Pennsylvania to the Pennsylvania Board of War, says that "Depreciating is really become a trade here, and even the friends of liberty are induced, nay almost necessitated, to adopt the hard measure. The Mennonites refuse to sell their produce unless for hard cash, and when they bring any market stuff to town, will carry it from house to house and sell it very low for hard cash, but will carry it home again rather than sell it for congress currency." As a check to this growing evil, he recommended the appointment of a trusty and spirited person who had no connections there, to reside there and take cognizance of all those matters. "Let him cause a party of soldiers to seize any person accused of depreciating or refusing the congress currency, whether in buying or selling. Let him immediately after seizing such person, take an inventory of the person's estate real and personal, and transmit the inventory to any board the law might direct. And let the person so seized be immediately sent to the state prison, there to remain without bail till tried for misprision of treason, or call it felony, if judged proper, and let the punishment be equal to the crime. I confess the measure looks violent, but if something equally so is not immediately done, I am firmly persuaded the cause will be materially hurt."[2]

[1] June 22, 1777, Penn. Archives, vol. v. p. 396.

[2] Paper money did not circulate in Philadelphia in October, 1777. Penn. Hist. Soc. Coll., vol. i. p. 173.

Violent indeed was the measure; but was not almost any measure justifiable to save the Union?

The value of Continental money was not so easily shaken in the South as in the Northern portion of the Union. Several months passed, after Congress issued it, before any reached South Carolina; and so scarce was it there in the summer of 1777, that a premium of ten per cent was paid to procure it " for the accommodation of persons travelling to the northward."[1] Probably Laurens, when making his speech in opposition to issuing foreign bills of exchange, which has been given in a previous chapter, was thinking of the wants of the South in affirming there was a deficiency rather than surplus of paper money.[2]

Among the worst sufferers were the Quakers. They refused to accept paper money issued by Congress, grounding their refusal on a religious principle maintained by the sect. As a consequence of their fidelity to it, they were fined, imprisoned, and banished; their

---

[1] Observations of English Commissioners, Nov. 25, 1780, Almon's Rememb., 1781, part 1, pp. 214, 215.

[2] Ante, p. 60. Ramsay says that "the depreciation began at very different periods in different states; but in general about the middle of the year 1777, and progressively increased for three or four years. Towards the last of 1777, the depreciation was about two or three for one; in 1778 it advanced from two or three for one to five or six for one: in 1779 from five or six for one to 27 or 28 for one; in 1780 from 27 or 28 for one to 50 or 60 for one, in the first four or five months. Its circulation was afterwards partial, but where it passed it soon depreciated to 150 for one. In some few parts it continued in circulation for the first four or five months of 1781, but in this latter period many would not take it at any rate, and they who did, received it at a depreciation of several hundreds for one." — *Hist. of Am. Rev.*, vol. ii. p. 128.

stores were robbed ; and their property was confiscated. Perhaps they suffered more severely than any other class of people. " All this upon public opinion so fickle that it was deemed a crime in 1781 to say this paper money should be redeemed at its full value, a public opinion which had in 1777 denounced as a criminal, any person who should receive it for a less amount than was expressed upon its face." [1]

There were those, however, who believed the opposition to paper money displayed by the Quakers was inspired quite as much by love for money as by religious principle. [2] This was the belief of Gouverneur Morris, who issued an address, directed chiefly to them, in which, after showing the futility of their hopes of the enemy's ultimate success, he adds " as little ground have you for hope in the depreciation of the continental money." He then proceeds to state the causes of its depreciation, for the purpose of showing how much paper money was really worth, and why it ought to be refused no longer by any class or sect. " You know that [the depreciation] is in a great degree to be attributed to the acts of interested men, whose efforts to acquire it show their conviction of its value. I know it hath been a fashionable doctrine, that after the emissions should amount to a certain sum, the bubble, as the phrase was, would burst. But the absurdity of this to men acquainted with human nature, was evident. The reasons are needless, because we may appeal to experience, to

[1] Phillips, p. 73.

[2] Phillips says, that, before the Revolution, the Quakers would as readily accept bills issued for war purposes as for any other, p. 37.

show whether there is the least danger of this event. When two emissions were called in, and every method, consistent with justice and good faith, taken to stop their circulation, those who had principally contributed to depreciate the money, were the very persons who continued to receive the vicious emissions. For as soon as it became a question, whether they should not lose the value, but merely the use of so much money, they made every effort to uphold the credit of it. A few days ago when a report prevailed of the arrival of some favorable intelligence from Europe, such of you as are in this city cannot but remember the rapid fall of every article, specie not excepted. Hence the deduction is clear, that the money issued by congress is intrinsically worth what they contend, but is depreciated by the quantity in some degree, and more by the arts of engrossers. Take the familiar proposition, that a country will easily bear taxation to the amount of some given part of the circulating medium, suppose a tenth, though in fact one-fifth may be raised among a free people, and you will see that, let the paper medium be increased to any degree, it may be sunk in a short period."[1] Plausible as was the reasoning of Morris, the Quakers, Mennonites, Bethlemites, and other religious sects, and of course the Tories, refused to accept Continental paper money whenever they could escape doing so, thus embarrassing the General Government, and hastening the day when its paper issues would be refused by every one.

Toward the close of 1777, John Adams,[2] writing from

[1] Almon's Rememb., 1779, p. 249.   [2] Works, vol. ix. p. 469.

Braintree to Gerry, who was then one of the most efficient members of the Board of Treasury, said, "I find the same perplexities here that we felt at Yorktown, a general inclination among the people to barter, and as general an aversion to dealing in paper money of any denomination; guineas, half joes, and milled dollars in as high estimation as in Pennsylvania. The moneyed men, I am informed, generally decline receiving paper for their debts; many refuse; and it is said all will, very soon. There is a whispering about among the richer sort that an act is necessary for allowing a depreciation or an appreciation, as the case may be, upon specialties; and the poorer sort look cunning, and give hints that the rich are aiming at a depreciation."

Adams then depicts some of the evil consequences to which the depreciated money had given rise, and his feelings about the matter. "The rapid translation of property from hand to hand, the robbing of Peter to pay Paul, alarms and distresses me beyond measure. The man who lent another a hundred pounds in gold four years ago, and is paid now in paper, cannot purchase with it one quarter part in pork, beef, or land, of what he could when he lent the gold. This is fact, and facts are stubborn things in opposition to speculation." Having declared that the depreciation would prove a serious perplexity even to Gerry, he continues, "It will not ruin our cause, great as the evil is, and if it was much greater. But it torments me to see injustice both to the public and to individuals so frequent. Every man's liberty and life are equally dear to him; every man, therefore, ought to be taxed equally for the defence of his life and liberty. That is, the poll tax should be equal. Every man's property is equally dear both to himself and to the public; every man's property ought to be taxed for the defence of the public in proportion to the quantity of it. These are fundamental maxims of sound policy. But instead of this every man who had money due to him. at the commencement of this war, has been already taxed three-fourth parts of that money, besides his tax on his poll and estate in proportion to other people. And every man who owed money at the beginning of the war, has put three-fourth parts of it in his pockets as clear gain. The war, therefore, is immoderately gainful to some, and ruinous to others. This will never do." Everywhere was the depreciation recognized, giving rise to serious evils which were alarming and painful to all good men.

In Massachusetts a new plan was originated for enhancing the value of the Continental money. At a public meeting in Boston, it was proposed that Congress should redeem all the State issues with Continental money, charging each State for the sum received, and then replacing these latter issues with loan-office certificates as rapidly as possible.[1] In this way it was thought the volume of paper money might be contracted and appreciated, while all the States would be equally interested in maintaining its value.

The army spent the winter of 1777 and 1778 at Valley Forge, — an event to be forever remembered on account of the dreadful sufferings endured by the soldiers. By foraging, the troops were able to procure at best only a

---

[1] Boston Gazette, June 2, 1777.

precarious living. Meanwhile, as the British commissary department paid in gold, the farmers were tempted to sell their produce to their enemies, rather than to the American camp. To prevent this, a guard was placed along the Schuylkill, to stop supplies from reaching the British army.

Once more Congress[1] addressed the people, the derangement of finances constituting the chief topic of explanation and discussion. Congress sought to strengthen the faith of the people by the inquiry, " Is there a country upon earth which hath such resources for the payment of her debts as America? such an extensive territory? so fertile, so blessed in its climate and productions? Surely there is none. Neither is there any to which the wise Europeans will sooner confide their property. What, then, are the reasons that your money hath depreciated? Because no taxes have been imposed to carry on the war: because your commerce hath been interrupted by your enemy's fleet: because their armies have ravaged and desolated a part of your country : because their agents have villanously counterfeited your bills: because extortioners among you, inflamed with the lust of gain, have added to the price of every article of life: and because weak men have been artfully led to believe that it is of no value. How is this dangerous disease to be remedied? Let those among you who have leisure and opportunity, collect the moneys which individuals in their neighborhood are desirous of placing in the public funds. Let the several legislatures sink their respective issues, that so, there being but one kind of bills, there may be less

---

[1] May 8, 1778.

danger of counterfeits. Refrain a little while from purchasing those things which are not absolutely necessary, so that those who have engrossed commodities may suffer (as they deservedly will) the loss of their ill-gotten hoards, by reason of the commerce with foreign nations, which fleets will protect."

Of course, the country abounded in Solons, having specifics which would effect a speedy and complete cure, if Congress could be persuaded to use them. It would not be uninteresting to describe some of them; but we have space to set forth only one, the simplicity of which is in marked contrast with several of the schemes presented.[1] "My scheme is a deep scheme," begins the writer. "The depreciation certainly arises from torture. Many a poor cur has been destroyed by the cry of mad dog, that was a good honest cur if he had been let alone. — Leonidas, I wish you had been prescribing for the bite of a mad dog, when you told us that life might as well survive in a furnace as truth or honor in the neighborhood of certain bills. — No matter, Sir, torture, vile torture, is the source of all the mischief. If these creatures will but let the public credit alone, my life for it, it will revive." His panacea, as the reader may suspect, was for his "brother schemers" to stop writing, and leave the currency to the operation of other principles than those which are so easily woven by the imagination. A good point, doubtless; yet his "brother schemers" continued to ply their pens as vigorously as ever.

The newspapers of the day were prolific with essays showing the certainty of the redemption of the Con-

---

[1] Penn. Packet, Jan. 6, 1780.

tinental money, because independence was assured. "Whatever else America may be tempted to, she never can be brought to a violation of her own faith,[1]" is a fair illustration of the kind of argument they employed to prop the leaning credit of the government.

During the year 1778 an alliance was formed with France; in June, Howe evacuated Philadelphia; and, on his way to New York, Washington fought the battle of Monmouth; the British fleet narrowly escaped battle, and probable capture by the French squadron: yet the courage of the people, though roused by these events, was somewhat depressed by the indecisive military operations of the summer and autumn.

Notwithstanding the plentifulness of almost every kind of goods, it was difficult to purchase them, except for hard money. "The state of our currency is really serious," Jay writes to Washington.[2] "When, or by what means the progress of its depreciation will be prevented is uncertain. The subject is delicate, but the conduct of some men really indicates at least great indifference about it." To which Phillips[3] adds, "The fluctuating currency, with the opportunities it afforded for speculation and for oppression, was too much loved by the dishonest for them to readily permit any measures to be taken for its improvement." What a striking parallel was seen in this country during the recent civil war!

How depreciation was regarded at this time by Washington[4] may be seen from the following extract contained

---

[1] Penn. Packet, Jan. 26, 1779.

[2] April 26. 1779, Jay's Life of Jay, vol. ii. p. 48.

[3] Cont. Paper Money, p. 115. [4] Sparks's Washington, vol. vi. p. 161.

in a letter to the committee of Congress: "The great impediment to all vigorous measures, is the state of our currency. What prospects there are of relieving it, what is to be expected from the measures taken to that effect, the committee to whom the subject is familiar, and by whom it is best understood, will judge. But I fear their operations will be too slow to answer the purposes of the next campaign; and, if the vast expenditures necessary to the plan under consideration were to be made, I should have little hope of the success of any project for raising the value of the currency that can be adopted." Subsequently he writes, "that a wagon load of money will scarcely purchase a wagon load of provisions."

Congress again implored the people to aid in preserving the value of the rapidly-sinking money.[1] The enemy's only hope was the bankruptcy of the government; but, as Phillips[2] remarks, this "was of a most paradoxical kind, as it ensued from superabundance, and not the want of money." "Were it possible," remark a committee appointed by the citizens of Philadelphia, in June, 1779, "that the property of America could fail, her lands become barren, her rivers dried up, agriculture extinguished and population extinct, the currency would then want a foundation for its credit, and ability for its redemption; because in those cases it would be a representation of nothing. Having said thus much on the subject we shall conclude with recommending it to our sister states to concur with us in measures absolutely necessary at this time, for redeeming and supporting the credit of our currency, and of consequence individual

---

[1] May 26, 1779.   [2] Cont. Paper Money, p. 127.

prosperity. We wish to see committees formed in every state and county, whose immediate business it shall be to watch against the depreciation, and promote the value of the money." [1]

In October of the same year the Rev. John Clarke [2] informs Timothy Pickering, "We can procure nothing, sir, for money; barter is the only method of commerce which now prevails. You will therefore readily believe that the circumstances of such as have neither salt, sugar, etc., beggar all description. It is my firm belief that we are the wretchedest people under heaven. We have depraved every virtuous principle, and, was Britain to remove her troops and leave us to our independence, it seems to me we should be incapable of enjoying it."

Two months earlier, in August, Washington [3] instructs his agent, Lund Washington, not to receive any longer Continental money at par for debts. "I have considered the matter in every point of view in which my judgment enables me to place it, and am resolved to receive no more old debts (such I mean as were contracted and ought to have been paid before the war) at the present nominal value of the money, unless compelled to do it, or it is the practice of others to do it. Neither justice, reason, nor policy requires it. The law undoubtedly was well designed. It was intended to stamp a value upon, and to give a free circulation to, the paper bills of credit; but it never was nor could have been intended to make a man take a shilling or sixpence in the pound for a just

[1] Penn. Packet, June 29, 1779.
[2] Pickering's Life of Pick., vol. i. p. 242.
[3] Sparks's Washington, vol. vi. p. 321.

debt which his debtor is well able to pay, and thereby involve himself in ruin. I am as willing now, as I ever was, to take paper money for every kind of debt, and at its present depreciated value for those debts, which have been contracted since the money became so; but I will not in future receive the nominal sum for such old debts as come under the above description, except as before specified. . . . If it be customary with others to receive money in this way, that is, sixpence or one shilling on the pound for old debts; if it is thought to be promotive of the great cause we are embarked in for individuals to do so, thereby ruining themselves while others are reaping the benefit of such distress; if the law imposes this, and it is thought right to submit, I will not say aught against it nor oppose another word to it. No man has gone, and no man will go further to serve the republic than myself. If sacrificing my whole estate would effect any valuable purpose, I would not hesitate one moment in doing it. But my submitting in matters of this kind, unless the same is done by others, is no more than a drop in the bucket. In fact, it is not serving the public, but enriching individuals, and countenancing dishonesty; for sure I am, that no honest man would attempt to pay twenty shillings with one, or perhaps half of one. In a word, I had rather make a present of the bonds, than receive payment of them in so shameful a way."

Of course, it was to be expected that the enemy would exaggerate, and report the depreciation as much as possible. Accordingly, "The London Morning Post," in February, 1779, declared that depreciation was seven hundred per cent. Twenty paper dollars were given for a silver one; and the Dutch were warned not to assist the French by loaning them money, since the finances of the rebellious Colonies were in such an extremely low condition.[1]

Depreciation of the currency was now everywhere acknowledged, Congress alone refusing to recognize the fact. During the year the depreciation had increased from eight dollars to forty-one dollars and a half for one.[2]

The next year saw the end of Continental paper money. The bill passed in March, 1780, declaring forty dollars in paper equivalent to one in specie, destroyed what little faith the most confiding had retained in the bills. Not all discussion concerning their redemption was yet over; but their end, nevertheless, had come. There were those who declaimed loudly against this measure. Dr. Witherspoon of New Jersey, one of the most prominent members of Congress, could not reconcile himself to so flagrant a breach of promise.[3]

France was deeply stirred by this action of Congress. The Count de Vergennes[4] addressed several letters to Adams and Franklin upon the subject, the chief concern expressed in them relating to the effect of the measure upon French subjects. He very plainly declares they ought to have been exempted from the operation of the Act, which should have applied to Americans alone.

[1] Newspaper Cuttings, vol. v. pp. 191, 261, N. Y. Hist. Library.

[2] Phillips, p. 145.

[3] He made an eloquent speech in Congress in favor of maintaining the public faith. Waln's Life of Witherspoon, Biog. Signers to the Dec. of Indep., vol. v. pp. 143, 149.

[4] June 21, 1780, J. Adams's Works, vol. vii. p. 100; June 30, 1780, ibid., p. 212.

Adams replied[1] that it was just to redeem the bills according to their value, as they had been received in the same way.[2]

At the same time the Forty-for-one Act was passed, Congress resolved to pay the holders of loan-office certificates as much as paper money was worth at the time the certificates were issued. The publication of this resolution, for some reason or other, was delayed for a considerable period after its enactment. Had the two been given to the public simultaneously, the alarm occasioned in Europe when the first Act was known might have been averted, because nearly all the interest of European merchants in American funds centred in the loan-office certificates.[3] The paper money in the possession of foreign agents residing in America had been, for the most part, received at a greatly reduced rate;

[1] June 22, 1780, ibid., p. 193; July 1, 1780, ibid., p. 213.

[2] Gen. Greene expressed his opinion of this Act in a letter to Morris, from which the following is an extract: "The tender laws and the plan of redeeming the continental money, forty for one, have been replete with every kind of mischief. Credit and reputation are much alike, either in public or private life. Once lost they are very difficult to be regained, and no advantage gained at the expense of our credit or reputation can compensate for the loss of them. It was ever my opinion, that we ought to have supported the old continental money, and I am persuaded it would have afforded us the best medium of any plan we had it in our power to adopt. The hopes of benefiting by its appreciation would have supported its credit. If the states could have been prohibited from making money, and the taxes kept in motion, the continental money would have afforded a tolerable medium for business of all kinds." (GREENE's *Life of Greene*, vol. iii. p. 371.) The letter was dated Aug. 18, 1781.

[3] Letter of John Adams to Count de Vergennes, June 20, 1780, Works, vol. vii. p. 188.

and the Forty-for-one Act did not make the legal valuation less than the actual depreciation.

In truth, enormous as was the rate of depreciation established by law, it did not express the whole amount. Adams declared the real depreciation to be twice as much.[1] Thacher writes,[2] two months after the bill had passed, that he had just seen in a newspaper an advertisement offering for an article forty dollars per pound, or three shillings in silver.

The following extract from a London letter[3] is a striking picture of the condition of the country at that time, though perhaps too highly colored in some respects.

" £10,000 Maryland currency worth £6,000
  10,000 Continental currency worth   .   .   .   100
                                                      ____
  Difference £5,900

This was the exchange at Philadelphia in June, and as they had not then heard of Gates's defeat, it must be now lower. Actions commenced for considerable sums by creditors, have been obliged to be withdrawn, or a non-suit suffered; a lawyer of eminence, not opening his mouth, in a trial of consequence, under a fee of one thousand pounds, though the legal fee is about forty, and the debt, if recovered, being paid in continental money, dollar for dollar, worth now but a penny, the difference between a penny and 4s. 6d. sterling, is lost to the receiver. The Congress having called in the

---

[1] Works, vol. i. p. 314; ibid., appendix, p. 654.

[2] May, 1780, Thacher's Military Journal, p. 231.

[3] November, 1780, Newspaper Cuttings, vol. vi. p. 145, N. Y. Hist. Library.

former emissions, forty dollars for one, and giving that one in paper, cuts off every hope it will hereafter appreciate.

"Instead of the creditor pursuing the debtor with an arrest, the debtor pursues the creditor with a tender of continental money, and forces the bond out of his hand. Hence it appears what the best of fortunes in that country are reduced to, — an unpleasing reflection it must be; for time, which lightens all other losses, aggravates the loss of fortune. Every day we feel it more, because we stand more in the want of the conveniences we have been used to. On the other hand, new fortunes are made on the ruin of old ones. War which keeps the spirits in motion, has diffused a taste for gayety and dissipation. The French resident gives a rout twice a week to the Philadelphia ladies, amongst whom French hair-dressers, milliners and dancers, are all the *ton*. The Virginia jig has given place to the cotillon, and *minuet de-la-cour*. The congress are fallen into general contempt, for their want of credit and power; the army is absolute, and has declared it will not submit to a peace made by congress; the people grumble, but are obliged to surrender one piece of furniture after another, even to their beds, to pay the taxes." The correspondent closes with a reflection, which, however hopeful and pleasing it may have been to his countrymen when first received, did not prove to be true. "After all, a power drawn from such distant and dissonant parts cannot form a perfect Union." Nor was he less certain of his country's ultimate triumph.

The new emissions, issued with much confidence by Congress upon the credit of the States, did not meet everywhere with a welcome reception. Josiah Quincy[1] wrote not long after to Washington, "Our new paper money, issued by recommendation of congress, no sooner began to circulate, than two dollars of it were given for one hard one. To restore the credit of paper, by making it a lawful tender, by regulating acts, or by taxes, are political manœuvres that have already proved abortive, and for this obvious reason, — that, in the same proportion as ideal money is forced into currency, it must, from the nature of every thing fraudulent, be forced out of credit. . . . I am firmly of the opinion, and think it entirely defensible, that there never was a paper pound, a paper dollar, or a paper promise of any kind, that ever yet obtained a general currency, but by force or fraud, generally by both. That the army has been grossly cheated; that creditors have been infamously defrauded; that the widow and fatherless have been oppressively wronged and beggared; that the gray hairs of the aged and the innocent, for want of their just dues, have gone down with sorrow to their graves, in consequence of our disgraceful depreciated paper currency, — may now be affirmed, without hazard of refutation; and, I wish it could be said, with truth, that the war has not thereby been protracted. May it not, therefore, be safely concluded that no kind of paper currency is adequate to the purpose of collecting and combining the forces of the United States for their common defence?"[2]

---

[1] Nov. 27, 1780, Sparks's Letters to Wash., vol. iii. p. 157.

[2] Charles Petit, acting quartermaster-general, wrote from Philadelphia, July 13, 1780, "The new money of this state circulates but slowly, and as yet heavily, but it is working its way and gaining some

The General Assembly of Massachusetts, by resolving to pay the new emissions at one and seven-eighths exchange for hard money, sowed such a distrust among the people of the intention of the State to disregard its new promise, that Sullivan[1] wrote in August of the same year, "The money is now no more a currency than the ragged remains of a kite." He then proceeds to criticise intelligently, but with no slight severity, the policy of the government. "There is not hard money enough to carry on commerce, and a tax is ordered, which will call in all the new emissions. But when this is in the treasury, it will be of no avail to the support of the army. And the authors of this distressing measure do not pretend that there will be any other fruit of it than the sinking of the new emission. So that, while our army are disbanding themselves for want of necessaries, we are loading the people with taxes to redeem bills of credit that were not to be redeemed until the end of six years, and exhausting our treasury of hard money to support the credit of a currency which is dead as an almanac of the last century; dead beyond all the powers of resuscitation."

strength. Tradesmen and common people are shy and fearful of it, and therefore it does not obtain so ready a currency in small affairs as was expected. Were it ever so flippant in its passage, the whole amount is far short of the supplies expected from this state, and the money arising from taxes has so many other pores to supply that we are hardly sensible of any benefit from it." (GREENE's *Life of Greene*, vol. ii. p. 313.) President Reed wrote to the commissaries of purchases, "We have now full confidence that this money will pass as gold and silver and therefore direct you not to exceed upon any account the gold and silver price" (*Penn. Archives*, vol. viii. p. 277).

[1] Aug. 4, 1781, Amory's Life of Sullivan, vol. ii. p. 380.

Indeed, the new emission fell so rapidly in value that no computation could accurately mark the decline. A bushel of wheat was worth at one period seventy-five dollars; coffee was sold for four dollars a pound, and sugar for three-fourths of the latter sum.[1]

It was useless to repeat experiments in this direction. As Pelatiah Webster[2] says, " The people of the states had been worried and fretted, disappointed and put out of humor by so many tender acts, limitations of prices, and other compulsory methods to force value into paper money, and compel the circulation of it, and by so many vain funding schemes, declarations, and promises, all which issued from congress, but died under the most zealous efforts to put them into operation and effect, that their patience was all exhausted. . . . They appeared heartless and almost stupid when their attention was called to any new propositions." Faith in paper money was gone, Congress had forced it upon the people for four years in spite of continual depreciation; but the time had come when Congress could do so no longer. The day of paper money, with all its dreadful evils, the worst of which are yet to be related, was over, never to re-appear, as those worthy fathers thought, but which, contrary to their hopes, and in spite of their most determined, efforts to prevent it, was revived a century later, attended by the same inevitable, though perhaps not equally distressing results.

Paper money continued to circulate to some extent among the people through the greater part of 1781, and,

---

[1] Amory's Life of Sullivan, vol. i. p. 121.
[2] Political Essays, p. 116, note I.

by the government was received for a still longer period.[1] The old emissions were refused by the army in September, 1780,[2] and toward the close of May the next year, a mercantile house[3] in Boston informed an individual in Philadelphia that "Continental paper still passes with some people and a great speculation might be made, if any one had a large quantity of paper by them, but not else as no credit is given even for an hour." Thus, credit had been completely paralyzed and destroyed by using paper money. The people would have their eyes open, ere long, the correspondent affirmed, and then it would not pass at all with any, except at the Philadelphia exchange.

About the same time, William Cooper,[4] writing from Boston, to his brother in Philadelphia, says, "The old

[1] Gerry writes from Marblehead, Mass., May 20, 1781, "Since Tuesday last the old emissions have not the least circulation in this state." A considerable sum he had recently exchanged through an agent at seventy-five. Almon's Rememb., 1781, part 2, p. 112.

[2] Saffell's Records of Rev. War, pp. 77, 78. "The Penn line desire to have their depreciation made up, and that at 60 instead of 40 for 1, and to receive money that other people will take from them, and in such quantities that it may answer some purpose. Nothing but the general's order would induce some of the regiments to take it." (*Extract from Letter of John Pierce, Paymaster, dated Peekskill, Aug.* 1, 1780, SAFFELL, p. 75.) Pierce writes, Sept. 1, the same year, "I have paid the army as far as the money has gone for Jan. Feb. and March; my cash is now exhausted, and I want about 400,000 dollars to complete the payment. The army would not receive it but on account, which was accordingly entered into the warrants to be so, agreeable to a resolve of congress of the 10th of April last." (SAFFELL, p. 77.)

[3] John R. Livingston & Co., May 23, Almon's Rememb., 1781, part 2, p. 115.

[4] May 19, 1781, Ibid., p. 116.

bills, so called, are within this week greatly depreciated, owing to large quantities of that money poured into this state from Philadelphia. Goods are much risen, and I suppose they must be also at Philadelphia. Dollars, till lately were seventy-five for one, the southern gentry have offered one hundred and twenty of the old bills for one hard dollar, and indeed, I scarce know what. We are at present in great confusion; the takers refuse it, and this morning there is a cry for bread." To such a deplorable condition had paper money finally brought the people.

In September, 1781, Sullivan [1] wrote from Springfield, " Paper money is not even mentioned in trade ; but one is given for four, in order to pay the present state tax. There is, however, a scarcity of silver that reduces the price of goods very fast, and it seems the general opinion that there shall be no more paper currency. However, the treasurer pays it out as fast as it comes in, and unless the general assembly puts a stop to that, it will again be in circulation, and again depreciate."

The final blow was given by merchants and brokers in the Southern States, who, apprehensive of the approaching fate of the paper currency, pushed immense quantities of it suddenly into New England, making enormous purchases with it, whereupon " instantly the bills vanished from circulation." [2] For several years after their circulation ceased, the holders regarded them as a part of the national debt, which would be paid in gold and silver ; not the amount indeed expressed on the face of the bills, but what they were worth in specie at the

---

[1] To Benjamin Lincoln, Amory's Life of Sullivan, vol. ii. p. 382.

[2] Noah Webster, Coll. of Essays, p. 191.

time they were received by the holders, with interest at six per cent per annum. Most of the French possessing paper money deposited it with the French minister or council at New York, that payment might be demanded whenever Congress should appropriate funds for that purpose. Speculators, however, purchased the bills, as well as every other form of public indebtedness, expecting, of course, to reap a rich reward in due time from the operation.[1]

Occasionally, paper money was exchanged, even as late as 1782, to a very small extent, at an enormous discount, but merely to serve special local purposes.[2]

Having exhausted the magical power of the printing-press, the reader may be somewhat curious to learn how the people supplied themselves with money, or whether they made exchanges without the intervention of a circulating medium. President Reed of Pennsylvania, one of the leaders of the Revolution, — and whose correspondence and official papers containing reference to the financial questions of the time evince a mastery of them, — communicated to Mr. Searle,[3] who was then abroad trying to negotiate a loan for that State, "The paper money has at length found its *ne plus ultra;* a total loss of confidence and credit, arising from a variety of causes, to some of which you cannot be a stranger, gave it an honorable, and, what you will,

---

[1] Jefferson's Letter to Morliene, June 3, 1786, Works, vol. i. p. 578. In the same letter he declared that it was six years since the paper money of New England had ceased to circulate as money.

[2] Writings of Madison, vol. i. p. 60.

[3] "In the spring of 1781," Reed's Life of Reed, vol. ii. pp. 293, 295.

perhaps, think more extraordinary, a peaceful exit about three months ago. I believe the history of the world affords no instance of such a transition. At this time all dealings, and commerce of every kind are carried on in gold and silver; paper having, in its turn, become a merchandise, and kept for some time at an exchange of four or five for one. You will naturally ask how this has been effected, and where have you found a sufficient and ready substitute. I answer, it was effected really and truly by the people themselves gradually depreciating the money till the exchange rose to two hundred and fifty and three hundred for one. Ostensibly it was occasioned by a declaration of the Supreme Executive Council that it should be received in public payments at a ratio of one hundred and seventy-five for one. At once, as if by that force which, in days of ignorance, would be ascribed to enchantment, all dealings in paper ceased. Necessity forced out the gold and silver — a fortunate trade opened at the same time to the Havana for flour, all restrictions were taken off, and the Mexican dollars flowed in by thousands; this supported the sinking spirits of those who would have been discontented and uneasy, and in a few days, specie became the universal medium, and so continues. Every one is surprised at the change. Our enemies, both external and internal, who promised themselves tumults, insurrections and revolt, hang their heads in despondency and despair. A general system of economy and frugality will be a natural consequence of the money finding a settled value, and we may with reason hope soon to find ourselves on the same principles as other nations."

The truth of the sketch here given of the peaceful exit of paper money and the sudden re-appearance of specie is amply confirmed by other testimony. Evidently the principles governing the circulation of money were a perplexing mystery to most of our revolutionary fathers; and even now the haze has not entirely cleared away before every eye.

CHAPTER X.

STATE VERSUS CONTINENTAL ISSUES.

THE Colonies had issued paper money long before any one dreamed of a Confederate Government. Massachusetts was the first Colony to embark in the business; and, though the experiment partially failed, it was successful enough to inspire constant repetition. It was well known, before the paper money of Congress appeared, that, whenever any Colony issued more than a very limited amount, it always depreciated: therefore, to sustain the credit of the Continental bills, the issues of the States, for the time at least, should have been stopped.[1] The two issues were in direct conflict, and, if the States continued to send forth their supplies as though Congress had no thought of doing the same thing, of course the values of both kinds would decline more speedily. Yet the needs of the Colonies were so pressing, that, before the close of 1775, every one of them, from Massachusetts to Georgia, had joined in swelling the stream of paper money.

[1] Madison entertained an intelligent view of the causes affecting the value of paper money. "It depends on the credit of the state issuing it, and on the time of its redemption; and is no otherwise affected by the quantity than as the quantity may be supposed to endanger or postpone the redemption." Written prior to March, 1780. Writings, vol. iv. p. 462.

Not content with issues of the States and the General Government, private issues of tokens, certificates, &c., for small change, were sent forth by individuals, which debased still more the quality of the paper flood. The evil grew so alarming in New York, that the Committee of Safety resolved not to receive such money, and warned the people against accepting it.[1] Virginia declared it to be a penal offence to issue or receive such tickets, and other Colonies took similar action.[2]

Congress doubtless saw in the beginning how the value of Continental money was affected by the action of the States in issuing bills of credit; but whether this body dared not recommend the States to stop, or whether the evil was not sufficiently alarming to render such a recommendation necessary, or whether, after all, the members were very slow in seeing how the State and Continental issues clashed, no effort was put forth to prevent the evil until Feb. 15, 1777, when Congress recommended the States to stop issuing bills, recall those already emitted, and rely wholly upon the paper money which Congress should provide for the country. This was wise action surely, and it was one of the very few recommendations of Congress which the States either wholly or in part followed. All of the States ceased to emit any more paper money; and some of them remained true to the recommendation of Congress nearly four years.[3] How far, however, they went in contracting or redeeming their issues, we have been unable to discover.

On the 22d of November, 1777, Congress repeated the

---

[1] Am. Archives, fourth series, vol. vi. p. 996.   [2] Phillips, p. 46.
[3] Arnold's Hist. of R. I., vol. ii. p. 458.

recommendation, and urged the States to refrain from emitting any more bills of credit, and, where a sufficient quantity of Continental bills existed to serve as a circulating medium, forthwith to recall by loan or taxes their State issues, and to cancel them, small bills less than a dollar excepted, which were needed for change.

As associations had been formed in some places for preserving the value and credit of bills issued by the Colonies sustained by the British crown, thus lessening the value of the Continental issues and those of the States not relying on any such authority, Congress finally recommended[1] the States to call in all notes issued by them prior to the 19th of April, 1775, and to declare such as were not delivered within a reasonable time to be irredeemable.

[1] Dec. 3, 1777.

CHAPTER XI.

COUNTERFEITING.

THE bills of credit sent forth by Congress would have rapidly sunk by reason of the enormous quantity issued, even if they had not been weighted in any other manner; but, not long after the appearance of the first issues, counterfeits found their way among the people, the effect of which was to hasten the depreciation and fall of paper money. The subject first received the attention of the New-York Provincial Congress, as the offenders principally flourished within the jurisdiction of that State. Their headquarters were at Cold Springs, on Nassau Island, where they were captured; but the destruction of this nest of counterfeiters by no means effectually ended the practice. The Jersey delegation presented to Congress a number of counterfeits, which doubtless created gloomy forebodings in that body, and led to the appointment of a committee to consider what remedy could be effectively applied. The Legislatures were recommended[1] to pass laws against counterfeiting, and, content with this action, Congress took no further steps for a considerable period.

Although the States promptly complied with the recommendation of Congress in respect to counterfeiting, the

---

[1] June 24, 1776.

counterfeiters continued their unhallowed occupation, for doubtless their gains were large and tempting. Counterfeiting, however, was not confined solely to individuals. The British Government also embarked in the business. Gen. Howe abetted and patronized those who were engaged in making and pushing these spurious issues into circulation. In the same papers which published British official documents and proclamations might be found advertisements like the following: —

Persons going into the other colonies may be supplied with any number of counterfeited congress notes for the price of the paper per ream. They are so nearly and exactly executed that there is no risk in getting them off, it being almost impossible to discover that they are not genuine. This has been proved by bills of a very large amount which have been successfully circulated.[1]

"A shipload of counterfeit continental money," says Phillips,[2] "coming from Britain, was captured by an American privateer. Persons accompanying an English flag of truce are known to have largely made use of the opportunity for disseminating the fraudulent notes; emissaries from New York endeavored to obtain from the mills, paper similar to that used by congress for its emissions."

Many in Great Britain and elsewhere believed, that, if Continental paper money could be destroyed, the Americans would be obliged to submit, from lack of funds to

[1] H. Gaine's Gazette, April, 1777, cited in Moore's Diary of the American Rev., vol. i. p. 440.

[2] Cont. Paper Money, p. 71.

maintain their cause. This is why the British Government promoted so extensively the business of counterfeiting. But Gen. Clinton wrote truthfully, in January, 1780, "Every day teaches me the futility of calculations founded on its failure." Great Britain had not yet fathomed the depth of American patriotism, what the people were willing to suffer to acquire. independence; nor had the mother-country reckoned accurately the aid which France was to bestow. Clinton, who was on the ground, saw with more discerning eyes: the Revolution was not to fail, even if the nation did become bankrupt.[1]

[1] This entire letter discloses the clearness of his vision and judgment: "No experiments suggested by your Lordship; no assistance that could be drawn from the power of gold, or the arts of counterfeiting have been left unattempted. But still the currency, like the widow's cruise of oil, has not failed the congress. My hopes on this head, I must acknowledge, were much higher twelve months since than to-day. With the appearance of an enormous quantity, still it is all the debt which the people have to struggle with; and in this view, and when compared with that of other nations, it shrinks into a very inconsiderable sum. The people begin to be sensible of this; but on the other hand, all men, even the friends of the British government, residing in the Rebel states, would be unwise sufferers, did the money fall to the ground without a substitute. The different acts of the states, which made it a lawful tender, forced it into every pocket. The continuance of the war; the almost total disappearance of specie, and the necessity there was for employing some medium for trade, or auxiliary, in the way of barter, assisted further in its general promulgation, till at length every individual found it his interest, so closely connected with its value, that it is candidly my sentiment, no efforts of ours can make it less. If it is to be destroyed at all, it can only be by congress; and in this case, it will undoubtedly be succeeded by some substitute more valuable and permanent." Willing, nay, eager, to do any act which would be likely to weaken America, he concludes, "I shall, nevertheless, my Lord, continue assiduous in the application of those means intrusted to my care;

Nevertheless, large quantities of the forged paper were circulated, and once more was the attention of Congress called to the subject. No further action, however, was taken to protect the issues of the government: perhaps Congress was unable to devise any method for suppressing the evil.

Nor did the State issues escape the attention of the counterfeiter.[1] The wife of John Adams writes to him on the 9th of May, 1777,[2] "A most horrid plot has been discovered of a band of villains counterfeiting the Hampshire currency to a great amount. No person scarcely but what has more or less of these bills." Adams in his reply alludes to "a counterfeit continental bill abroad, sent out of New York," but adds that "it will deceive none but fools, for it is a copper plate, easily detected, miserably done."[3]

Although the forgeries were poorly executed, so many counterfeits were pushed into circulation, especially of the bills dated May 20, 1777, and April 11, 1778, that Congress resolved[4] to retire these two emissions. They were to be received for taxes, and in exchange for other bills, until a certain period, after which they were to be irredeemable. The notes thus withdrawn were disfigured, effectually preventing their further circulation; while the time fixed for receiving and exchanging them,

---

if they cannot work its destruction, yet they can embarrass government, and make the carrying on the war more precarious, burdensome and less energetic." — ALMON's *Rememb.*, 1780, part 2, p. 40.

[1] A person was convicted at Middletown, Conn., for counterfeiting the bills of that State, and sentenced to "four years confinement in New Gate prison." Continental Journal, Jan. 30, 1777.

[2] Familiar Letters, p. 269.   [3] Ibid., 278.   [4] Jan. 2, 1779.

which was the 1st of June, 1779, was afterward extended to 1780. To facilitate their withdrawal, the managers of the lottery were directed to receive them, and the paymasters of the army to exchange them; associations of citizens also were formed for the same purpose.[1]

The effect of this measure was probably a surprise to every one, and is a fine illustration of human inability to foresee the quality of fruit which public measures enacted with the best motive and apparently soundest wisdom may sometimes bring forth. Counterfeiting these emissions had become so general, that this seemed a very easy and practical way of circumventing the forgers, simply by withdrawing them. But what happened in consequence of doing this? The immediate effect was to discredit all notes bearing these dates, — the genuine as well as the spurious issues. It is true that merchants and others possessing unsalable property were willing to take the bills by way of exchange, and the newspapers of the day teemed with advertisements containing offers of this character. The way in which this order was received is spiritedly depicted in the following letter : —

" How comes it that congress, by their resolve, relative to the two emissions of May, 1777, and April, 1778, have set the country in such a ferment, and given room for a set of speculating people who are enemies to the real good of their country, to take occasion from it to depreciate the value of those two emissions in the manner they have done, and are now daily doing. . . . There are a set of them here very busy in this matter; and by their man-

---

[1] Penn. Gazette, Jan. 21, 1779.

agement within this day or two it is rendered twenty-five p. cent worse than the other emissions, which God knows were sunk low enough before. . . . Our butchers, bakers, and farmers begin to refuse it entirely, owing to the stories propagated about it. Must people, who have this money, either lose a fourth of it or starve? and when the time comes for exchanging it, must they spend half of the value of the little they have in taking it to Philadelphia to place it in the office? and after that wait sixty days and attend a second time for payment? Indeed, I think the resolve is not one the wisest, and wish to see these evils speedily remedied. . . . The merchants, or rather hucksters, of Philadelphia, are playing the game there. Surely, congress can call in these or any other emissions in a manner less injurious to the country."[1]

Robert Rutherford[2] also wrote to Washington from Virginia, "It is with much concern I find the resolve of congress, respecting the money emissions of May 20th, 1777, and April 11th, 1778, giving great and general alarm, tending to depreciate the currency, as the holders of these emissions are really deprived of the use of their money for six months, as it in a great measure ceases to pass here in payments; . . . Assuredly Congress have not taken the whole matter into the account, and I am informed that large sums of this money are now in possession of the subjects of Spain upon the Mississippi, they being enjoined by the governor of Orleans to receive it, not to mention many other obvious objections; so that I am sensible it will be consistent with the wonted jus-

---

[1] Penn. Archives, vol. vi. p. 212.
[2] Sparks's Letters to Wash., vol. ii. p. 252.

tice and prudence of that august body, without loss of time, to revise and greatly change the terms of that resolve."

Another evil attending the measure was the loss to exchangers from the depreciation of their money during the period required to effect exchanges. Several months elapsed before these could be made by persons living far away from Philadelphia: as paper money was now rapidly depreciating, of course the loss must have been very considerable.

The case would not have been quite so bad if the genius and enterprise of the counterfeiters had been wholly expended in making bogus paper money. But they were not content with working in that direction: hard money, also, was subjected to ruinous manipulation. In one of the newspapers [1] published during that period the following bit of news is given: "The unnatural enemies of this country, not satisfied with their frequent but fruitless attempts to destroy the credit of our paper currency, have, at length, introduced large sums of Counterfeit *Half Joes* and *Dollars* among us, in order to buy up the paper money and thereby stamp a discredit upon it; but, thank God, this villany has been detected in its bud, though the perpetrators of the same are still unknown. The *Half Johannes* are admirably well imitated, and require the nicest observation to distinguish the genuine from the counterfeit."

Great Britain was very confident, that, by ruining the circulating medium in America, the people would return to their allegiance: hence the desperation with which

[1] Penn. Packet, March 13, 1779.

counterfeiting was practised by the British agents. The depth of the determination of the people to achieve independence had not been accurately sounded across the ocean. The cause would not be lost, even if the value of Continental paper money sank out of sight. Yet so long as paper money possessed any value, counterfeiters were busy. Although counterfeiting was branded a crime by all the States, and a reward of two thousand dollars was offered by Congress to persons who should " take and prosecute to conviction " all who forged or knowingly attempted to pass counterfeit money, the practice assumed larger and more alarming proportions until paper money ceased to have any value.[1] Counterfeiting was not the chief cause of the depreciation of paper issues; but it greatly aggravated the evils springing from their use, and hastened their extinction.

[1] Even Morris's own notes were extensively forged. See Lieut.-Col. Smith's Letter to Washington, July 15, 1783, New York in the Am. Rev., p. 142. Almon's Rememb., 1783, part 1, p. 126.

CHAPTER XII.

LIMITATION OF PRICES.

CONGRESS had not issued paper money many months before the prices of all commodities began to rise, exciting alarm, producing uncertainty, and disturbing every calculation. The rise of prices was regarded a terrible evil; and Congress sought to prevent this inevitable effect of the over-issue of paper money by a measure, which in the light of these days looks puerile enough, but which at that earlier period found numerous supporters.[1] The plan was to fix the prices of all commodities, both domestic and imported, by legal enactment. This was in no sense a novel conception; for, at an early period in New-England colonial administration, the experiment had been tried; the prices of labor,[2] and of almost every thing forming the subject of sale or exchange, having been established by law. It was a New-England idea, therefore; and, when prices had risen to a considerable height, representatives of the New-England States assembled at Providence, and formed a tariff, which was

[1] Yet Noah Webster wrote, not long after the Act limiting prices was passed, "These regulating acts were reprobated by every man acquainted with commerce and finance." — *Coll. of Essays*, p. 192.

[2] The regulation of prices began in the Massachusetts Colony as early as 1633. Winthrop's Hist. of New England, vol. i. p. 138, new edition, and Felt's Hist. of Mass. Currency, Index, Prices of Articles and Labor.

adopted by all the States represented in the convention.[1] The plan was eagerly seized by Congress, and recommended[2] to other States for imitation, in order " to prevent the present fluctuating and exorbitant prices."

A week before this action of Congress, Adams wrote to his wife, that " the attempt of New England to regulate prices is extremely popular in congress; " but " for my own part," he continues, " I expect only a partial and temporary relief from it, and I fear that after a time the evils will break out with greater violence. The matter will flow with greater rapidity for having been damned up for a time," the truth of which opinion was quickly seen in the swift march of events.

The rapid increase of prices was generally condemned as immoral and unpatriotic, and deserving severe punishment. A French officer,[3] writing from Philadelphia, undoubtedly expressed the truth when he remarked, " The country people are so exasperated at the high price every thing bears, that unless some change soon takes place, they threaten not only to withhold provisions from the town, but to come down in a body, and punish the leaders."

Yet a few, at least, clearly saw why prices were rising. The reason was, because the value of the money by which the prices of things were measured was declining. There was no advance in prices previous to the issue of paper money; but when the issues were greatly

<hr>

[1] For report of Committee of Convention which met at Providence, Dec. 31, 1776, to fix prices, see Conn. Courant, Jan. 27, 1777.

[2] Feb. 15, 1777.

[3] Baron de Bonstellin, Newspaper Cuttings, vol. v. p. 215, N. Y. Hist. Lib.

multiplied, and no adequate provision was made for their redemption, the prices of commodities increased.[1] This truth did not seem so obvious to all as it did to Webster, who published his opinion concerning the measure in a very clear and cogent manner soon after the action of Congress above mentioned. A writer in " The Boston Gazette "[2] declares that the depreciation of the currency "as to its degree, has been more, a great deal the effect of art than nature, and with a view to give greater scope to the operations of that avarice, which, if not laid under restraint, will be the ruin of the country. 'Tis a real truth, that an insatiable thirst after gain, and not the depreciation of the currency is the grand cause of that enormous height to which the prices of things has arisen." This opinion was shared by many others; and even Congress, when addressing the public, professed to believe that paper money had really not depreciated, but that prices had risen through the action of speculators who were accounted the enemies of the government. The real causes for advancing prices were as completely overlooked by that body as they were by Lysias when prosecuting the corn-factors of Greece. As the Greek orator wholly attributed the dearness of corn to a combination among the factors, so did Congress ascribe the enormous advance in the price of things to the action of those having commodities for sale.

Nor were the persons few who believed in the justice and efficacy of the measure limiting prices. An innocent

---

[1] Webster, Political Essays, pp. 11–18.

[2] April 6, 1778; see Letter of Soldier, Ibid., June 25, 1779.

writer in " The Connecticut Journal "[1] maintained that prices ought to be fixed at what they were before the war, and kept so until the conflict was over. No weak believer was he in the power of the State to regulate prices ; yet he merely expressed the prevailing sentiment of the time.[2]

Webster, however, was not alone in maintaining that trade should be left to regulate itself ; for several members of Congress entertained a similar opinion.[3] Says a writer in " The Connecticut Courant,"[4] " As to the scheme of supporting the money and regulating the price of things by penal statutes, it always has and ever will be impracticable in a free country, because no law can be framed to limit a man in the purchase or disposal of property, but what must infringe those principles of liberty for which we are gloriously fighting." By President Reed the experiments were pronounced the " effusions of honest but intemperate zeal to sustain the credit of the paper money."[5] Many other persons echoed the same opinion.

---

[1] Oct. 14, 1778.

[2] Phillips declares that the same opinion was held in all the departments of the States and of the Confederacy. " No considerations of justice, honor, religion or policy, or even the experience of the utter inefficiency of such measures could eradicate it from the public mind " (*Cont. Paper Money*, p. 84). " It seemed to be a kind of obstinate delirium," said Webster, " totally deaf to every argument drawn from justice and right, from its natural tendency and mischief, from common sense and even from common safety." To which he added the very truthful and forcible observation, " It is not more absurd to attempt to impel faith into the heart of an unbeliever by fire and fagot, or to whip love into your mistress with a cowskin, than to force value or credit into your money by penal laws " (*Political Essays*, p. 128, note, and p. 132).

[3] Bradford's Hist. of Mass., vol. ii. p. 172.   [4] May 12, 1777.

[5] Reed's Life of Reed, vol. ii. p. 140.

One of the earliest fruits of this measure was the secreting of goods by their owners.[1] This was an unexpected result; but a quick though extremely rough and characteristic remedy was found for what was generally regarded a violation of the spirit of the law. Stores were opened, and the goods were sold at fixed prices by self-constituted committees. The owners were accused of conspiring to raise the price of commodities and to depreciate the currency; and Tories, speculators, engrossers, and forestallers, enemies of their country, and many other names of a similar character, were liberally applied to them.[2]

The measure soon encountered bitter opposition. Adams writes from Philadelphia,[3] "The merchant scolds, the farmer growls, and every one seems wroth that he cannot grind his neighbor." The law from the beginning was very generally disregarded. On the 20th of April, 1777,[4] Abigail Adams informs her husband, "The Act which at first was in some measure regarded and stemmed the torrent of oppression, is now no more heeded than if it had never been made." This was only two months after Congress had recommended the other States to adopt the measure. Yet, as the law was broken so openly and quickly in Boston and vicinity, the home of its inception, no one could reasonably hope for a better execution of it elsewhere.

The law did not fail through lack of effort to enforce it in several, at least, of the States. In Pennsylvania especially, severe measures were devised and executed

[1] Phillips, p. 83.   [2] Webster, Political Essays, p. 11, note.
[3] Feb. 8, 1777, Familiar Letters, p. 243.   [4] Familiar Letters, p. 262.

for enforcing the Act. A public meeting was held at Philadelphia in May, 1779, at which it was resolved unconditionally to " insist and demand that the advanced or monopolized price of the present month be instantly taken off," and a committee were appointed to determine and publish, from time to time, fixed prices for goods and commodities. Even Morris did not escape visitation from a committee who were appointed to execute the law. A ship arrived, laden with goods consigned to him, but which were really for the use of the French fleet. Notwithstanding Morris's explanation, "the people," says Phillips, "chose to believe that they were for the use of the monopolizers and forestallers." [1]

In other parts of the country similar experiments were tried in enforcing the law. In Boston, on the 17th of June, 1779, the following handbill was seen, having been posted during the preceding night: [2] —

SONS OF BOSTON! SLEEP NO LONGER!

Wednesday, June 16, 1779.

You are requested to meet on the floor of the Old Scotch Meeting House to-morrow morning, at 9 o'clock, at which time the bells will ring.

Rouse and catch the Philadelphia spirit; rid the community of those *monopolizers* and *extortionators*, who, like *canker worms*, are gnawing upon your vitals. They are reducing the currency to waste paper, by refusing to take it for many articles; the infection is dangerous. We have borne with such wretches, but will bear no longer. Public *examples*, at this time would be public *benefits!* You then that have articles to

---

[1] Cont. Paper Money, p. 124.　　　　[2] Phillips, p. 128.

sell, lower your prices; you that have houses to let, refuse not the currency for rent; for inspired with the spirit of those heroes and patriots, who have struggled and bled for their country, and moved with the cries and distresses of the widow, the orphan and the necessitous, Boston shall no longer be *your* place of security! Ye inhabitants of Nantucket, who first introduced the accursed crime of refusing paper money, quit the place, or destruction shall attend your property, and your persons be the object of   VENGEANCE.

N.B. Lawyers, keep yourselves to yourselves. It is our determination to support the reputable merchant and fair trader.

The merchants of Boston were alarmed. At a meeting held the same day the above handbill appeared, they agreed not to advance prices, and, after the 15th of July, to reduce them.[1] They resolved to buy neither silver nor gold, nor to make any payment in these metals; to expose all persons who transgressed the regulation, and to bring to justice all persons concerned in monopolizing and forestalling. In the town of Milton, near Boston, it was resolved to take gold and silver at the same rates as paper money.[2]

In Albany the same spirit broke forth. A committee were chosen to regulate prices; and two transgressors who had sold rum for more than the established price were publicly cried through the city by order of the committee "as having incurred the just indignation of the

---

[1] Penn. Packet, June 29, 1779.

[2] For similar action of the county of Fairfield, Conn., see Conn. Journal, Aug. 25, 1779. In respect to taking gold and silver at the same valuation as paper, see hotel bill of Lieut. Anberry, Travels through the Interior Parts of America, vol. ii. p. 487.

people. The inhabitants ordered them immediately to appear before them, being met at the market place, where, by falling on their knees on a scaffold they acknowledged themselves guilty, and promised to abide by and assist the orders of the committee, upon which they were discharged." "The Pennsylvania Packet" of Philadelphia, which published the foregoing incident, adds, "hard money is not to pass here any more; we have lately hung up and burned in effigy a dollar in hard money.[1]" Notwithstanding the punishments inflicted, and indignities heaped upon individuals, for selling above legal prices, the law was constantly evaded.[2] The importer attempted to justify himself because of the great risk incurred in getting his goods into the country, and the farmer justified himself in raising the price of his commodities because the merchant had done the same thing, and all having any thing to sell who violated the law pleaded a similar excuse.[3]

The object of the measure was to prevent a great calamity, the depreciation of the currency; "but unfortunately," as a correspondent declared in one of the newspapers of the day, "it has a powerful tendency to bring on us the very misfortune it was designed to prevent, at least it would have, if strictly observed."[4] Adams[5] writes as early as September, 1777, before the experiment had been tried a year, "That improvident Act for limiting prices has done great injury, and in my sincere

---

[1] Penn. Packet, June 29, 1779.

[2] Bradford's Hist. of Mass., vol. ii. p. 135.

[3] Conn. Courant, Oct. 21, 1777; Dec. 2, 1777.

[4] Ibid., May 26, 1777.   [5] Familiar Letters, p. 307.

opinion, if not repealed, will ruin the state and introduce a civil war. I know not how unpopular this sentiment may be; but it is sincerely mine." Nor will any one question the truth of the assertion who has ever investigated the subject. The regulation of prices by law had precisely the opposite effect to that intended; for prices were increased rather than diminished by the adoption of the measure.

To what extent prices were raised by the operation of this Act cannot be ascertained, because it was only one of several co-operating causes, and it would be impossible to show the precise extent to which each cause contributed in swelling prices. One newspaper correspondent[1] affirmed that the high prices prevailing at the time he wrote were occasioned by three causes, — the plentifulness of money, the cessation of trade, and the obstruction of courts of justice, whereby debts were not discharged. Another affirmed that high prices were caused, first by a " want of credit or means of redemption in the emitters, second, a flood or great number of bills emitted. The first admits of no remedy, and must assuredly not only depreciate but annihilate a currency so ill supported. The last is no more incident to a paper than to a gold or silver currency." Money had not depreciated, he thought, but things were higher because money was so abundant.[2] On the other hand, Watson gave as a reason for raising the price of "The Courant," that " things in general were raised about fifty per cent by the regulating Act."[3] One thing is certain, the rise in prices was not wholly covered by the depreciation in

---

[1] See also Conn. Courant, Dec. 30, 1777.   [2] Ibid., May 12, 1777.   [3] Ibid.

paper money; for at one time the prices of articles in hard money were on an average three times higher than they had formerly been, measured by the same standard.

Congress, seeing the futility of the measure, on the 8th of October, 1778, voted "that all limitations of prices of gold and silver be taken off," though the measure was carried by only a bare majority. This was not long after the French alliance, when the prospect had brightened, and many indulged the belief that the war would come to a speedy close. The States, however, did not heed this latter recommendation; for they continued to regulate prices nearly three years longer.

Even Congress, more than two years afterward, was led to ask the executive power of the several States to prepare and transmit to the Treasury Board a list of the commodities usually sold within each State during the year 1774, with the prices received therefor, for the purpose of guiding the commissary-general and his assistants in making purchases.[1]

Just before Congress made this request,[2] a convention, composed of delegates from the New-England States and New York, had assembled at Hartford to regulate prices, which recommended a general convention of all the States as far south as Virginia, to meet for the same purpose at Philadelphia, in January the following year.[2] This action received the warm approval of Congress;[3] and the States were earnestly recommended to enact laws for establishing and carrying into execution a general limitation of prices in their respective jurisdictions on the following

[1] Jan. 1, 1780.   [2] October, 1779.   [3] Nov. 19, 1779.

principles, and to commence applying them from the first day of February, 1780.

Articles of domestic produce, farming, and common labor, the wages of tradesmen and mechanics, water and land carriage, were not to exceed twenty-fold the prices current through the various seasons of the year 1774.

Articles imported from foreign parts were to be in due proportion with labor and the articles as above stated, making a proper allowance for freight, insurance, and other charges. Salt and military stores, however, whether of home manufacture, or imported from abroad, were to be excepted from any limitation of price.

The several States were also recommended to enact strict laws against engrossing and withholding, and to take the necessary steps for securing the efficient execution of the same; and officers and agents employed in making purchases for the United States were directed to conform strictly to the State regulations upon the subject.

Thus Congress failed to recognize the real difficulty: perhaps it was not seen; anyhow, it was suffered to remain.[1]

---

[1] The following extract illustrates Gen. Marion's idea concerning the enforcement of the Act regulating prices: "Every article that is brought in for sale, I wish to have regulated, that it may not be sold at too extravagant prices, giving such a generous profit to the importers as to encourage the trade as much as possible. Salt must not be more than four hard dollars per bushel. Every article that is or may tend to luxury may be at whatever price the seller pleases, and my meaning is to regulate nothing but what may be absolutely necessary for the support of life, such as salt, sugar, coffee, tea and medicines." — *Order to Col. Horry*, March 7, 1782, GIBBES's *Doc. Hist. of Am. Rev.* in 1781 and 1782, p. 204.

When paper money ceased to circulate, and prices were measured in specie, they speedily fell, and no one felt the need of calling on the States to regulate them. As soon as a sound money was employed, the general dissatisfaction respecting the inflation of prices immediately ceased. The true remedy for high prices was found at last; but in the mean time a vast deal of evil and suffering had been experienced.

In August, 1779, which was only a few days before the action of Congress just described, the merchants of Philadelphia petitioned the city to repeal the Act limiting prices, to which petition a committee composed of thirteen persons made an elaborate reply. The two papers [1] contain an interesting summary of the reasons both for and against the measure, and it is within the line of our inquiry to pass them briefly under review.

The memorialists claimed that the limitation of prices in principle was unjust, because it invaded the laws of property by compelling a person to accept less in exchange for his goods than he could otherwise obtain, and therefore operated as a tax upon a part of the community only. To this claim the committee replied, that claiming a right to an unlimited extortion such as prevailed before the limitation took effect, and ability to enforce the claim because foreign necessaries of life were in the hands of a few, and wanted by many who could not otherwise procure them, nor conveniently subsist without them, was a principle far more unjust; and therefore, admitting the position to be true (which was not), and determining between two evils by a comparison of

---

[1] Published in Penn. Packet, Aug. 10, 1779.

causes and consequences, the committee were led to prefer the least evil as the wisest choice.

Nor could the committee subscribe to the doctrine that the limitation of prices was in principle unjust. The limitation of prices where extortion might otherwise be easily practised had been the custom, not only of our own, but of other countries in particular times and cases. Limiting the interest of money by law to prevent extortionous usury was an application of the same principle. The limiting of town expenses, porters' and carriers' charges, ferriages, and numerous other matters, were founded on the probability, that, if no such restraints were imposed, the persons practising those employments would take an unjust advantage of the immediate necessity of others, and compel them to pay just what they pleased; yet merchants had never been known to declare that the principle thus applied to their advantage was unjust.

The memorialists not only claimed an unlimited right of setting what price they pleased on their commodities, but admitted, that, from the present situation of trade, they had it in their power to enforce those prices. The right without the power of course would produce no ill effect, as might be seen in times when trade is free, open, and plentiful; but, as the present situation of trade had introduced a union of the right with the power, therefore it was dangerous, so the committee declared, and required that kind of restraint which should remove the danger.

To the claim that limitation of prices tended to injure public credit, the committee replied, " The defect cannot be in the money itself, neither can it be in the want of ability in the states to redeem it when they please, but in the little value which has lately been set upon it by those who have endeavored to get great sums into their hands for small quantities of goods. And we wish the memorialists to see, that if the value of the money should be still farther impaired by an advance of prices, it seems to us reasonable to apprehend that it will scarcely be worth the redeeming, and that the easiest, cheapest, and most expeditious method to sink it will be for every man to consent to lose that portion of it which he possesses, whether in bills or loan-office certificates. For we are free to declare that the late depreciated state of the currency has introduced such a practice of speculating upon its future probable value as is not only disreputable to the national character of the country but dangerous to her real and public interest, and that unless the value of it can be so supported as to become of equal and universal advantage to the community, it had better not be supported at all."

The committee further contended, that it was impossible to oppose an argument of words against an argument of facts. "We have had the experience of four years without limitations or regulations; the consequence of which had very nearly been the total ruin of the currency, and resting it here, we prefer this single case to all the arguments that can be produced against it."

Another argument urged by the merchants was, that they had subscribed liberally to the public funds, which, as previously explained, were the loan-office certificates. The reply of the committee on this point was not less true than, perhaps, unexpected: "We are by no means satisfied that the public funds, on their present footing, are any benefit to the United States, neither are we of opinion that borrowing paper money on the credit of paper certificates is an eligible system of finance, and that for the following reasons:

"The country is thereby burthened with an interest of six per cent, without receiving a proportionate advantage therefrom; because an emission of certificates is as much an emission of money as if the same quantity had been struck in dollars; therefore the six per cent is paid for nothing, and the same sum which the certificates represent might as well have been struck in dollars without interest as in certificates with it, for on a full consideration of the case we have numerous reasons to believe, that the sums which have been borrowed by congress and represented a second time in certificates, and those certificates negotiated in payment add as much to the quantity of money in circulation as if the same sum had been struck which has been borrowed. Neither do we conceive it possible that the quantity of dollars which have been emitted should be a sufficient reply considering the present annoying high prices, were not some other species of money circulating in large payments; and therefore the importer by changing his dollars into certificates and trading with those certificates, in the same manner he would with the dollars, receives the same mercantile advantages under one shape as another, and an interest of six per cent into the bargain, which we conceive to be a mode of funding and financing the country will not be able to bear."

Such, in brief, were the main arguments advanced by friends and opponents to this scheme of a legal regulation of prices. Patriotic arguments could certainly be framed in support of the measure; other plausible ones were not wanting: none, however, could live in the sunlight of experience. Tried by facts, the measure was a total failure in achieving the end proposed by its authors, and ultimately had not a defender.[1]

[1] Ineffectual and unwise as the measures of Congress and of the States were for regulating prices, it is worth while to note the fact, that, while the British occupied New York, the prices of wheat, rye, corn, flour, and meal, were fixed by Sir Henry Clinton, on the ground that it was "highly unreasonable that those who may stand in need of those articles, should be left at the mercy of the farmer." The rates at which the farmers were selling their produce were declared to be too high, in other words, "do vastly exceed in proportion the advanced price of those articles which the farmer stands in need of purchasing;" and still further, the farmers were directed to thresh their grain within certain times stated in the proclamation. If the order were disobeyed, his whole crop of grain or quantity of manufactured flour or meal was to be seized and confiscated. Proclamation issued Dec. 20, 1777, Almon's Rememb., 1778, p. 57. Also, when Sir William Howe was in possession of Philadelphia, the prices of porters and draymen were fixed by proclamation on account of "the exorbitant prices they demand for their services." Proc. dated May 13, 1778, Ibid., p. 210.

CHAPTER XIII.

THE LEGAL TENDER LAWS OF THE REVOLUTION.

AMONG other expedients to preserve the value of Continental paper money was the enactment of laws by Congress and the States, making bills of credit a legal tender in discharge of all pecuniary obligations. As paper money had formerly been a legal tender in Pennsylvania, this measure was not an original one with the Continental Congress. Rhode Island was the first State to heed the recommendation of Congress; and in August, 1775, the Assembly declared the Continental bills to be a legal tender in payment of all debts, and threw over them the same protection from the arts of the counterfeiter as had been devised for the preservation of the State issues.[1] The Assembly also resolved that any person who refused such money ought to be considered an enemy to the credit, reputation, and happiness of the Colonies, and wholly destitute of the regard and obligation which he owed to his country; that he should be regarded as wanting in zeal to the cause of liberty, and be debarred from communication with all good citizens. Virginia followed next in enacting laws of a similar import: these examples were shortly afterwards imitated

---

[1] Staples, Hist. of R. I. in the Cont. Cong., p. 49.

by New Hampshire and New Jersey, and ere long all the States had taken action theron.

The laws of the States were not in every respect similar; for in some of them the bills were made a legal tender only for the interest of former debts, but not for the principal. In New Hampshire, on the other hand, if a creditor refused to receive the bills when offered, the whole debt was legally cancelled. Congress, desiring uniformity of action on the part of the States, passed the following resolution in January,[1] 1777 : "*Resolved,* That all bills of credit, emitted by authority of Congress, ought to pass current in all payments, trade, and dealings, in these states, and be deemed in value equal to the same nominal sums in Spanish milled dollars; and that whoever shall offer, ask, or receive more in the said bills for any gold or silver coins, bullion, or any other species of money whatsoever, than the nominal sum or amount thereof in Spanish milled dollars, or more, in the said bills, for any lands, houses, goods, or commodities whatsoever, than the same could be purchased at of the same person or persons in gold, silver, or any other species of money whatsoever; or shall offer to sell any goods or commodities for gold or silver coins, or any other species of money whatsoever, and refuse to sell the same for the said continental bills; every such a person ought to be deemed an enemy to the liberties of these United States, and to forfeit the value of the money so exchanged, or house, land, or commodity so sold or offered to sale. And it is recommended to the legislatures of the respective states, to enact laws inflicting such forfeitures and other penal-

---

[1] Jan. 14.

ties on offenders as aforesaid, as will prevent such pernicious practices." Congress further recommended the Legislatures of the States to pass laws making the bills of credit issued by Congress a lawful tender in payment of public and private debts, and a refusal thereof an extinguishment of the same.

Thus, by action of the States and Congress, paper money was endowed with a legal tender attribute. The disastrous consequences of this legislation will now be related.

A historian who lived in those times has given a vivid description of the miseries which flowed from this truly iniquitous measure. "The aged who had retired from the scenes of active business, to enjoy the fruits of their industry, found their substance melting away to a mere pittance, insufficient for their support. The widow who lived comfortably on the bequests of a deceased husband, experienced a frustration of all his well-meant tenderness. The laws of the country interposed, and compelled her to receive a shilling, where a pound was her due. The blooming virgin who had grown up with an unquestionable title to a liberal patrimony, was legally stripped of every thing but her personal charms and virtues. The hapless orphan, instead of receiving from the hands of an executor, a competency to set out in business, was obliged to give a final discharge on the payment of 6d. in the pound. In many instances, the earnings of a long life of care and diligence were, in the space of a few years, reduced to a trifling sum. A few persons escaped these affecting calamities, by secretly transferring their bonds, or by flying from the presence or neighborhood of their debtors."

The debtor, however, leaving out the wrecking of his conscience, was the gainer. "A hog or two would pay for a slave; a few cattle for a comfortable house; and a good horse for an improved plantation. A small part of the productions of a farm would discharge the long outstanding accounts, due from its owner. The dreams of the golden age were realized to the poor man and the debtor, but unfortunately what these gained, was just so much taken from others."

The candor of history requires the fact to be stated that paper money was "at all times the poor man's friend. While it was current, all kinds of labor very readily found their reward. In the first years of the war, none were idle from want of employment, and none were employed, without having it in their power to obtain ready payment for their services. To that class of people, whose daily labor was their support, the depreciation was no disadvantage. Expending their money as fast as they received it, they always got its full value. The reverse was the case with the rich, or those who were disposed to hoarding. No agrarian law ever had a more extensive operation, than continental money. That for which the Gracchi lost their lives in Rome was peaceably effected in the United States, by the legal tender of these depreciating bills.

"That the helpless part of the community were legislatively deprived of their property, was among the lesser evils, which resulted from the legal tender of the depreciated bills of credit. The iniquity of the laws estranged the minds of many of the citizens from the habits and love of justice. The nature of obligations was so far changed, that he was reckoned the honest man, who from principle delayed to pay his debts. The mounds which government had erected, to secure the observance of honesty in the commercial intercourse of man with man, were broken down. Truth, honor, and justice were swept away by the overflowing deluge of legal iniquity, nor have they yet assumed their ancient and accustomed seats." So wrote Ramsay in 1789.[1]

The newspapers of the period were filled with bitter complaints of the injustice of the measure and of the losses to which persons were subjected in consequence of it. The following letter, addressed to Mr. Dunlap, the printer of "The Pennsylvania Packet,"[2] reflects very truthfully the sentiment of the time: —

If something is not done to prevent trustees and guardians from taking advantage of the times, in defrauding helpless widows and orphans, great numbers who have lived in opulence before the death of their husbands or parents, and had what was thought a competency left them after their death, will be reduced to a state of indigence. I am an only daughter of an indulgent father, who died about six years ago, and left me a pretty fortune in ready cash, which he placed in the hands of a neighbor, whom he trusted would administer strict justice towards me. The interest arising from it has, till of late, enabled me to live in a genteel style of life, but in our country's present distress, only affords a scanty pittance; but that is not the worst, sir! I am just arrived at age, and my guardian insists on paying me the principal. Is not this cruel hard in the present state of our money? I appeal to the guardians of our country, I appeal to the heart of every honest man,

---

[1] Hist. of Am. Rev., vol. ii. p. 134, *et seq.*   [2] April, 1779.

whether this be acting the faithful guardian, and whether laws ought not to be enacted to prevent such undue advantages being taken of the widow and orphan. I am a female whig, Mr. Dunlap, and my hopes and wishes warm for my country's success; but why am I to be thus the sufferer? My guardian appropriated my fortune to his own use six years ago, for which he has now a real estate which would sell for ten times the price it cost; but he says, it was your father's will that you should receive your fortune in money. Thus, you see, what advantages our laws give to bad men, who aggrandize themselves at the expense of the helpless orphan. I have had a hint from a friend, that he would pay me half the amount in hard money, if I would give a receipt in full. How base such an offer! How deserving the contempt of a much injured, helpless woman! No, sir, all I desire is, to see laws enacted empowering widows and orphans, in such cases, to refuse receiving payments until our money is reinstated in its original value; which, I trust, it will ere long; thereby rendering those incapable of taking an advantage who have not honesty enough to do as they would be done by. For though there are laws in force making our money a legal tender in all payments, sure there might be exceptions in such cases as these, the justice of which, at the present time, must be obvious to every honest man, obliging all trustees and guardians, who were possessed of money on trust before certain dates, to be obliged to retain such moneys in their hands until the conclusion of the present glorious revolution; and so confident am I that such a measure must take place, that I shall absolutely refuse to take my fortune at present.

A writer in "The Connecticut Journal"[1] affirmed, that

---

[1] Conn. Jour., Nov. 11, 1778; see Continental Journal, Jan. 7, 1779; also Ibid., Feb. 25 and April 15, 1779.

in consequence of the resolutions of Congress and of the States, making the currency a tender in law, nine-tenths perhaps, at least, of the debts outstanding in 1775, had been paid in Continental bills. People took advantage of the times, and almost universally settled accounts with creditors who would accept these bills in payment. All such debts were once as good as gold and silver. A very considerable part of them were originally in hard money lent out on interest. Great sums were debts of merchants, contracted when goods sold at the lowest rates, some of which, probably, had been on book for years, without interest. Other debts were fortunes, or lesser inheritances, originally paid in hard money, or in obligations for it ; or they were funds for the support of public schools and seminaries of learning. The losses accruing to nearly all creditors of this description were irreparable.

It is easy enough to see how the debtors were benefited ; but how could creditors be by the operation of a law, as one of them pithily put it, which declared " denominations and sounds to be equivalent for real substance " ?

Had the legal tender regulations been framed with reference to future contracts, while deploring the measure as unwise, no one could have complained of their operating unjustly. But, in endowing such legislation with a retroactive operation, the grossest injustice was perpetrated. The fraudulent debtor took advantage of the law to cheat his creditor ; while the latter could not save himself, except by privately transferring the written obligation, or by refusing payment, which, indeed, was done at a risk of losing the debt. Nevertheless, creditors did occasionally refuse to accept payment, believing, that, at some future time, justice would triumph, and the iniquitous law be repealed. Husbandmen who lived remote from the scene of hostilities were able to preserve their property. Hawkers and monopolizers, "who crept from obscurity and assumed the name of merchants," waxed strong and rich during these distressing times. But those whose property was held in trust, or whose living depended on fixed salaries, or who could not descend to practise knavery, though established by law, experienced severe suffering.

These laws, notwithstanding their well-known operation, remained in force until 1780, when Congress urged the States to amend them in "such a manner as shall be judged most conducive to justice in the present state of the paper money."[1] Then arose a new set of difficulties to confront debtors whose obligations had been incurred while paper money was passing swiftly through the era of depreciation. The several States acted upon the recommendation of Congress, and repealed the legal tender laws; but in most cases the situation of both the debtor and creditor classes was viewed in the clear light of justice, and such laws were enacted as displayed a fine perception of the rights and equities of all parties.[2] Rhode Island was among the first States to act, and her legislation is worthy of extended consideration.[3]

---

[1] March 20.

[2] The English commissioners, who had previously acted in South Carolina, recommended as just and equitable the payment of debts according to a scale of depreciation established by them, Almon's Rememb., 1781, part 1, pp. 216, 217.

[3] R. I. Col. Records, vol. ix. pp. 281–284.

All contracts made previously to the 1st of January, 1777, for bills of credit, either of that State or of Congress, were deemed equal to the same nominal sum in gold or silver, while all contracts made after that date, and previous to the Act we are now describing, which was passed in November, 1780, expressed or understood to be liquidated in paper money, were to be rated in Spanish milled dollars, or other money equivalent thereto, by a table of depreciation contained in the Act itself, extending over the years 1777–79, and the first four months of 1780, in which the depreciation varied from 105 in January, 1777, to 4000 in April, 1780.

It was also enacted that all private contracts made before the 1st of May, 1777, "and all special contracts made for silver or gold after that time, between individuals, shall be paid in gold or silver only," and that all other private contracts made after that date might be discharged by paying "the just value of the currency contracted for in silver or gold, or in bills of credit of the United States, at the current exchange at the time of payment."

Provision was next made for executors, administrators, guardians, agents, clerks of courts, and other persons having trust funds in their possession. They were to be discharged from any demands of those for whom they had so acted, without the allowance of any depreciation thereon. If, however, they had used the funds thus confided to them on their "own private account," they were required to "account therefor upon the principles of justice and equity, in the same manner as other persons."

While paper money was depreciating, as we have previously shown, a class of persons refused to receive it in payment of obligations due to them.[1] The Legislature provided, that in such cases, if the creditor brought an action to recover his debt, the Court should refer the matter to indifferent persons to determine the same in the way appearing to them "just and equitable, taking into account all the circumstances thereof."

"As the widow, the infant and the orphan, at all times, ought, in a special manner, to receive the support of the laws, in the protection of their persons and property," it was enacted that the refusal of any executor, administrator, guardian, or agent, to receive paper money due to them in their capacities as trustees, should not operate to the prejudice of those for whom they were acting, but they should "be allowed the whole depreciation in such debt notwithstanding."

In respect to partial payments of notes and other obligations, the Act further provided, that the sums thus paid should be allowed, without any deduction on account of the depreciation of paper money; while adequate provision was also made for the just settlement of all accounts, including book debts, thus covering all claims of debtors and creditors who were likely to be affected in any way by the repeal of the legal tender laws.

No one in that State, or any other, seems to have questioned the propriety, either of repealing the legal tender laws, or of adjusting the liability under contracts and obligations incurred during the three years and more during which paper money was depreciating prior

---

[1] Ante, p. 180.

to the repeal of the legal tender laws by the standard of justice.

The example of Rhode Island was imitated by all the States, with more or less variation. Its essential feature, however, is found in the legislation of all the other States; namely, of adjusting contracts made while the legal tender law was in operation, in such a way as to render to the creditor a fair equivalent for what, in the beginning, was received by the debtor. Besides, creditors were generally prevented from bringing actions for a year or two, or even a longer period, to recover their debts, and, in cases where judgments had been rendered, the courts were directed to suspend issuing executions. The purpose of these stay laws was to give the Legislatures time to enact measures for determining the rights of all parties, which were devised, in most cases, within a year from the time Congress recommended a repeal of the tender laws.

Virginia did not take action upon repealing the legal tender law till June, 1781; and even then the legal tender function attached to it for a year longer, while it was continued without limit in respect to paying paper money for taxes. The law provided that all debts and contracts made in the current money of the State for the six years inclusive, between the 1st of January, 1777 and 1782, or of the United States, "excepting at all times contracts entered into for gold and silver coin, tobacco or any other specific property," remaining due and unfulfilled, should be liquidated in accordance with a scale of depreciation established by the Legislature; "that is to say, by reducing the amount of all such debts and contracts to the true value in specie at the days or times the same were incurred or entered into; and, upon payment of said value so found in specie or other money equivalent thereto, the debtors or contractors shall be forever discharged of and from the said debts or contracts, any law, custom, or usage to the contrary in any wise notwithstanding." In all cases of part payment of any debt, the debtor was allowed full credit for the nominal amount.

The action of Maryland is worthy of note from its striking difference to the other modes related. The old Continental issues were declared to be no longer a legal tender, except at the exchange of £166 13s. 4d. current money for £100 sterling; but the new emissions were to be "current and a legal tender in payment discharge" of any obligation incurred thereafter: if, however, they did depreciate, the chancellor and judges of the General Court were to ascertain the amount of their depreciation, and the liquidation of debts was to be governed by the rule thus established.

Pennsylvania, alarmed at the novel situation, passed an Act forbidding all persons to bring suits to recover debts for two years, because of the scarcity of specie.[1] The first attempt in March, 1780, to suspend the operation of the legal tender laws, so far as they related to the Continental currency, failed; but two months later a bill was passed depriving these paper issues of their legal tender quality. In June the same year, the Assembly declared, "that from time to time all contracts should be made good according to the special nature of each."

[1] Penn. Packet, Dec. 3, 1782.

The question had not reached a final solution. The State issued more paper money, which at first every one was free to take at his own valuation; not long afterward, however, by a special Act, this new issue was declared to possess a legal tender function. Legislation on the subject grew bitter; but finally, in June, 1781, all the legal tender laws were repealed.[1]

We have not space to trace minutely the action of every State repealing its legal tender laws in accordance with the recommendation of Congress. As soon as the voice of Congress was heard in South Carolina, Gov. Rutledge issued a proclamation forbidding creditors to sue for the recovery of their debts until the meeting of the Legislature.[2] In his message addressed to that body he remarked, with reference to this subject, " You will now consider whether it may be proper to repeal those laws, and fix some equitable mode for the discharge of debts contracted whilst paper money was in circulation." This view prevailed throughout the States, and in a more or less perfect form was embodied in their legislation.[3]

A somewhat singular effect of the repeal of the legal tender laws was experienced in collecting fines imposed under enactments passed at various times prior to the repeal of the legal tender measures.[4] As the specie standard was now restored, it was necessary to collect

---

[1] The opinion of President Reed was, that "all contracts should be made good according to the special nature of each" (REED's *Life of Reed*, vol. ii. p. 289). See Ibid. for action of Pennsylvania on the subject, pp. 288-292, 296-299.

[2] Gibbes's Doc. Hist. of Am. Rev., 1781 and 1782, p. 105.

[3] Ibid., p. 233.   [4] Ibid., p. 104.

fines in specie; but it was manifestly unjust to collect a fine in specie for the written amount, when the legislators, at the time of prescribing the fine, supposed the collection of it would be made in paper, at an enormous depreciation compared with gold and silver. Gov. Rutledge wrestled with this vexatious question in a proclamation; and, doubtless, the judiciaries of other States were perplexed with the same question. Of course, it was easy enough to amend the statutes with reference to future fines; but it was very difficult to deal with those cases which had occurred before legislation could render any relief.

Congress, like the States, established a scale of depreciation of paper money, by which all contracts made by officials of the General Government during the time legal tender laws were in operation were to be settled. It was also necessary to pass numerous special acts upon the subject which it was quite impossible to cover by any general regulation.

Such were some of the chief consequences flowing from the enactment as well as the repeal of the legal tender laws. Their enactment proved a benefit to the debtor and the working-classes; creditors of every description were injured or ruined; and the foundations of morality were sadly undermined.[1]   In repealing these

1 " The whole history of this continental paper is a history of public frauds. Old specie debts were often paid in a depreciated currency, and even new contracts for a few weeks or days were often discharged with a small part of the value received. From this plenty and fluctuating state of the medium, sprung hosts of speculators and itinerant traders, who left their honest occupations for the prospect of immense gains, in a fraudulent business, that depended on no fixed principles, and the

regulations, the States sought to do justice to all who had incurred obligations while the currency was depreciated, and labored honestly and effectually to that end. In making paper money a legal tender, neither Congress nor the States designed to perpetrate the ill effects which followed. Until the year 1780, it was believed by Congress and the people generally, that the whole paper flood would improve 'in quality until it was worth as much in specie as it purported to be. The legal tender laws were established, said "The Freeman's Journal" in 1782, in reviewing their history in Pennsylvania, "with the approbation of every one who wished to be considered as devoted to independence and liberty, and whatever may be said against the enforced tender of this sort of money, yet to these tender laws, under God, must the political salvation of the country in the years 1776, 1777 and 1778 be ascribed."[1]

When the present Constitution was framed, its authors, fresh with the recollection of the terrible losses and iniquities which had sprung from the legal tender laws, endeavored to guard as strongly as possible against the perpetration of so grave an injustice in the future; but, within a hundred years, the barriers set up in the Con-

profits of which could be reduced to no certain calculation." — NOAH WEBSTER, *Coll. of Essays*, p. 192.

[1] Thomas Paine wrote with reference to paper money, "Every stone in the bridge, that has carried us over, seems to have a claim upon our esteem. But this was a corner-stone and its usefulness cannot be forgotten. There is something in a grateful mind, which extends itself even to things that can neither be benefited by regard, nor suffer by neglect; — but so it is, and almost every man is sensible of the effect." — *Letter addressed to the Abbé Raynal*, p. 26.

stitution have been broken down, and the deed sanctioned, not on the ground of a necessity greater than the preservation of the Constitution itself, — a defence which many would have regarded as justifiable, — but upon the ground, forsooth, that the act was indeed within the meaning of the organic law, which if read in the light of history, especially the debate thereon at the time of its creation, nothing can be clearer than that the framers of that marvellous instrument meant and said just the opposite to that which the Supreme Court of the United States affirm they said and intended.

CHAPTER XIV.

TAXATION.

IN several ways, as we have seen, did Congress seek to obtain funds for maintaining the government, and carrying on the war. There was another mode, however, that of taxation, which ought to have proved the most efficacious of all, but which, for various reasons, yielded only slight relief.

When the first issues of paper money appeared, no one supposed the quantity would be very great; and for several months their value was maintained at par with gold and silver.[1] "The United States," says Ramsay, "for a considerable time derived as much benefit from this paper creation of their own, though without any established funds for its support or redemption, as would have resulted to them from the free gift of so many Mexican dollars." Probably no one was so sanguine as to believe that any large quantity could be maintained at par with the precious metals; and accordingly, Congress, as soon as the first two issues were authorized, consisting

---

[1] It is true that some persons in Philadelphia, as early as November, 1775, refused to receive Continental bills, or even those of Pennsylvania (STAPLES's *Hist. of R. I. in the Cont. Cong.*, p. 50); but, doubtless, they were either Tories, Quakers, or individuals wearing some other religious cloak.

of three million dollars, prepared an assessment based upon the supposed population of the Colonies, and apportioned this sum among them, expecting they would raise the quotas assigned to them by taxation. Congress did not possess the power to tax the States directly; and, even had such an authority been granted, the exercise of it in the beginning of the war would doubtless have proved an unpopular proceeding.[1] Congress prudently left this matter to the States, believing they would promptly devise measures for raising their quotas. But they hesitated to act, perhaps fearing evil consequences if a tax were thus early imposed upon the people.

There was one person at least, who, at the very outset of issuing paper money, saw the necessity of taxing the people for the purpose of paying it. This was Webster. Writing to " The Pennsylvania Evening Post,"[2] in October, 1776, he remarks, " Payment in promises or bills of credit is a temporary expedient, and will always be dangerous, where the quantity increases too much, at least it will always have the consequences of a medium increased beyond the necessities of trade, and whenever that happens, a speedy remedy is necessary, or the ill effects will soon be alarming, and, if long neglected, will not be easily remedied. The remedy or rather prevention of this evil I take to be very easy at present."

Having shown the effects of issuing a greater quantity of paper money than required by trade, he points out the remedy, which consisted in " lessening the quantity of circulating medium." This could be done in three

---

[1] Franklin, Letter to Morris, Dec. 25, 1783, Dip. Cor., vol. iv. p. 187.
[2] Political Essays, p. 2.

ways; the last of which was by a tax, which, he affirmed, "never can be paid so easy as when money is more plenty than goods, and of course, the very cause which makes a tax necessary, facilitates the payment of it."[1] A writer in "The Boston Gazette"[2] held a similar view. He declared there was too much money, and that a tax ought to be laid, and not a light one either. "Money without credit is no money," he correctly observed.

[1] Ibid., p. 3.

Webster continues the consideration of the subject by declaring that "the tax ought to be equal to the excess of the currency, so as to lessen the currency down to that quantity which is necessary for a medium of trade, and this, in my opinion, ought to be done by every state, whether money is immediately wanted in the public treasury or not, for it is better for any state to have their excess of money, though it were all gold and silver, hoarded in a public treasury or bank, than circulated among the people, for nothing can have worse effects on any state than an excess of money. The poverty of the states of Holland, where nobody can have money who does not first earn it, has produced industry, frugality, economy, good habits of body and mind, and durable and well-established riches, whilst the excess of money has produced the contrary in Spain, i.e. has ruined their industry and economy, and filled them with pride and poverty.

"But there is, besides this general principle, a special reason in our case, why we should pay a large part of our Continental debt by a present tax; the great consumption of our armies, and stoppage of our imports, make a great demand for the produce of our lands, the fabrics of our tradesmen and the labor of our people, and of course raises the prices of all these much higher than usual, so that the husbandman, tradesman and laborer get money much faster and easier than they used to do, and it is a plain maxim, that people should always pay their debts when they have a good run of business, and have money plenty, many a man has been distressed for a debt when business and money were scarce, which he had neglected to pay when he could have done it with great ease to himself had he attended to it in its proper season; this applies to a community or state as well as to a private person."

[2] Feb. 2, 1778.

Early in January,[1] 1777, Congress recommended the Legislatures of the several States to pass resolutions making provision for withdrawing and sinking their respective quotas of the bills emitted by Congress at the several periods fixed by that body, and to " raise by taxation in the course of the ensuing year, and remit to the treasury such sums of money as they shall think will be most proper in the present situation of the inhabitants, which sums shall be carried to their credit and accounted in the settlement of their proportion of the public expenses and debts, for which the United States are jointly bound." Thus all the authority possessed by Congress in respect to taxation was early and fully exercised. This recommendation Congress renewed whenever the States were asked to furnish more money.

When the Articles of Confederation were adopted, no additional power was conferred upon the General Government to levy and collect taxes, though the necessity of enlarging its scope in this direction must have been very apparent. The Eighth Article merely provided that all charges of war, and other expenses incurred for the common defence and general welfare, should be defrayed out of a common treasury, which should be supplied by the several States, in proportion to the value of all land and the buildings and improvements thereon, within each State, belonging to any person. As though this provision did not sufficiently guard the States against Federal usurpation, the article further provided that " the taxes for paying that proportion shall be laid and levied by the authority and direction of the legislatures of the several

---

[1] Jan. 14.

states." This was one of the worst defects in the Articles of Confederation, from which the government was to suffer in the future. The States, however, were so jealous of their rights, notwithstanding their slowness to exercise them, that no larger concessions could be obtained; and afterwards, during Morris's administration, when this defect was generally seen, an attempt to amend the Articles, and grant the government power to collect taxes upon importations, signally failed after repeated attempts to secure the adoption of such an amendment.[1]

Throughout the entire period from 1774 to 1789, only very small sums flowed into the general treasury from the State coffers. As the power to tax belonged to the States, Congress dared not attempt such a thing; nor would the experiment at any time have been a prudent one to try. Congress, it is true, did stretch their authority in several directions, slowly and with judicious care; but the right of taxation was regarded by the States with peculiar jealousy. Having thrown off allegiance to Great Britain mainly because she assumed the right to tax the Colonies without their consent, the people were in no mood to substitute the General Government for Great Britain in this regard. From first to last, the States insisted upon retaining the power to tax, and consequently Congress was obliged to trust wholly to them for funds raised in this manner. Unlike the states of the Hellenic Confederation, which raised money, and placed it under the control of Attica, the stronger state, to be used in making preparation for resisting future Persian invasions, the States of the American Union neither contributed as they

---

[1] March 20, 1783; April 1, 1783; Aug. 28, 1783.

should to sustain the National Government, nor raised much to support their own local organizations.

There is no weaker spot in the financial history of these times than the unwillingness or failure of the States to tax at once and deeply, as soon as the first issues of paper money were sent forth by Congress. In the addresses of that body the States were urged in the strongest way to levy and collect adequate taxes for the purpose of retiring the paper circulation, and raising funds to support the government. In the address issued in November, 1777, after describing the depreciation of the currency and the consequences to be apprehended from the event, the tendency to the depravity of morals, the decay of public virtue, a precarious supply for the war, debasement of the public faith, injustice to individuals, and the destruction of the honor, safety, and independence of the United States, Congress added, " Loudly therefore are we called upon to provide a reasonable and effectual remedy. Hitherto spared from taxes let them now with a cheerful heart, contribute according to their circumstances."

In May, a year afterward, Congress issued another address, in which the necessity of taxation was considered. " Is there," says Congress, " a country upon earth which hath such resources for the payment of her debts as America? such an extensive territory? so fertile, so blessed in its climate and productions? Surely there is none. Neither is there any to which the wise Europeans will sooner confide their property. What then are the reasons that your money hath depreciated?" What reply did Congress give? " Because no taxes have been imposed to carry on the war," to which other reasons of a minor character were added. In this address, Congress urged the States in the strongest manner to sink their bills by taxation; and in many other addresses of Congress was the necessity of State taxation clearly set forth. Notwithstanding these appeals, the States failed utterly to collect only a very small sum for the benefit of the General Government.

The need of taxation was quite as clearly seen by individuals as by Congress. John Adams wrote in August, 1777,[1] about redressing the evils of paper money, " Taxation as deep as possible is the only radical cure." The same doctrine was echoed in the newspapers throughout the country.[2]

[1] Familiar Letters, p. 293.

[2] A person wrote in Penn. Packet, March 5, 1782, " Artful men have endeavored to spread an opinion that the taxes are too heavy, and weak men are inclined to a belief in their assertion; but if seeing is believing, we are bound to believe the direct contrary. It is possible enough that the taxes are unequal, and that amendment might be made in the mode of levying and collecting them; but as to the amount, it is but trifling compared with the taxes we have actually paid."

A writer in the Boston Gazette says, " As our debt is large, we must be willing to pay a large tax; and it is not for me to say how large; but it must be in proportion to the bills we have emitted. This, and this only, will prevent the great difficulties that we labor under, and have long been complaining of. For, as heretofore. both merchants and farmers have been fond of keeping their goods, because they found that was the best way to make the most of them, as they were continually rising in their hands; or rather, if they took the money for them, that would be falling and depreciating in their hands. So now, if we are taxed in some good measure equal to our debt, and the people are hereby convinced that the money is to be made good, and the credit thereof punctually maintained, they will immediately find, that, in-

It is true the States did not wholly omit to levy and collect taxes during the early period of the war; but they were much lighter than they should have been. A writer in "The Connecticut Courant"[1] affirmed toward the close of 1776, "As to taxes, there have been none, or next to none, for some time. True, they begin now in a low degree to take place." The neglect of the States in this regard was a grave mistake which could not easily be repaired.

Heavy taxes were indeed laid by the States after considerable delay; but the omission to levy them earlier, paved the way for dilatoriness in their collection and payment.[2] People everywhere complained of the weight of taxes,[3] yet too often evaded the duty of paying them.[4] Great as was the burden, there were individuals who bore it without a murmur. " I hope you will pay every

stead of articles of merchandise or provisions rising in their hands, they will begin to fall. And as the scarcity that has appeared, has not been altogether real, but artificial, we shall soon see many things exposed to sale, and the price falling as fast as it rose, and we shall have reason to think and hope, that things will soon come to right and standard." Feb. 2, 1778.

[1] Dec. 27, 1776, see Ibid., Jan. 3, 1777, and Jan. 13, 1777.

[2] Ellery and Collins, delegates from Rhode Island, made a shrewd suggestion on one occasion, when they were requested to get the sum apportioned to that State by Congress reduced: "The more we pay now, the less we shall have to pay hereafter, when the money may be appreciated." It was March 2, 1779, when they thus wrote to the Governor of Rhode Island. STAPLES's *Hist. of R. I. in the Cont. Cong.*, p. 210.

[3] See Letter of Pickering, Sept. 22, 1782, Life of Pickering, vol. i. p. 375.

[4] Sparks's Franklin, vol. x. p. 45; Wells's Life of S. Adams, vol. iii. pp. 163-165.

tax that is brought you," wrote John Adams to his wife,[1] "if you sell my books or clothes, or oxen, or your cows to pay it." At one time she informs him, "rates high; that, I suppose, you will rejoice at, so would I, did it remedy the evil."[2] In October, 1780, she writes again about "enormous taxes."[3] The more patriotic undoubtedly paid; but many certainly did not, for, if they had, there would not have been such a dearth of funds in the public treasury.

If the people were unwilling to pay taxes directly to redeem a sinking currency, they could not escape paying them in another form infinitely worse, because they were more unequal. Depreciation was a constant tax upon all who received paper money. A merchant receiving bills of credit would lose a portion of their value before he could part with them. This loss operated as a tax upon him, and in many cases it was a very unequal and unjust one. The loss to the creditor class, especially to those who had loaned gold and silver, and were paid in almost worthless paper, was fearful. Livingston[4] concluded that because this tax, though unequal, had been borne by the people of the States, and had not produced national ruin, the States had sufficient resources to bear the burden; which was correct reasoning, no doubt: nevertheless the losses to some individuals and associations supported by trust funds were enormous.

As secretary of foreign affairs, Livingston wrote in February, 1782, to the governors of the States,[5] " From the

---

[1] Familiar Letters, p. 293.   [2] Ibid., p. 365.   [3] Ibid., p. 388.
[4] Letter to Jay, Nov. 1, 1781, Dip. Cor., vol. vii. p. 508.
[5] Feb. 19, Dip. Cor., vol. xi. p. 225.

time that the depreciation of the continental bills of credit
began, till they were no longer current, the states that
received them paid a tax equal to all the expenditures
of the army, and a very considerable one beyond it;
for if we suppose ten millions of dollars, in specie, a
year, to be necessary for their support, then the expense,
till the close of the campaign of 1779, must have
amounted to upwards of fifty millions, exclusive of the
supplies from Europe; and yet, in March, 1780, the
whole national debt contracted in America did not, in
fact, amount to five millions; so that forty-five millions
were paid by the United States in those five years of the
war, when they had the least commerce and agriculture,
and when they were most distressed by the enemy; and
this tax, too, was the most unjust and partial that can
be conceived, unless we except that, by which we have
since raised much more from the people, without giving
so much to the public; I mean the laws for impressing,
&c., which placed the greatest burden of the war upon
the shoulders of a particular order of men in particular
states only."

Yet John Adams regarded depreciation as a real advantage.[1] Not so thought the clearer-minded Webster.[2]
Having shown how all the expenditures of the war for
the first three years, except foreign debts and internal
loans, had been paid in depreciation of the currency,
which was perhaps the most inconvenient method of
levying public taxes that could be invented, he then
proceeds, by fact and argument, to prove his point so

[1] Letter to Capellen, Jan. 21, 1781, Works, vol. vii. p. 357.
[2] Political Essays, p. 29.

clearly that none could question it. "I imagine," he says, "it will not be disputed that the depreciation for three years past has been at least fifty per cent per annum, i.e. that one hundred pounds at the end of the year, would not buy more goods than fifty pounds would have purchased at the beginning of the year. Try it for the year past: in August, 1778, fifty pounds would have purchased sixteen hundred of flour, fifty bushels of Indian corn, five hundred of bar iron, one and an half hundred of sugar, twelve pounds of hard money, &c. See if one hundred pounds will buy as much now. This is arguing on fact, which is stubborn and yields to the prejudice of no man."[1]

[1] "It appears then that a man who has kept one hundred pounds by him for the space of one year, is to all intents in the same condition he would have been in, if the hundred pounds had kept its value undepreciated, and he had paid one half of it in a tax, i.e. in both cases he would have had fifty pounds and no more left. He has then, to all intents and purposes, paid a tax of fifty pounds for the year towards the depreciation, and has now fifty pounds less money than he would have had if no depreciation had taken place, as much in every respect, as his cash would have lessened fifty pounds by paying a tax of that sum.

"I have heard that this plea was made use of by the Agents of the New England colonies, when the matter of reimbursements to those colonies, for their great expenditures in the two last wars, was debated and granted in the British Parliament, and the argument allowed to be a good one. The question was, what sums those colonies had emitted for the service of the wars, and what was the value of the bills to be redeemed? the Agents pleaded, that the value was to be estimated at the time of emission, not at the time of redemption of those bills; for when bills of credit depreciate in any country, the depreciation is as much a tax on the inhabitants as the depreciated sum would be, if levied in the usual way of assessment on polls and estates. The argument is indeed a demonstrable one, and supported and justified by plain fact in every view; yet there is such a subtle and strong delusion in the

There were many who regarded depreciation very differently from Webster. Said a plausible writer in " The Pennsylvania Packet," [1] " There is at present no absolute necessity for high government taxes, the natural unavoidable tax of depreciation is the most certain, expeditious, and equal tax that could be devised. Upon the scale which has lately existed, every possessor of money has paid a tax for it, in proportion to the time he held it. Like a hackney coach it must be paid for by the hour." Having shown that the two hundred millions of paper issued by the government were equivalent to forty-eight millions of specie, had the latter been employed in making payments, he asserts that forty-three millions of the latter sum have been paid by the tax of depreciation, leaving only five millions to be discharged. " Now I would ask the best financier amongst us, whether in four years he could have levied a tax of forty three millions of hard dollars, in a more equal or less expensive way? There have been no commissions to pay, no embezzlements, no public defaulters, and no appeals, except by the possessors of old contracts, who have been ungenerously and unjustly paid off in current nominal value, under sanction of laws, which ought long ago to have been repealed."

The truth was, paper money having depreciated enor-

depreciation as obscures the subject, and will almost cheat a man who views it under full conviction, and feels the effects of it; and this tends to render the mischief more ruinous than otherwise it would be, because people who feel it, often mistake the cause, and adopt from thence remedies altogether ineffectual, and sometimes very hurtful, and which often tend rather to increase than cure the evil."

[1] Jan. 20, 1780.

mously, and all remedies having proved hopeless, the
only course left for the leaders of the Revolution was to
lay the most pleasant colors they could find upon the
experiment. Happily the idea arose in the public mind
of regarding depreciation as a tax, and this thought
did much in softening the bitterness of many toward
the industrious workers of the paper-money printing-
press. This view of the matter was not altogether un-
sound: it contained enough truth to satisfy many, and
make them feel that depreciation, notwithstanding its
great evils, had also brought an unexpected, though none
the less welcome, blessing.

Of all the writers discerning the advantages attending
the depreciation of paper money, none saw so many, nor
saw them so clearly, as Thomas Paine. During the
American Revolution an elaborate work appeared in
Paris, entitled "The Political and Philosophical History
of the European Settlements in the East and West Indies," written by the Abbé Raynal, which gave him a
sudden, world-wide, and truly dazzling reputation that
astonished no one probably so much as the author himself. The work, in truth, was very superficial, and is
now never sought for any information entombed within
its pages; and the heavy coating of dust lying upon the
buried volumes in the great libraries speaks mournfully of
the utter extinguishment of the reputation of the author.
When the Forty-for-one Act was passed by Congress, in
March, 1781, the details of which have been already
described, Raynal wrote a letter upon the finances of
America, criticising the administration of them in severe
terms. Among other matters discussed by him was

the above-mentioned Act and the depreciation of paper
money. Paine answered this communication, prefacing
his own letter with the remark that paper money, though
issued by Congress under the name of dollars, was not
all of equal value. The issues of the first year were
equal to gold and silver; those of the second year were
worth less; and so, for five years, the issue of each year
was of less value than that of the preceding year, until
the end of the fifth year. "I imagine," says Paine,[1] "that
the whole value at which Congress might pay away the
several emissions, taking them together was about ten
or twelve million pounds sterling."

As it would have taken ten or twelve millions sterling
of taxes to carry on the war for so long a period; "and
as while this money was issuing, and likewise depreciating
down to nothing, there were none, or few valuable taxes
paid; consequently the event to the public was the same,
whether they sunk ten or twelve millions of expended
money, by depreciation, or paid ten or twelve millions by
taxation; for as they did not do both, and chose to do
one, the matter which, in a general view, was indifferent.
And, therefore, what the Abbé supposes to be a debt, has
now no existence; it having been paid, by everybody
consenting, to reduce at his own expense, from the value
of the bills continually passing among themselves, a sum,
equal to nearly what the expense of the war was for five
years."

Paper money, however, had now ceased, and so, of
course, had the depreciation of it, while gold and silver
had resumed their former sway. The war was to be

---

[1] Letter addressed to the Abbé Raynal, Phil., 1782, p. 26.

maintained by taxation, which, happily, Paine affirmed, would take from the public a smaller sum than depreciation drew; "but as while they pay the former, they do not suffer the latter, and as when they suffered the latter, they did not pay the former, the thing will be nearly equal, with this moral advantage, that taxation occasions frugality and thought, and depreciation produced dissipation and carelessness."

Paine had now reached a pinnacle of reasoning sufficiently high to fly easily in almost any direction. Accordingly he ventures forth in this fashion: "If a man's portion of taxes comes to less than what he lost by the depreciation, it proves the alteration is in his favor. If it comes to more, and he is justly assessed, it shows that he did not sustain his proper share of depreciation, because the one was as positively his tax as the other.

"It is true," he continues, "that it never was intended, neither was it foreseen, that the debt contained in the paper currency should sink itself in this manner, but as by the voluntary conduct of all and of every one it has arrived at this state, the debt is paid by those who owed it. Perhaps nothing was ever so universally the act of a country as this. Government had no hand in it. Every man depreciated his own money by his own consent, for such was the effect, which the raising the nominal value of goods produced. But as by such reduction he sustained a loss equal to what he must have paid to sink it by taxation, therefore the line of justice is to consider his loss by the depreciation as his tax for that time, and not to tax him .when the war is over, to make that money good in any other person's hands, which became nothing in his own.

"Again, the paper currency was issued for the express purpose of carrying on the war. It has performed that service, without any other material charge to the public, while it lasted. But to suppose, as some did, that, at the end of the war, it was to grow into gold and silver, or to become equal thereto, was to suppose that we were to get two hundred millions of dollars by going to war, instead of paying the cost of carrying it on."

The effect produced upon the Abbé's mind by Paine's answer was never known. But one thing is certain, the answer displayed as much wisdom as the Abbé's discussion of American finances, and far more ingenuity. In those days, when financial questions were not probed so deeply nor thoroughly as they are now, it is highly probable that Paine's answer was by many deemed as complete as it was consoling. That depreciation operated as a tax, which all paid in varying proportions, was, doubtless, to many, an unexpected revelation; but it was not for that reason any the less readily and joyfully accepted by them as true and satisfying.

CHAPTER XV.

PLEDGES AND ARGUMENTS.

IF it be possible to maintain the value of paper money by solemn pledges of redemption, surely the paper emissions of the Continental Congress ought to have been maintained; for the faith of that body was pledged repeatedly to the faithful fulfilment of their monetary obligations. The following vote of Congress is a fair specimen of the action of Congress on the subject: "Whereas a report hath circulated in divers parts of America, that Congress would not redeem the bills of credit issued by them to defray the expenses of the war, but would suffer them to sink in the hands of the holder, whereby the value of the said bills hath, in the opinion of many of the good people of these States, depreciated; and lest the silence of Congress might give strength to the said report; resolved that the said report is false and derogatory to the honor of Congress." This was in December, 1778,[1] and as paper money depreciated more and more, the pledges of Congress in respect to its redemption were more frequent, and intense in form **of** expression. In addresses issued, as well as in special resolves, Congress heaped pledge upon pledge; and this practice was continued until nearly all value was gone out of the bills, and

____
[1] Dec. 29.

within a very short period of the time when Congress passed the Forty-for-one Act, which was a direct violation of the entire stream of promises that had been unceasingly flowing from nearly the beginning of the creation of paper money.

In September, 1779,[1] Congress sent forth a spirited address portraying the situation, in which, among other questions, was the following: "whether, admitting the ability and political capacity of the United States to redeem their bills, there is any reason to apprehend a wanton violation of the public faith?" To this question Congress uttered a disdainful negative; yet six months had scarcely passed, when that body declared[2] that the United States having been driven into a just and necessary war at a time when no regular civil governments were established of sufficient energy to enforce the collection of taxes or to provide funds for the redemption of such bills of credit as their necessities obliged them to issue, and before the powers of Europe were sufficiently convinced of the justice of their cause, or of the probable event of the controversy, to afford them aid or credit, in consequence of which their bills increasing in quantity beyond the sum necessary for the purpose of a circulating medium, and wanting at the same time specific funds to rest on for their redemption, had daily sunk in value, notwithstanding every effort that had been made to support the same, insomuch that they were then passed by common consent in most parts of the United States at least thirty-nine fortieths below their nominal value, and still remained in a state of depreciation, whereby the

---

[1] Sept. 13.   [2] March 18, 1780.

community suffered great injustice, the public finances were deranged, and the necessary dispositions for the defence of the country were much impeded and perplexed; and whereas, effectually to remedy these evils, for which purpose the United States had now become competent, their independence being well assured, it was necessary speedily to reduce the quantity of the paper medium in circulation, and to establish and appropriate such funds as should insure the punctual redemption of the bills: — for these reasons it was resolved to receive silver and gold in payment of the quotas assigned to the States at the rate of one Spanish milled dollar in lieu of forty dollars of the bills then in circulation.

Let no one imagine that this Act of Congress was passed without opposition, or that the news of it was received by the country without surprise. There were many who believed that in no event would Congress violate the public faith.[1] Yet the act was done: "the safest possible currency," "the only currency which would not take to itself wings and disappear," was disappearing at a fearful rate, and in a short time would utterly vanish.

Indeed, in a few years, public sentiment had changed so rapidly, that the rejoicing was very general over the disappearance of Continental money. Webster[2] declares this to be the fact, nor is there any reason for questioning the truth of the statement.

Many arguments were used showing the security for the ultimate payment of paper money; perhaps the most favorite argument was the one used by Webster.[3] It

---

[1] Ante, p. 131.   [2] Political Essays, p. 4, note.
[3] Political Essays, p. 4, note b.

was "a debt of great honor and justice, of national honor and justice, not barely empty honor, but that essential honor and credit in which the safety of the state is comprised, and therefore by concession of everybody must be punctually and honorably paid in due time: otherwise all security arising from public credit must be lost, all confidence of individuals in our public councils must be destroyed, and great injustice must be done to every possessor of our public currency, to the detriment of all, and ruin of many who have placed most confidence in our public administration; and nothing but shame, scandal and contempt can ensue for which nothing but most inevitable necessity can be any reasonable excuse." This was written in 1776: several years afterward, when his essays were republished in a volume, he says, that, at the time of writing the foregoing observations, he "had no conception that the Continental money could continue to be a quick currency at five hundred for one, and finally run itself out to nothing, and die, not only without any tumult, but with the general satisfaction of the people." It was found out, that, after all, paper money did not constitute a lien upon the real estate and other property of the country which could not be released whenever Congress chose. Paper money was fiat money; Congress made it, and Congress could destroy it: it was impossible for that power or any other to offer a security which could not be taken away, or make a pledge which could not be broken.[1]

---

[1] See Memorial of Public Creditors addressed to Congress Dec. 20, 1790, Am. State Papers by Lowrie and Clarke, Finance, vol. i. p. 76, in which the history of that body in dealing with the public creditors is set forth.

CHAPTER XVI.

SPECULATION, CORRUPTION, AND REPUDIATION.

SOME of the evils growing out of the use of paper money have been shown in previous chapters; but the worst effects upon the morals of the people yet remain to be described. This work would not be complete without reviewing these: moreover, the lessons to be learned from them are of deep significance.

The first effect worthy of note is the speculation to which paper money gave rise. Just as the depreciation of paper money during the late war unsettled prices, and thus inaugurated an era of extraordinary speculation, so, in the period under review, paper emissions, by upsetting the former range of prices, gave a wonderful impetus to speculation, which acted as a terrible blight upon the prosperity and morals of the people.[1]

A vast deal of speculation was carried on by govern-

[1] "The first visible effect of an augmentation of the medium and the consequent fluctuation of value, was, a host of jockeys, who followed a species of itinerant commerce; and subsisted upon the ignorance and honesty of the country people; or in other words, upon the difference in the value of the currency, in different places. Perhaps we may safely estimate, that not less than 20,000 men in America, left honest callings, and applied themselves to this knavish traffic. A sudden augmentation of currency flattered people with the prospect of accumulating property without labor." — NOAH WEBSTER, *Coll. of Essays*, p. 105.

ment officials in those days.[1]   James Lovell,[2] writing for the committee of foreign affairs to the foreign commissioners, remarked, " The manners of the continent are too much affected by depreciation of our currency ; scarce an officer,[3] civil or military, but feels something of a desire to be concerned in mercantile speculation, from finding that his salary is inadequate to the heavy demands, which are made upon him for the necessaries of life, and from observing, that but little skill is neces-

[1] See letter in Penn. Archives, vol. vi. p. 212. A very depressing, but we fear altogether too common, picture of the way the affairs of the army were managed is given by President Reed during a tour of investigation through Pennsylvania with reference to the collection of revenues in that State. The account is contained in a letter dated from Bethlehem, Oct. 5, 1780, to George Bryan. " The abuses of the quarter-master's department are great and many. A practice has obtained here to sell continental property by appraisement, and it has proved a very convenient mode to gratify a friend with a good team or horse, at one-third the value. Here is a commissary, on pay, rations, and forage, with a waiter, to supply six Hessians, who work about the town, but I should rather say was, as I have sent to Easton to-day to cashier about eight or ten of them. A mulatto in the county has acquired a very handsome fortune under Mr. Hooper, as deputy comissary, some say £10,000 specie. Now the influence is removed, the people speak out, and pretty loudly too, but I fear it is almost too late. There have been at one time twelve deputy quartermasters in this county only, on pay, rations, and with clerks, &c. Had a suitable inspection taken place twelve months ago, I am sure we should have saved many thousands, if not millions." — REED's *Life of Reed*, vol. ii. p. 283.

[2] March 24, 1778, Dip. Cor. vol. i. p. 375.

[3] Among other abuses which crept into the army was the appropriation of public horses to private use. Says Gen. Greene, " There was scarcely an officer in the cavalry who had not from one to three public horses, which he felt at liberty to exchange or sell at will." — GREENE's *Life of Greene*, vol. iii. p. 455.

sary to constitute one of the merchants of these days. We are almost a continental tribe of Jews; but I hope heaven has not yet discovered such a settled profligacy in us as to cast us off, even for a year."

Other individuals also engaged in speculation. Before the States had received their new money, or called in their old, speculation in Boston by Tories and others depreciated the old money to eighty-five, and even a hundred and ten, for one in that city. Nor was this all: those who had hoarded specie speculated upon foreign bills, so that twenty-five per cent was lost on all the money borrowed from France.

Extravagance is the legitimate child of speculation; and, notwithstanding the Puritan severity of the revolutionary times, the weeds of extravagance rankly flourished, not only in the management of public business,[1] but in the affairs of private life. Hancock, as chief magistrate of Massachusetts, led the way in that State "in a series of routs, balls, and glittering re-unions, entirely incompatible with the stern spirit of republicanism which had produced and sustained the Revolution."[2] Franklin wrote in 1779,[3] "The extravagant luxury of our country, in the midst of all its distresses, is to me amazing. When the difficulties are so great to find remittances to pay for the arms and ammunition necessary for our defence, I am astonished and vexed to find upon inquiry, that much the greatest part of the congress interest bills come to pay for tea, and a great part

---

[1] Letter of Robert Morris, Dec. 21, 1776, Dip. Cor., vol. i. p. 238.

[2] Wells's Life of S. Adams, vol. iii. p. 157, see Ibid., p. 156.

[3] Oct. 4, Dip. Cor., vol. iii. p. 116.

of the remainder is ordered to be laid out in gewgaws and superfluities." What else could be expected when money had become cheap and plentiful, and the old-fashioned ways of making money slowly had been very generally discarded for the more exciting, but less healthy methods of speculation![1]

[1] Col. Pickering, quartermaster-general of the army, wrote to a committee of Congress Nov. 22, 1779 : "I am aware of the public embarrassments on account of the currency, and that many, like ourselves, are suffering in the public service; and, were public virtue generally apparent, as at the beginning of the contest, we would with pleasure devote our time and all we possess to the public service, nor ask a recompense. But, while some servants of the public are amassing fortunes, and all ranks of people pursuing, with so much avidity, only their private gain, we are unwilling, for their sakes, to reduce ourselves to beggary." (PICKERING's *Life of Pick.*, vol. i. p. 245.) Henry Marchant, a delegate from Rhode Island, wrote to Gov. Greene, "We have scarce to fear but from the inordinate extravagance of the times, a lawless thirst for riches, and a spirit of monopolizing and speculation, big with more evils than all the armies of Europe could afford." (Aug. 3, 1778, STAPLES's *Hist. of R. I. in the Cont. Cong.*, p. 102.) Said a writer in a Boston paper, "The articles of rum and tea alone, which are drank in this country, would pay all its taxes." (PORCUPINE's *Works*, vol. i. p. 61.) "The scarcity of money is the only thing that will save this people. This alone can produce industry and economy, without which no people can be virtuous and happy. This is an universal truth, applicable to all people in every country." (*Extract from Sermon*, PORCUPINE's *Works*, vol. i. p. 65.) "Speculation ran riot. Every form of wastefulness and extravagance prevailed in town and country, nowhere more than at Philadelphia, under the very eyes of congress; luxury of dress, luxury of equipage, luxury of the table. We are told of one entertainment at which eight hundred pounds were spent in pastry. As I read the private letters of those days, I sometimes feel as a man might feel if permitted to look down upon a foundering ship whose crew were preparing for death by breaking open the steward's room and drinking themselves into madness. . . . The zeal which had blazed forth with such energy at the beginning of the

Beside speculation there was a vast deal of corruption growing out of the use of paper money. Even government officials were seriously infected. The system of purchasing encouraged it. The commissaries of the army received a percentage upon the amounts expended, and of course, the larger the purchases, the greater were the profits. They were not slow to take advantage of the system under which they were authorized to make purchases. "Peculation and minor thieving were the order of the day."[1] Even Gen. Arnold attempted to perpe-

war was fast sinking to a fitful, smouldering flame. Individual interests were again taking the precedence of general interests. The moral sense of the people had contracted a deadly taint from daily contact with corruption. The spirit of gambling, confined in the beginning and lost to the eye, like Le Sage's Devil, had swollen to its full proportions, and, in the garb of speculation, was undermining the foundations of society. Rogues were growing rich; the honest men, who were not already poor, were daily growing poor. The laws that had been made in the view of propping the currency, had served only to countenance unscrupulous men in paying their debts at a discount ruinous to the creditor. The laws against forestallers and engrossers, who, it was currently believed, were leagued against both army and country, were powerless, as such laws always are. Even Washington wished for a gallows as high as Haman's to hang them on; but the army was kept starving none the less."—GREENE's *Hist. View of the Am. Rev.*, pp. 160, 164.

"The articles of rum and tea alone, which are drank in this country, would pay all its taxes. But when we add, sugar, coffee, feathers, and the whole list of bawbles and trinkets, what an enormous expense! My countrymen are are all grown very tasty! Feathers and jordens must all be imported! A Hampshire man, who drinks forty shillings worth of rum in a year, and never thinks of the expense, will raise a mob to reduce the governor's salary, which does not amount to three pence a man per annum."—NOAH WEBSTER, *Coll. of Essays*, p. 129.

[1] Phillips, 106.

trate a gross fraud upon the people.   He had run a long career of profligate dissipation at Philadelphia, and was desirous of covering his deficiencies by making a claim on the government.   A very slight inspection showed the claim to be fraudulent, and it was disallowed.   The affair produced a great sensation at the time.[1]

Henry Laurens[2] wrote to Gov. Houston of Georgia, from Philadelphia, at the time he was presiding over Congress: "Were I to unfold to you Sir, scenes of venality, peculation and fraud which I have discovered, the disclosure would astonish you, nor would you Sir, be less astonished were I by a detail which the occasion would require prove to you that he must be a pitiful rogue, who, when detected, or suspected, meets not with powerful advocates among those who in the present corrupt time ought to exert all their powers in defence and support of these friend-plundered, much chagrined, and I was almost going to say, sinking, states."[3]

Paper money was indeed bringing forth evil fruits in great abundance.   Washington[4] wrote: "Speculation, peculation, engrossing, forestalling, with all concomitants, afford too many melancholy proofs of the decay of public

[1] Austin's Life of Gerry, vol. i. pp. 316, 317.

[2] Aug. 27, 1778, Hist. Mag., vol. i. p. 66, second series.

[3] See further Hamilton, Hist. of Repub., vol. i. p. 567; Address of Congress, 1777; Letter of Arthur Lee, May 21, 1779; Dip. Cor., vol. ii. p. 244.   The frauds discovered in the medical department were of a peculiarly distressing character.   Stores needed for sick and wounded soldiers were sold, and the money was retained by the perpetrators of the fraud.   Two of the chief officers in the medical department were implicated in these frauds, — Drs. Morgan and Shippen.   See supra, p. 79, and Penn. Packet, Sept. 19, 1780.

[4] Sparks's Washington, vol. vi. p. 210.

virtue. . . . . Nothing, I am convinced, but the depreciation of our currency, proceeding in a great measure from the foregoing causes, aided by stock-jobbing and party dissensions, has fed the hopes of the enemy."

Creditors to a very alarming extent swelled their accounts to obviate losses arising from depreciation. The Treasury Board were in constant collision with public creditors who sought to swindle the government in this manner.[1]

On every hand it was acknowledged that from paper emissions had flowed the most serious immoral consequences. Says a discriminating writer in "The New-Jersey Journal,"[2] "I do not say that the abundance of money is the only cause of the decay of virtue or increase of vice, but I say it is a very principal cause, it operates more this way than any other, yea, than all other causes put together. An abundance of money creates idleness, pride, dissipation, avarice, and these co-operate with the money in the quick production of luxury, debauchery, gambling and every species of prodigal extravagance."

Webster, in one of his essays, — having shown how paper money defrauded the army of their pay, discouraged enlistments, and promoted desertions, rendering it more difficult also to obtain supplies, "because few men are fond of carrying the fruits of their year's labor to the army, to be sold for a perishing medium, which every day grows worse and worse," — continues to remark, " The whole system is grounded in injustice, is contrary to the first maxims of upright dealing, and corrupts the whole

[1] Austin's Life of Gerry, vol. i. p. 316.   [2] May 27, 1779.

course of trade and commutative justice, and of course
will soon destroy all principles of morality and honesty
in trade, among the people; for here it is to be considered,
that money is not only the instrument or means by which
trade is carried on, but becomes a sort of common measure of the value of all articles of trade; and therefore I
should conceive it would be as dangerous to adopt any
measures which would alter its value and render it fluctuating, as to alter the standard weights and measures, by
which the quantity of goods sold in market is usually
ascertained: — as for example, to shorten the standard
yard, lessen the standard bushel, or diminish the standard pound weight, or adopt any measures that tend to
this, and will probably affect it. We can easily see the
dangerous consequences." [1]

Having corrupted the morals of individuals everywhere,
the insidious poison finally ate into the very vitals of
the leaders of the nation itself, and led them to perpetrate the crowning scheme of dishonesty, that of repudiation.   Washington was among the first to be beguiled
by reasoning in this wise: "The sponge," [2] he writes to
President Reed, "which you say some gentlemen have
talked of using, unless there can be a discrimination, and
proper saving clauses provided (and how far this is
practicable I know not), would be unjust and impolitic
in the extreme. Perhaps I do not understand what
they mean by using the sponge. If it be to sink the
money in the hands of the holders of it, and at their
loss, it cannot in my opinion stand justified upon any
principles of common policy, common sense, or common

<hr>

[1] Political Essays, p. 32.   [2] Sparks's Washington, vol. vi. p. 331.

honesty. But how far a man, for instance, who had possessed himself of twenty paper dollars by means of one, or the value of one, in specie, has a just claim upon the public for more than one of the latter in redemption, and in that ratio according to the periods of depreciation, I leave to those, who are better acquainted with the nature of the subject, and have more leisure than I have, to discuss."

In this way the Russian financiers have reasoned several times since respecting the paper issues of their government; and this is precisely the ground taken by Russia whenever she has redeemed her paper emissions, not at their nominal, but at their market value, — a policy which is very likely to be repeated with respect to the paper money now in circulation in that empire. M. Horn, manager of "The Journal of St. Petersburg," said during a spicy discussion of the subject at Paris in September, 1878, "Russia has at this moment a circulation of twelve hundred million roubles worth sixty per cent of their nominal value, that is to say, only worth seven hundred and twenty millions. The depreciation has been borne; everybody has been equally affected by it. The Imperial Government must now ask itself, whether there is any thing better to do than to squarely accept the fact of the depreciation of its paper, and better still, to profit by it as a means of escaping the bad predicament it is in, by unloading itself by a stroke of internal bankruptcy." An easy way surely of escaping from debts. But the moral obligation to pay is not thus easily discharged.

Doubtless the mode of reasoning in which Washington

indulged was not in the least peculiar to him: it was the common thinking of the day. The people, therefore, by degrees prepared themselves for repudiation, which finally came in the Forty-for-one Act, the provisions of which have already been considered.[1]

"Wherever the species is much debased, the people are so too," said John Evelyn[2] nearly a century before, the truth of which saying was again impressively verified. How long prior to this Act of repudiation did Congress, in a stirring address to the people, declare that a bankrupt, faithless republic would be a novelty in the political world, that it would appear "like a common prostitute among chaste and respectable matrons"? Yet within ninety days from the time of uttering these sentiments, the United States, by act of Congress, became a "common prostitute," and the novelty of a bankrupt and faithless republic was exhibited to the full blaze and glare of the civilized world. No doubt

---

[1] The tide of speculation, having once set in, could not easily be turned. Long after the war had closed, speculation still continued. "The country swarms with speculators," says Webster, "who are searching all places, from the stores of the wealthy to the recesses of indigence for opportunities of making lucrative bargains. Not a tavern can we enter, but we meet crowds of these people who wear their character in their countenances. . . . It is remarked by people very illiterate and circumscribed in their observation, that there is not now the same confidence between man and man, which existed before the war. It is doubtless true; this distrust of individuals, a general corruption of manners, idleness, and all its train of fatal consequences, may be resolved into two causes: The sudden flood of money during the late war, and a constant fluctuation of the value of the currencies." — NOAH WEBSTER, *Coll. of Essays*, p. 107.

[2] Discourse on Medals, p. 11, ed. 1697.

the pressure upon Congress was great; but no pressure ought to have been thought sufficient to sink a nation into the mire of dishonesty. Its faith, its promises, should have been kept at every hazard; their fulfilment should have been prevented only by the death of the nation itself. The American nation could have lived and fulfilled its promises, or have obtained at least partial voluntary relief from them, had such a concession been necessary. There was enough patriotism in those days to have made almost any arrangement for the suspension of payments, or to have obtained whatever relief in the way of postponement or acceptance of a portion of the public indebtedness was required by the government. The repudiation of the debt was as dishonest as it was unnecessary; though it may be said, in slight extenuation of the course of members of Congress, they perhaps saw no other way out of the difficulties which so darkly surrounded them. Had they looked with clearer eyes, determined in no event ever to dishonor the nation just then emerging into life, they would have surely found a way; for it cannot be that the paths of truth and honesty, if steadily, and if need be heroically, followed, shall ever fail to lead men and nations through the forests, however dark, into the clear spaces beyond.

CHAPTER XVII.

FOREIGN LOANS.

HAVING shown how the finances were managed until Morris's retirement from office, let us go across the Atlantic, and ascertain what financial assistance was rendered by foreign nations, and what impressions were created there by the early efforts of the revolutionary fathers in the untrodden field of public finance.

When revolution grew to be the inspiring yet daring thought of Congress, that body looked abroad for aid, especially from France, because she felt keenly the disastrous peace of 1763 with Great Britain, and was eagerly waiting for an opportunity to wreak successful revenge. How closely, therefore, did she bend her ear to hear every sound of discontent proceeding from the English Colonies in America! and how gladly did she welcome the news of revolution! But the hour was not yet come when she could openly espouse the cause of Congress: nevertheless, she secretly proffered assistance. For several months, aid came through a private channel from a person less known in commerce than in politics and society, — the discreet yet enthusiastic confidential agent of the French ministry, Beaumarchais. For the more perfect concealment of his designs, the business was conducted under the name of Roderique

Hortalez & Co.   Within a few years, something has
been done to rescue the history of his well-meant and
valuable efforts from oblivion; and, while the record is
incomplete, enough has been preserved to show that
he was an efficient if not always true friend of the
republic.

The two leading spirits in the French cabinet at the
outbreak of the Revolution were Turgot, the minister of
finance, and Vergennes, who held the post of secretary
of state.   The former, from the beginning, was strenuously opposed to furnishing any aid whereby the peace
between France and Great Britain would be endangered.
Doubtless his policy was the wisest for France, as her
prosperity was dependent upon peace: war might indeed
increase her glory, and swell her pride, but only at the
expense of life and property, which in Turgot's eyes were
of far greater account.   Vergennes, though equally cool,
and withal a discreet minister, was not so harmoniously
endowed by nature, as he burned for revenge and the
humiliation of Great Britain; yet he was possessed of
sufficient caution to wait until France could strike a
decisive blow.   The king's feelings were akin to those of
Vergennes; and so, while he admired Turgot as much as
a person of such inferiority is capable of appreciating a
great superior, his policy was determined by the minister
of foreign affairs, and Turgot's influence was lost.

Negotiations with France on the side of the Colonies
emanated for a long period from a committee of secret
correspondence, appointed by Congress,[1] and composed of
five members.   In April,[2] 1777, the name was changed to

____

[1] Nov. 29, 1775.   [2] April 17.

that of Committee of Foreign Affairs, by which they continued to transact the foreign affairs of the government until the appointment of Robert R. Livingston as secretary of foreign affairs, in August,[1] 1781. While the committee were in existence, like all the other committees of Congress, their business was poorly performed: letters often remained unanswered when prompt replies should have been sent; the records of their proceedings were very imperfectly kept; and Franklin had urged the appointment of a secretary of foreign affairs long before Congress waked up to the necessity of the measure. With the appointment of Livingston, order was established; all correspondence received prompt attention; and the records of the office were faithfully and intelligently preserved.

The committee of secret correspondence soon after their appointment authorized Arthur Lee, who was then in London, to ascertain, if possible, the intentions of the British Government, as well as to obtain supplies for the use of Congress; and early in 1776 Silas Deane was sent by the same authority to Paris as commercial and political agent. These two commissioners were successful in opening negotiations with Beaumarchais, with whom an agreement was made for munitions of war and other supplies needed by the Colonies. One million livres were paid by Vergennes to Beaumarchais[2] for the benefit of the American Colonies, with which he purchased munitions of war

---

[1] Aug. 10.

[2] June 10, 1776; see letter of Franklin to Charles Thompson, June 27, 1787, Dip. Cor., vol. iv. p. 226; Lyman's Diplomacy of the U. S., vol. i. p. 28, 2d ed.

secretly from the royal arsenals.   Shortly afterward[1] a sum equally great was sent by the Court of Spain to Vergennes, to be appropriated by him in the same manner.[2]   In return, Beaumarchais expected to receive the produce of the country, for the importation of which every facility was to be furnished by the French Government.[3] It was confidently believed that this system would prove mutually advantageous; though the French Government prudently reserved the right to modify or suspend the plan, if such a step became necessary.[4]

The plan worked well in the beginning; but ere long the rumor reached America that Deane and Beaumarchais were jointly engaged in swindling the American Government by receiving cargoes from that country, while the munitions sent thither were the gift of the king, and not the property of Beaumarchais.   The effect of this rumor was to delay the shipment of cargoes, and finally none were despatched in payment of the materials thus furnished.   Vergennes, fearing that the British Government might learn of the transaction, denied to the committee of secret correspondence all participation therein on the part of the French Government, and admitted no more than that Beaumarchais had been allowed to make a portion of his purchases at the royal arsenals.   It is unquestionably true, whether the French Government ever

---

[1] Aug. 11, 1776.

[2] Pitkin's Polit. and Civil Hist. of U. S., vol. i. p. 411, ed. 1828.

[3] Pitkin says the French court did not expect to receive any produce in return for the money: the main object of this stipulation was to cover up the transaction, and make it look like a mercantile affair. Ibid., vol. i. p. 403.

[4] North Am. Rev., vol. lxxxiv. p. 137.

advanced Beaumarchais any funds secretly to be used for the benefit of America or not, he did spend a very much larger sum than it was ever known or supposed the French Government advanced to him, and justice required that this excess at least should be repaid. Congress, however, partly from the belief, no doubt, that Beaumarchais meant to perpetrate a fraud upon the country, and partly from want of means to pay him, delayed making a settlement for many years. He visited this country in the hope of inducing Congress to consider his claim, and pay him what was due; but the matter was kept open until 1835, when Congress finally paid to his heirs, in settlement of the claim, less than one-third of the balance declared by Hamilton to be due in 1793.[1]

Deane arrived in France in June, 1776, and two months[2] afterward gave a lengthy account of his efforts to obtain aid for his government. One of the persons desirous of furnishing arms, powder, and other war material, was M. Penet, who had collected these stores in fulfilment of a contract made with the committee of secret correspondence.[3] Deane urged him to send the supplies forward, and told him that he would certify to the merchants from whom Penet had made his purchases,

---

[1] See John Bigelow's article on Beaumarchais, Hours at Home, vol. xi. p. 160; American State Papers by Lowrie and Clarke, Claims, p. 433; North Am. Rev., vol. lxxxiv. pp. 134–139; Pitkin's Polit. and Civil Hist. of U. S., vol. i. p. 402, *et seq.* The claim of Beaumarchais was presented to Congress several times, and on one occasion especially an elaborate report was made thereon. March 15, 1814. State Papers, 13th Cong., second session. vol. ii. p. 84; see report also of March 23, 1812, Reports, &c., 12th Cong., 1st session, vol. ii.

[2] Aug. 18, 1776, Dip. Cor., vol. i. p. 9.   [3] Ibid., p. 10.

"that the Congress would pay for whatever stores they would credit them with, and in the mean time, advised him to proceed strictly agreeable to the letter of the contract," as he was "positive that the Congress would fulfil their part of it,"[1] whereupon he departed for Nantes, to ship the goods the next day. This reply well represents Deane's loose method of doing business; for, under cover of the authority granted him, there was no limit to the frauds which Penet might have perpetrated upon the American Government. Nor was it long before Deane found his accounts in such confusion that he was never able to explain them satisfactorily to Congress. From M. Chaumont, Deane obtained a credit for the Colonies "to the amount of one million livres;" and he also adds in the same letter, that he has "in treaty another credit," which, with the other, would be sufficient to purchase the things mentioned in his letter of instructions. This credit was to run until the next May, before which time he hoped to receive remittances.[2] Notwithstanding these credits, and his assertions respecting funds to complete his purchases, he asks the committee of secret correspondence to consider his situation, "with only 6,000 or 7,000 pounds to complete a contract of forty," while bills for his private expenses had been protested.[3] Thus Deane, in the beginning of his representative career, was a poor proof of the financial ability of his countrymen. At a later period he alludes to a quantity of stores which were soon to be shipped, that would amount to a large sum; and in September he writes to Robert Morris, who was then serving as one of the members of the com-

---

[1] Dip. Cor., vol. i. p. 11.   [2] Ibid., p. 21.   [3] Ibid., p. 21.

mittee of secret correspondence, of receiving the promise of supplies of clothing in October for thirty thousand men, beside a large quantity of ammunition, which was to come from the royal arsenals.[1] At that time the debt which the Colonies were likely to incur by carrying on the war was a common topic among ministerial writers; but Deane was certain, that, if American liberties were established, the demand for land in America would more than compensate for the whole expense of the struggle. The people of France were eager for news from the revolutionary Colonies; and Deane was prosecuting his cause with great zeal, even if not according to knowledge. "Surely," he says to the committee, "you will put me down as one of the first in the roll of American heroes, when you consider my situation, plunging into very important engagements, which I can by no means avoid, yet without funds to support them."[2] He adds, that he had met with every possible encouragement from every person he had seen, whether in or out of office, — a remark showing very clearly the drift of public sentiment in Paris regarding the contest between Great Britain and America.[3]

After independence was declared, Deane was appointed one of the three commissioners (the other two were Dr. Franklin and Arthur Lee) to negotiate treaties, and procure assistance from the nations of Europe. Early the next year[4] they applied to Vergennes for ships, men, and

[1] Sept. 17, 1776, Dip. Cor., vol. i. p. 40.

[2] Aug. 15, 1776, Ibid., p. 33; Letter to John Jay, Dec. 3, 1786, Ibid., p. 91.

[3] See Letter of Commissioners, Jan. 17, 1777, Ibid., p. 253.

[4] Jan. 5, 1777, Ibid., vol. ii. p. 21.

munitions of war; but this application was refused. France was not yet ready to engage in the contest, and, of course, granting such aid would have been construed as an act of war. They had been directed also to procure a loan of two million pounds (a suggestion emanating from Deane), in the effort to obtain which they were partly successful. Money could be furnished without the knowledge of Great Britain: war-ships could not be. At first it was proposed to obtain money from the farmers-general, to be repaid in tobacco, of which they wanted a large quantity. As it was difficult to settle all the terms, the Crown granted two million livres, of which sum one-quarter was paid in advance, and the balance in three payments of equal amount, in April, July, and October. The king exacted no promise of repayment, but required absolute silence respecting the transaction.[1]

Though this sum was only a small portion of what they were directed to borrow, the commissioners wrote hopefully concerning their ability to raise enough money to pay the interest upon twenty million dollars of paper money which Congress had issued, and might be obliged to borrow, in order to preserve the credit of all the Continental emissions. They also offered the suggestion, that, on "great or urgent occasions," Congress might venture to borrow even more, as they conceived it were better to do this than to pay interest on two millions sterling to foreigners.[2] They advised Congress to draw on them, for "sums equal to the interest of what they have borrowed, as that interest becomes due," allowing the

---

[1] March 12, 1777, Dip. Cor., vol. i. pp. 272, 273.

[2] April 9, 1777, Ibid., p. 276.

lenders, in the drafts, "five livres, money of France, for every dollar of interest;" which advice was speedily and gladly followed. They also ventured to make the same promise respecting future loans, without, however, mentioning the grounds of their expectation. Never relaxing their efforts to borrow money, they were compelled to write, about the time the last payment on the two million French loan was made, that they saw no probability of obtaining another loan of two millions sterling from any money-holder in Europe until affairs in America were in foreign opinion more firmly established.[1] Nevertheless, the commissioners did succeed, before the year closed, in getting a second loan of three million livres from France, seventy thousand pounds of which were remitted in December.[2]

This loan was paid in quarterly instalments; and, when the last instalment had been received, the commissioners applied once more to Vergennes for money.[3] They regretted the necessity of asking for further assistance; but as the war had proved very expensive, and emissions of paper money had become indispensable, in order to pre-

---

[1] Oct. 7, 1777, Dip. Cor., vol. i. p. 335.

[2] Dec. 18, 1777, Ibid., pp. 357, 358. When the Act of Sept. 10, 1777, was passed, relating to the drawing of bills of exchange on France, Almon, in his Remembrancer, added the remark, "It has long been notorious, that the courts of France and Spain have supplied the Colonies, with arms, ammunition, artillery, clothing, &c. The above extraordinary resolution of Congress, demonstrates, that the Colonies are subsidized by these courts; and that being thus secure of having the interest of their public debt discharged in Europe, they can want no other assistance for the establishment of their independency, and the solidity of their national credit." 1777, p. 486.

[3] Aug. 28, 1778, Ibid., p. 429.

vent their depreciation, Congress had borrowed large quantities of this paper, and had promised the lenders that interest thereon would be paid out of European funds; and, consequently, the commissioners were expecting to hear of the arrival of vessels from America, bringing bills of exchange for the interest which was then due, and amounting to a large sum. They therefore hoped that the quarterly payment of seven hundred and fifty thousand livres might be continued; and Vergennes was assured, that, as soon as Congress could find other ways of answering their demands, they would not trespass upon the goodness of the French court.[1]

The commissioners also sought for permission to borrow two millions sterling in France, changing somewhat the purposes for which the money, if borrowed, would be applied, as they declared it would be appropriated to the express purpose of redeeming so many of the bills of credit in America as would be sufficient to restore the remainder to their original value.[2] Why this reason was given is apparent. The bills of credit had depreciated, and, of course, the European money-market was unfavorably affected toward the Colonies by this event; and the commissioners were anxious to restore American credit, which could be done in no other way than by retiring the surplus of paper money issued by Congress. They never ceased to do every thing within their power to maintain American credit abroad, though they have never received half the praise which justly belongs to them for their untiring efforts.

This loan of two millions sterling, therefore, was not

[1] Dip. Cor., vol. i., pp. 429, 430.   [2] Ibid., p. 430.

asked of the French Government. What the commissioners desired was permission to borrow any part of the sum in France, as they found opportunity. Larger interest was offered as a stronger inducement; yet, as they were competitors with the king in the money-market, and perhaps had an advantage over him by offering higher rates, they were politic enough to request him, if he found fault with the measure, to fix the rate of interest himself. This permission to borrow money in the French dominions a month later was declined, and then the application for a quarterly payment of three-quarters of a million livres from the French Government was renewed.[1] Beside the poor credit of the newly created republic in Europe, which prevented it from obtaining assistance, the principal European nations were arming for war, and all were borrowing money, while some of them offered much higher rates of interest than America. On the 17th of September[2] the commissioners wrote that "France, England, the Emperor, Spain, Russia, at least, are borrowing money, and there is not one of them that we can learn, but offers better interest than the United States have offered.[3] There can be no motive then but simple benevolence to lend us." So long as this condition of affairs existed, there was no hope of obtaining funds from individuals: these must come from governments, if at all, inspired either by benevolence, as the commissioners believed, or by the desire to humiliate the British crown.

[1] Sept. 17, 1778, Dip. Cor., vol. i. p. 445.   [2] Ibid., p. 446.

[3] The same condition of the European money-market remained for a long period. See Ibid., vol. ii. p. 182.

Nor were these the only causes affecting American credit. Deane, whose rash ways of doing business could not escape notice and unfavorable comment, had continued to make purchases in the most careless manner, until his accounts were in inextricable confusion; while the creditors of the government continually pressed him for a settlement. John Adams and Arthur Lee went through a "tedious examination" of them, but without satisfaction. "All that we can find is," Lee wrote, "that millions have been expended, and almost every thing remains to be paid for. Bargains have been made of the most extravagant kind. For example, the uniforms that are agreed for at thirty-seven livres might have been had here for thirty-two livres each, and equally good, which, being five livres in every suit too much, comes to a large sum upon thousands."[1] Numerous irregularities were found, amounting to a large sum, and these things seriously affected the credit of the country. Deane afterwards sought to satisfy Congress that he was guilty of no dishonesty or impropriety in his purchases; but he failed to convince that body of the regularity of his transactions. It does not appear from any evidence that has ever come to light that Deane was dishonest;[2] but

[1] June 1, 1778, Dip. Cor., vol. ii. p. 163.

[2] Deane's conduct gave rise to much heated discussion at the time; nor are writers yet perfectly agreed concerning the light in which his transactions are to be regarded. To us both Lee and Deane appear to have been honest men, and exceedingly ambitious to serve their country; while each in obtaining aid for America was jealous of the success of the other. Moreover, Lee's hatred of Deane undoubtedly arose, in part, from the fact that the latter was a Connecticut schoolmaster, while the former belonged to the high bloods of Virginia. Deane had strong enemies and friends: among the latter was Robert Morris, who, in

that he did conduct the public business in a reckless and wasteful manner, thereby injuring the public credit, cannot be questioned.

When the commissioners assured Congress of their ability to pay the interest upon the sums borrowed at home, they "did not dream" of Congress drawing upon them for other purposes. Yet in a short time they paid drafts to returned officers to the amount of 82,211 livres, and feared the receipt of many more orders of the same kind. Mr. Bingham, one of the members of the committee of secret correspondence, sent drafts for a hundred thousand livres more. "This has among other things," wrote Franklin, "made me quite sick of my Gibeonite office, — that of drawing water for the whole congregation of Israel. But I am happy to learn from our minister of finance, that after the end of March next no further

turn, was assailed, for defending Deane, by Thomas Paine with no little severity. See letters of Deane, November, 1778, Almon's Rememb., for Year 1778 and beginning of 1779, p. 185, and from Robert Treat Paine, Thomas Paine, Robert Morris, and other persons, Ibid., pp. 369–390; also Lee's Letter, April 5, 1778, Dip. Cor., vol. ii. p. 150; and especially Wells's Life of S. Adams, vol. iii. pp. 60–63; Deane's Reply to Lee's Letter of June 1, 1778, Dip. Cor., vol. ii. p. 162, Oct. 12, 1778, Dip. Cor., vol. i. p. 139. Franklin entertained a good opinion of Deane, March 31, 1778, Dip. Cor., vol. i. p. 120; July 22, 1778, Ibid., vol. iii. p. 52. Oct. 17, 1779, Franklin wrote to James Sewell, "I had and have still a very good opinion of Mr. Deane, for his zeal and activity in the service of his country; I also thought him a man of integrity. . . . As yet, I think him innocent" (Dip. Cor., vol. iii. p. 120). Campbell in his History of Virginia, while strongly taking the side of Lee, says with reference to Deane, "He certainly rendered the Colonies great service at one time, and found a strong party in Congress in his support, including men of both sections and high character." P. 703.

drafts shall be made on me, or trouble given me by drafts on others." Well might Franklin and his colleagues write, "If you reduce us to bankruptcy here, by a non-payment of your drafts, consider the consequences." The following advice of Franklin was certainly sound: "In my humble opinion, no drafts should be made on us without first learning from us that we shall be able to answer them."[1]

When the three million loan was filled, Franklin desired the king to continue to make his quarterly payments of seven hundred and fifty thousand livres; and Gerard announced, on the 9th of February, that the king had consented to advance seven hundred and fifty thousand livres more.[2]

Congress continued to draw bills of exchange upon the commissioners, which were accepted and paid so long as they were in possession of any funds belonging to the government. But they suffered "the utmost anxiety," so they wrote, "lest we should be obliged to protest bills."[3] They had done every thing within their power to obtain money for Congress; but their efforts had been only partially successful. They now begged for supplies from home, and were unable to send the arms, ammunition, and clothing which Congress had ordered, because they had no funds to pay for them.

Franklin never wearied in his efforts to obtain assistance for his country, when the prospect of success would have disheartened a less patient and courageous soul. In

[1] July 22, 1778, Dip. Cor., vol. iii. p. 58.
[2] Feb. 9, 1779, Ibid., vol. x. p. 268.
[3] Nov. 7, 1778, Ibid., vol. i. p. 492.

various ways and through different channels did he lay
before the ministry "the distressed state of our finances
in America." All seemed to be willing to help, except
the comptroller, Neckar, who, Franklin affirmed,[1] was supposed to embarrass every measure containing grants of
money. The king was favorably disposed; for he promised to be security for the payment of interest upon
three million livres, if such a loan could be obtained in
Holland. Meanwhile, the loan obtained at home, the
interest upon which the commissioners expected to pay,
had been increased beyond the original sum of five million livres; while they were drained in other ways by
Congress. Moreover, the cargoes sent over to re-im-
burse a portion of the advances made by Beaumarchais
and others met with a poor fate, as some of them
were "run away with by the seamen," or taken by the
enemy, or, when arrived, had been applied toward the
payment of debts, — the tobacco to the farmers-general,
in fulfilment of the contract made with them; and the
rice and indigo to Beaumarchais, in part payment of the
advance received from him.[2]

Unlike Deane, Franklin kept an intelligent account of
his expenditures, and informed Congress what disposition
was made of the money received from the French Government. He endeavored to borrow money in Holland;
and, though two eminent houses in Amsterdam attempted
to negotiate a loan in accordance with the French king's
promise of payment, yet the great demand for money by
Germany and England, raising the rate of interest above

[1] May 26, 1779, Dip. Cor., vol. iii. p. 85.
[2] May 26, 1779, Ibid., p. 86.

what Franklin was authorized to offer, coupled with the
success of the British arms in destroying French trade,
together with the reported divisions in Congress (which
were, of course, greatly magnified by the British Government), and the pressure of several of the American States
for separate loans, — all these things rendered the Dutch
bankers sceptical of the ability of America to repay
loans, if they were made. The applications of separate
States were, indeed, serious obstacles in the way of procuring assistance for the General Government. This was
especially true in those cases in which the agents were
empowered to offer higher rates of interest, or were possessed with unlimited powers.[1] Notwithstanding the evil
effects of the practice of the States, they did not cease
from "running all over Europe, asking to borrow money,"[2] which shadowed forth such a belief in the distress
and poverty of the country, as to render all foreigners
afraid to incur deeper obligations for the benefit of
America.[3]

But there was one individual who dared come forward
and offer a loan to the downcast and well-nigh bankrupt
republic. M. Neufville was a banker whose ambition
and pretensions far exceeded his capacity for executing
the great plans he so glibly proposed. Neufville is the
type of a numerous class who have flourished in the
financial world during the last twenty years: indeed,
probably some of them are always to be found in every

---

[1] May 26, 1779, Dip. Cor., vol. iii. p. 91.

[2] May 31, 1779, Ibid., p. 144.

[3] See Letter of John Trumbull, agent for Connecticut, July 20, 1781,
Trumbull's Autobiography, p. 336.

country. Let us hear Dr. Franklin tell the story of his intercourse with this pretentious banker : —

" A Mr. Neufville[1] came from thence to me last spring, proposing to procure great sums, if he might be employed for that purpose, and the business taken away from the house that had commenced it. His terms at first were very extravagant, such as that all the estates real and personal in the thirteen Provinces should be mortgaged to him ; that a fifth part of the capital sum borrowed should every year, for five years, be laid out in commodities, and sent to Holland, consigned to him, to remain in his hands till the term (ten years) stipulated for final payment was completed, as a security for the punctuality of it, when he was to draw the usual commissions ; that all vessels or merchandise coming from America to Europe should be consigned to him or his correspondents, &c. As I rejected these with some indignation, he came down to the more reasonable one of doing the business as it was done by the other house, who, he said, could do no more, being destitute of the interest which he possessed.

" I did not care abruptly to change a house, that had in other respects been very friendly and serviceable to us, and thereby throw a slur upon their credit, without a certainty of mending our affairs by it and therefore told Mr. Neufville, that if he could procure and show me a list of subscribers, amounting to the sum he mentioned, or near it, I would comply with his proposition. This he readily and confidently undertook to do. But after three months, during which he acquainted me from time to

---

[1] This man must not be confounded with the Neufville with whom Adams transacted business. — LYMAN's *Diplomacy*, vol. i. p. 74, 2d ed.

time, that the favorable moment was not yet come, I received, instead of the subscription, a new set of propositions, among the terms of which were an additional one per cent, and a patent from Congress, appointing him and his sons[1] Commissioners for Trade and Navigation, and Treasurers of the General Congress and of every private State of the thirteen United States of North America, through the seven United Provinces,[1] with other extravagances, which I mention, that it may be understood why I have dropped a correspondence on this subject with a man, who seemed to me a vain promiser, extremely self-interested, and aiming chiefly to make an appearance without solidity, and who I understand intends applying directly to Congress, some of his friends censuring me as neglecting the public interest in not coming into his measures."[1]

Franklin had indeed no expectation of raising funds in Holland; since the interest paid by other nations was so much higher, while their credit was better than that of America. The American States also offered a more generous rate of interest than Congress; and this tended to sink the credit of the General Government. "My sole dependence," says Franklin, "now is upon this Court; I think reasonable assistance may be obtained here, but I wish I may not be obliged to fatigue it too much with my applications, lest it should grow tired of the connection."[2]

The year 1779 was drawing towards the end, and no loans had been obtained from France for more than a twelvemonth. Franklin had succeeded in honoring all

[1] Oct. 4, 1779, Dip. Cor., vol. iii. p. 109.
[2] Oct. 4, 1779, Ibid. p. 111.

the drafts sent by order of Congress, though he was living in constant apprehension of failure to meet all of them. Bingham complained because Franklin had refused to accept some of his drafts, as very hurtful to his credit; but he acknowledged that he had no authority from Congress to draw them; while Franklin's defence was unassailable, that he never undertook to provide for more than the payment of interest upon the first loan authorized by Congress. He declares, that if all the agents of Congress were permitted to run in debt, and draw upon him to support their credit, he would be utterly unable to fulfil their demands. Surely he could not pay drafts exceeding the amount he was able to raise by loans from France and other foreign countries.[1]

Congress still cherished the hope of obtaining another foreign loan. But Lee wrote[2] that there was not the least possibility, in the present situation of things, of getting any adequate loan in Europe; and he besought Congress not to let the vain expectation of obtaining one divert their attention from deriving aid from every resource at home. He continues, "It is necessary, that the impressions to our discredit, which have arisen from the unsuccessful attempts that have been already made, should be allowed to wear off, and some favorable event occur, such as the enemy being obliged to draw off their troops, before it will be possible to succeed in such a plan. In the mean time, the repetition of ineffectual attempts will only debase your credit more, and especially, if they are accompanied with the offer of more than ordinary interest,

---

[1] May 31, 1780, Dip. Cor., vol. iii. p. 144.
[2] Nov. 6, 1779, Ibid., vol. ii. p. 267.

which ever augments the suspicion of the insecurity of the principal, and that the borrowers are themselves conscious of their insufficiency."

During the next year France granted new loans; but Congress drew "bills extraordinary," on Franklin to the amount of nearly three hundred thousand dollars. He was sorely perplexed. Besides, the French ministry did not like the proceeding, as the revenues of the government were measured by its wants, and, consequently, there was no surplus to apply to new purposes.[1] To meet the last bills drawn by Congress, Franklin stipulated that his government should furnish provisions to the king's forces in America, in return for funds sufficient to pay the drafts, and immediately wrote to the president of Congress about the agreement.[2] Gerard had proposed the same thing in December, 1778, as a mode of discharging the indebtedness of Hortalez & Co. to the government. At the same time, Franklin urged the necessity of a strict compliance, on the part of Congress, of the assurance given him that no drafts would be drawn on him in the future, without first knowing whether he had funds in his hands for paying them.

As Congress greatly needed money, Franklin was instructed to apply for another loan;[3] and at the same time John Laurens was appointed a special minister to the Court of Versailles, as it was believed, that, coming directly from his country, he would know and feel its necessities more keenly, and press these with

---

[1] Dec. 2, 1780, Dip. Cor., vol. iii. p. 179.

[2] Dec. 2, 1780; Ibid., p. 180, Dec. 3, 1780, Ibid., p. 182.

[3] Letter of Instructions dated Nov. 29, 1780, Ibid., p. 176.

greater force upon the French ministry. But Franklin was by no means indifferent to his mission. As soon as fresh instructions from the committee were received, he obtained an interview with Vergennes, and laid the necessities of America before him. It was not until March,[1] 1781, that he was assured of the king's good will and of his willingness to grant more aid to the United States. The king, however, was not unmindful of the great expense he was incurring for his kingdom, and also of the fact how much the depreciation of Continental money had injured American credit in Europe. A loan in the king's dominions could not be favored, because it would interfere with the one he was trying to obtain himself to carry on the war; but, to give the States a signal proof of his "friendship," the king granted them the sum of six million livres, not as a loan, but as a free gift, a part of which was to be employed in making purchases in France, and the rest was to be sent to the United States with the view of re-establishing the credit of the government. The French Government had evidently learned the slow, wasteful, and inefficient ways of doing business by committees or boards established by Congress; and, as the gift was wanted more especially for the army, Washington alone was authorized to draw bills of exchange for it gradually, as the money might be wanted for that purpose. This was contrary to the usual mode of drawing them; and Franklin sought to have them drawn by the treasurer of the United States; but the ministry, with good reason, was inflexible on the point. Franklin, in his

---

[1] Letter dated March, 12, 1781, Dip. Cor., vol. iii. p. 192.

philosophic way, adds that there was no room for disputing this determination, as every donor has the right of qualifying his gifts with such terms as he thinks proper.[1]

A considerable portion of this gift was to be sent under the direction of Major Jackson, when Franklin, finding the engagements of Congress were accumulating, ordered the money to be stopped in the hands of the bankers; which event gave rise to a very lively correspondence between himself and Jackson. The latter claimed that Franklin had no control over the money, as it had been obtained by the efforts of Lee,[2] and threatened to take legal proceedings to get it if Franklin did not revoke his order. The latter, however, was not moved either by Jackson's representations, appeals, or threats. Franklin proved clearly that Lee had not been instrumental in obtaining the loan; and he certainly had not, as the correspondence of Lee shows. Jackson was compelled to return without the money; yet Franklin never accused him of exhibiting any other spirit than that of great and commendable zeal in the service of his country.

While Laurens had done nothing in the way of procuring this gift, he did succeed elsewhere in obtaining very substantial assistance. For a long time efforts had been put forth in Holland to raise loans there, but without success. Through the solicitation of Laurens, how-

---

[1] March 12, 1781. Dip. Cor., vol. iii. pp. 192–194.

[2] The loan was certainly due to Franklin's efforts: see Franklin's Cor., Dip. Cor., vol. iii. p. 230; also Lee's Letters, March 20, 1781, Ibid., vol. ix. p. 208; Sept. 2, 1781, Ibid., p. 235.

ever, it was determined to procure a loan in that country for ten million livres, the King of France agreeing to be security, and, if it failed, he was to supply the sum from his own treasury as soon as possible.[1] This sum, whether obtained from Holland or France, was to be repaid; and by the middle of May four millions of it had been given to Dr. Franklin to discharge bills of exchange drawn on him by order of Congress. Soon after obtaining this aid, Laurens returned home.

In November, Livingston, secretary of foreign affairs, wrote to Franklin, representing to him in strongest terms the necessity of procuring still further assistance from the king.[2] Three months later, Congress passed a resolution[3] to the same effect, fixing the amount of the loan authorized at twelve million livres. Morris had previously urged the same thing,[4] though his demand was for three millions more than the sum specified in the resolution of Congress. To these requests Franklin could make only one answer, and this was such as they had reason for expecting. Having granted the last loan with the " clearest and most positive assurances that it was all the king could spare," and that no more could be expected, " with what face," Franklin exclaims, " could I ask for another six millions? It would be saying, you are not to be believed, you can spare more; you are able to lend me twice the sum if you were but willing." Of course, he could not expect any further aid, and it would have been impolite in him to ask it.[5]

---

[1] Supra, p. 252.   [2] Nov. 20, 1781, Dip. Cor., vol. iii. p. 250.
[3] Feb. 8, 1782.   [4] July 13, 1781, Ibid., vol. xi. p. 377.
[5] June 25, 1782, Ibid., vol. iii. p. 308.

The same year the accounts between the United States and France were examined and settled. Dr. Franklin, in his communication upon the subject, remarks that "all the accounts against us for money lent, and stores, arms, ammunition, clothing, &c., furnished by government, were brought in and examined, and a balance received, which made the debt amount to the even sum of eighteen millions.[1] In this reckoning the loan of ten millions by Holland, which had been guaranteed by the French king, was excluded. In the same letter Dr. Franklin communicates the pleasing intelligence that the king had bestowed another gift of two millions, which, "added to the free gifts before made to us at different times, form an object

---

[1] Aug. 12, 1782, Dip. Cor., vol. iii. p. 494. When Dr. Franklin made a settlement with the French Government July 16, 1782, which was ratified by Congress Jan. 22, 1783, it was agreed that France had advanced the following sums under the various loans of 1778, 1779, 1780, 1781, 1782.

1778.	LIVRES.		1780.	LIVRES.	
28 February .	750,000		*Brought for'd* .	2,250,000	4,000,000
19 May . .	750,000		5 October .	750,000	
3 August .	750,000		27 November .	1,000,000	
1 November .	750,000				4,000,000
		3,000,000	1781.		
1779.			15 February .	750,000	
10 June . .	250,000		15 May . .	750,000	
16 September .	250,000		1 August .	1,000,000	
4 October .	250,000		15 August .	750,000	
21 December .	250,000		15 November .	750,000	
		1,000,000			4,000,000
1780.			1782.		
29 February .	750,000		10 April . .	1,500,000	
23 May . .	750,000		1 July . .	1,500,000	
21 June . .	750,000		5 July . .	3,000,000	
					6,000,000
Carried for'd .	2,250,000	4,000,000			18,000,000

of at least twelve millions, from which no returns but that of gratitude and friendship are expected." "These," Franklin adds, "I hope, may be everlasting."[1] He, at least, fully appreciated the benevolence of the king.

The next year another loan was granted of six million livres,[2] which was the final one, although the previous loan of the same amount the king had positively declared was the last pecuniary aid he could render. Franklin assured the French Government, that, under the administration of Morris, the finances at home had improved; and it was no doubt in consequence of his representations that the king was induced to grant another loan. Imagine Franklin's situation and feelings when finding his hopes turn into delusions, and of the unwelcome necessity of telling Vergennes that his previous assurances of better management at home had been too hastily given. This loan Franklin declares the king had not been able to make without great difficulties; and he says that he was "ordered to announce to Morris," to whom he was writing, "in the most positive manner, that it will be impossible for the king, under any supposition whatever, to procure new advances of money for Congress, for the next year."

It was at this time that Franklin wrote to Morris, who was now superintendent of finance, and authorized to negotiate foreign loans, that there was no prospect of procuring additional funds "until the United States shall have established a permanent public revenue, and the delay and repugnance, with which they proceed in doing

---

[1] Aug. 12, 1782, Dip. Cor., vol. iii. p. 494.
[2] April 15, 1783, Ibid., vol. iv. p. 103.

this, being known in Europe, the inclination for lending money to Congress, which may have existed, has disappeared; and the lenders make other investments; the speculations, which might have been directed towards the United States go further and further from them, and it will certainly be difficult to bring them back." He then repeats the substance of Vergennes' despatches: "Without the speedy establishment of a substantial public revenue, and without the vigorous execution of the engagements entered into by Congress, the hope of obtaining loans in Europe must be given up." The Colonists were unwilling to be taxed by Great Britain without representation, and having resisted taxation by the mother-country, and escaped payment of the burden, it was not easy to resume it, even when the establishment of the principle for which they contended was assured. They refused to be taxed, or rather were unwilling to pay taxes, even when represented, and so their credit suffered both at home and abroad; and the wonder is, that France was willing to grant as much assistance as she did. However pure were the motives which constrained her to furnish aid, the desire to diminish the pride and power of Great Britain must not be left out of sight. But, whatever her motives were, she fulfilled all her engagements, thereby setting an example to the new-born republic worthy of imitation, which, unhappily, was speedily forgotten.

Beside the pecuniary assistance rendered directly and indirectly by France, both Spain and Holland granted loans, the history of which may be briefly traced. One reason, and not the slightest, why European nations were willing to assist America, was to obtain a portion of her trade, nearly all of which had been previously monopolized by Great Britain. Holland wanted sugar especially, because she was largely engaged in refining it, and all the nations wanted rice, indigo, and tobacco. This was their opportunity, and they were willing to incur some risks to enhance their prospective gains. In February, 1777, the three commissioners appointed by Congress, soon after declaring independence, to attend to the affairs of the United States in Europe, resolved to separate: Dr. Franklin was to remain in France; Lee was to go to Spain; and Deane, to Holland; his early recall, however, preventing him from going thither. Lee proceeded to his destination, and soon opened negotiations with the Spanish Government for a loan. As the king was well disposed toward the United States, it was hoped that Lee might be successful in his mission. At first, things promised well, and he was assured that powder and clothing would be sent to New Orleans for the use of the government, and that a "credit on Holland" would be given.[1] In December[2] the three commissioners wrote from Paris, that Spain had promised to send three million livres in the course of the year, which was to be sent in specie from Havana to the United States. Spain was quite unlike the French court in her promises; for, notwithstanding the assurances of the Spanish ambassador at Paris ("a grave and wise man") to the American

---

[1] April 9, 1777, Dip. Cor., vol. i. p. 275.

[2] Dec. 18, 1777, Ibid., p. 357. Lee says, "Our friends in Spain" have promised to supply the three million livres. Jan. 15, 1778, Ibid., vol. ii. p. 125.

commissioners, that his court piqued itself on a religious observance of its word,[1] she advanced only a hundred and seventy thousand livres of the sum promised.[2]

Several times the promise of money was repeated.[3] Having abandoned the idea of sending funds from Havana, they were to be paid to the American banker in Paris in quarterly payments; but neither from Havana nor from the banker did Lee get any more money.[4] Spain was repeatedly pressed to supply stores; and orders were given for furnishing them: they were shipped from Bilboa, and were to be paid for out of the advances made

[1] Dec. 18, 1777, Dip. Cor., vol. i. p. 275.   [2] Ibid, vol. ii. p. 133.

[3] June 1, 1778, Ibid., vol. ii. p. 167.

[4] "Our joint despatches of the 28th of December, 1777, informed you," writes Arthur Lee, "that Spain had promised us three millions of livres, to be remitted to you in specie through Havana. This information we had through the French court. We have since been informed through the same channel, that it would be paid to our banker here in quarterly payments. Of this I apprised you in my letter of the 15th of January, 1778. Finding however that no payment was made, I applied lately to the Spanish ambassador here for an explanation. From him I learned, that by order of his court, he had informed the Court of France, that such a sum should be furnished for your use; but in what manner he was not instructed, nor had he received any further communication on the subject. He promised to transmit my application to his court without delay.

"The balancing conduct, which these courts have until very lately held towards us, has involved us inevitably in continual contradictions and disappointments. It is in this respect fortunate, that so many of our dispatches have miscarried, otherwise you would have been equally vexed, embarrassed and disappointed." (Feb. 28, 1778, *Dip. Cor.*, vol. ii. p. 138.) Lee's allusion to the date, "28th of December," is evidently a mistake. He meant the letter dated 18th of December, to which we have already referred.

by the Spanish Government.[1] When the United States authorized the first loan of two million pounds, Lee endeavored to get this sum "through the hands of a nobleman" residing in Madrid; but even his request to accept such a proposal was refused.[2] Lee then tried to negotiate a treaty for the cession of Florida in return for money and other assistance; but this plan, too, failed.[3] Finally Lee gave up the attempt of getting any thing from Spain, and withdrew.

John Jay succeeded him. His mission was just as unsuccessful as that of his predecessor. The history of his efforts can be summed up in a very short space, for it is not an inviting theme. For two years he continued at the Spanish court, suffering many embarrassments, delays, and cold treatment. Promises of money and other supplies were made to Jay, which were not fulfilled; and, had it not been for the aid furnished by Dr. Franklin, he would have been obliged to abandon his post. Bills were drawn on him from home, although he had no money to pay them; but Franklin came to his rescue on several occasions. Finally Jay was obliged to suffer bills to be protested, though not exceeding twenty-five thousand dollars. These were subsequently paid by Franklin. During Jay's long and patient negotiations he was able

---

[1] May 23, 1778, Dip. Cor., vol. ii. p. 162; June 15, 1778, Ibid., p. 173. The Spanish house of Gardoqui promised to send military supplies, and did send money, — at one time, 81,000 livres, and, at another, 106,500 livres. Dip. Cor., vol. ii. pp. 40, 45, 49. These sums were repaid out of the 170,000 livres advanced by the Spanish Government.

[2] Aug. 13, 1778, Ibid., p. 179.

[3] Aug. 20, 1778, Ibid., p. 180, and subsequent letters relating to the same subject.

to obtain one hundred and fifty thousand dollars. Such was the extent of the aid furnished by Spain.[1]

Let us turn to Holland, which at this time was one of the richest countries in Europe, whence surrounding nations drew fresh supplies for carrying on wars and other enterprises. In 1778 the American commissioners, who were then in Paris, resolved that one of their number should go to Holland with the view of procuring a loan there; and, before the close of the year, Arthur Lee wrote to the committee of foreign affairs, "Our affairs in Holland, both as to the treaty and loan, are in a promising state."[2] A month later Lee was still more confident. "If the irritation and ill-humor in Holland is continued by England's persisting in the interruption of their trade, they will lend us money out of revenge; and if England retracts, the Dutch will send us such plentiful supplies, and take in return our produce, as in a great measure to compensate for the want of funds."[3] After Deane's recall, Adams was sent to fill the vacancy. He proceeded to Amsterdam, whence he writes, in August, 1780,[4] that he was sure a loan could be obtained by any one having power from Congress to negotiate it. But, when full powers for that purpose arrived, he did not find the same willingness to loan America as he had found while he was without authority to enter into such an engage-

---

[1] Jay's Life of Jay, vol. i. pp. 109, 110; Dip. Cor., vol. vii. pp. 300, 304, 410; Ibid., vol. viii. pp. 49, 70, 71.

[2] Oct. 19, 1788, Ibid., vol. ii. p. 195.

[3] Nov. 15, 1778, Ibid., p. 202.

[4] J. Adams's Works, vol. vii. pp. 245, 246.

ment.[1] Before the year closed, he wrote to Franklin that there "was not a prospect of obtaining a shilling."[2]

Confiding in his earlier assurances, Congress drew bills of exchange upon Laurens, who had been previously designated for the Dutch post, but had been captured, and afterwards upon Adams. Had it not been for Franklin, these would have been dishonored, as Adams could procure no funds from any other source, not even enough to pay his own expenses. This change of feeling in respect to assisting America was due, in part, to severe military disasters; but Adams affirmed that it was also "due to fear of the English and the Stadtholderian party."

Early the next year, having failed to get any assistance from the government, notwithstanding his earnest and repeated solicitations, he opened a loan, which, however, some of his friends thought was ill-advised.[3] This proved a total failure, as only five thousand guilders were received, three thousand of which were paid upon the promise of Luzac, and the rest by M. de Neufville. His proposals for a loan, though well received by the public, Adams writes, have as yet had no success.[4] In October the situation had improved, and Adams informed Franklin of the fact. The same month he wrote to the president of Congress:[5] "It would fill a small volume to give a history of my negotiations with people of various stations and characters, in order to obtain a loan, and it would

----

[1] Nov. 17, 1780, J. Adams's Works, vol. vii. p. 330.

[2] Nov. 30, 1780, Ibid., p. 337.

[3] March 11, 1781, Ibid., p. 376.

[4] Note J. Adams's Works, vol. vii. p. 376.

[5] Oct. 15, 1781, Ibid., p. 472.

astonish Congress to see the unanimity with which they all have refused to engage in the business, most of them declaring they were afraid to undertake it. I am told that no new loan was ever undertaken here, without meeting at first with all sorts of contradiction and opposition for a long time; but my loan is considered not only as a new one, but as entering deep into the essence of all the present political systems of the world, and no man dares engage in it, until it is clearly determined what characters are to bear rule, and what system is to prevail in this country." In the same letter he regarded the situation so hopeless as to ask for his recall. While the loan which Adams had opened remained in suspense, Laurens, who had been appointed a special minister to France to obtain further assistance, succeeded in inducing the French court to open a loan in Holland for ten million livres, for the benefit of the United States, the payment of which was to be guaranteed by France. Unhappily, the Dutch flatly refused to countenance this; although Neckar, who was then the director-general of the French finances, supposed the grant would be obtained easily as there was double security for it. The security was not the obstacle in the way of its success, but the fear, that, if granted, it might embroil Holland in a war with Great Britain, and occasion the disturbance of business. France, however, came to the rescue, and agreed to make the advance herself, though she was able subsequently to obtain the money from Holland upon the security proposed in the beginning.

The skies began to brighten. Early the next year Adams received a promise from Capellen, secretary of state for Holland, of his intention "to place 12,000 florins in the American funds." [1] Adams was delighted to find that Capellen preferred to put the money in the loan he himself had proposed, rather than in the loan made with the warranty of France and the republic, because it was a more frank and manly acknowledgment of America's pretensions: it was treating America in her true character.

At this time Adams applied to a great banking-house in Amsterdam, which had traded with America for a hundred years, to undertake the loan. The answer received will interest the reader, because it shows the difficulties and subtleties in making loans in Holland at that period, —a curious revelation, truly, of the mysteries of finance then practised there. Adams was told the house would undertake the loan if it was found possible to succeed; "but there are four persons who have the whole affair of loans through the republic under their thumbs; these persons are united; if you gain one you gain all, and the business is easy; but without them, there is not one house in this republic can succeed in any loan." [2] The banker spent two days in exploring the field, after which time he called again on Adams, and narrated what he had done. First he had waited on one of the regency, and asked him if it was proper for him to put in a *requête*, and asked leave to open such a loan. He was answered he had better say nothing to the regency about it, for they would either give him no answer at all (which was most probable), or say it was improper for them to inter-

<hr>

[1] Letters Jan. 6, 14, 1782, J. Adams's Works, vol. vii. pp. 501, 502.

[2] Ibid., Letter to Franklin Jan. 25, 1782, p. 508.

fere; either of which answers would do more hurt than good. It was an affair of credit, which he might undertake without asking leave; for the regency never interfered to prevent merchants getting money. With this answer he went to one of the undertakers, whose answer was, that, at least until there was a treaty, it was impossible to get the money: as soon as that event should happen, he was ready to undertake it.

"I have been uniformly told," says Adams, "that these four or five persons had such a despotic influence over loans; I have heretofore sounded them in various ways, and the result is, that I firmly believe they receive ample salaries, upon the express condition that they resist an American loan. There is a phalanx formed by British ministry, Dutch court, proprietors of English stocks, and great mercantile houses in the interest of the British ministry, that support these undertakers and are supported by them.

"We may therefore reckon boldly that we shall get nothing here, unless in the form of the late five millions lent to the King of France, and warranted by the republic, until there is a treaty."[1]

On the 2d of May,[2] he again writes to Franklin, among other things, of trying to get a loan. He says, "It is true, I may open a loan for five millions, but I confess I have no hopes of obtaining so much. The money is not to be had. Cash is not infinite in this country. Their profits by trade have been ruined for two or three years; and there are loans open for France, Spain, England,

---

[1] Jan. 25. 1782, J. Adams's Works, vol. vii. pp. 508, 509.

[2] May 2, 1782, Ibid., pp. 580, 581.

Russia, Sweden, Denmark, and several other powers as well as their own national, provincial, and collegiate loans. The undertakers are already loaded with burdens greater than they can bear, and the brokers in the republic are so engaged, that there is scarcely a ducat to be lent, but what is promised. This is the true cause why we shall not succeed; yet they will seek a hundred other pretences. It is considered such an honor and such an introduction to American trade to be the house, that the eagerness to obtain the title of American banker, is prodigious. Various houses have pretensions, which they set up very high; and let me choose which I will, I am sure of a cry and clamor. I have taken some measures to endeavor to calm the heat, and give general satisfaction, but have as yet small hopes of success. I would strike with any house that would insure the money, but none will undertake it, now it is offered, although several were very ready to affirm that they could, when it began to be talked of. Upon inquiry, they do not find the money easy to obtain, which I could have told them before. It is to me, personally, perfectly indifferent which is the house, and the only question is, which will be able to do best for the interests of the United States. This question, however simple, is not easy to answer. But I think it clear, after very painful and laborious inquiries for a year and a half, that no house whatever will be able to do much. Enthusiasm, at some times and in some countries, may do a great deal; but there has as yet been no enthusiasm in this country for America, strong enough to untie many purses. Another year, if the war should continue, perhaps we may do better."

Negotiations were begun with the house of Willink; and in July [1] Adams had the pleasure of informing Congress that an agreement had been made to open a loan of five million guilders, which was to bear five per cent interest, redeemable in five years, with a commission of four and a half per cent for procuring the loan and all the charges relating thereto, as well as paying off the loan at maturity. At first, only three millions were to be put on the market, and, if this sum were taken, the other two millions were to be offered. In his letter to Secretary Livingston, announcing what he had done, he expresses his doubts of getting so much for a long time. "If we get a million and a half, by Christmas, it will be more than I expect." [2] Adams had lost faith by his long series of disappointments. Yet in little more than a month after writing this letter, 1,484,000 florins had been subscribed. By November the sum taken was between one million and a half and two million guilders. [3] At this time Dr. Franklin, who had paid Adams's salary and many of the bills which Congress had drawn upon their representatives in Holland, called upon Adams to pay the interest upon the ten-million loan of France, as well as bills of Congress drawn upon himself. Both Adams and Franklin were struggling hard to preserve the credit of Congress.

One reason why it was so difficult to raise money was the enormous demand for it by nearly all the nations of Europe. If America was a beggar, England was a far greater; while France and other countries were continu-

---

[1] July 5, 1782, J. Adams's Works, vol. vii. p. 509.   [2] Ibid.
[3] Nov. 6, 1782, Ibid., p. 657.

ally borrowing large sums. Money had grown scarce, even in opulent Holland; which country Franklin, adopting the language of another, was inclined to think was no longer "a nation, but a great shop," having no other sentiments or principles but those of shopkeepers.[1]

Bills were drawn more rapidly than the loan could be placed, and the bankers who were trying to negotiate it came very near protesting them to the amount of thirteen thousand guilders. Yet they did not despair of succeeding; for they proposed to open a new loan for four millions, as soon as this was filled, bearing six per cent interest.[1] Adams went to Holland in order to induce the bankers to put forth greater exertions; but all efforts on his part gave no promise of success. Finally, in order to save the bills from going to protest,[2] Adams consented to a new loan for two million guilders, bearing six per cent interest. While Adams was engaged in this perilous struggle to save the credit of his country, Franklin wrote to him that he did not wonder the regency in Holland had declined to come to the rescue, and save the bills, on account of the diversity of sentiment prevailing at home about the plan of impost which had been urged upon the States for their acceptance. "I hope these mischievous events," he says, "will at length convince our people of the truth of what I long since wrote to them, that the foundation of credit abroad must be laid at home."[3]

Yet this was not the only reason why the regency declined to assist Adams. It was the establishment of a

---

[1] Dec. 26, 1783, Jan. 24, 1784, J. Adams's Works, vol. viii. pp. 168, 170.

[2] Feb. 5, 1784, Ibid., p. 176.   [3] Ibid., p. 177.

dangerous precedent.   If they aided the United States when in a very tight place, by advancing money to pay bills drawn upon her minister, some other nation might ask a repetition of the same favor.

The efforts of Adams still continued successful in procuring funds for his government, although the condition of American finances in Europe at the close of 1784 were poor enough.   Beside the scarcity of money and the number of loans in the Dutch market, the divisions between Congress and the States, accounts of which came to Holland through English sources, and which were very greatly magnified, made an impression upon the money-lenders, "who," says Willink to Adams, "always incline to mistrust without cause, especially at a time when, through a great concurrence of loans, they are not at a loss with their money."[1]   Notwithstanding all these obstacles, lenders continued to loan money to the United States until the opening of 1785, when Adams had the pleasure of announcing that both his loans, the one for two million guilders and the other for five million guilders, were almost full, and that he had on hand nearly a million of guilders.[2]

Here let us cut this thread of our financial history, merely taking note of the fact that other nations in Europe, beside Holland, France, and Spain, were invited to loan money to the United States, though from no other sources than the three mentioned was any assistance derived.

[1] J. Adams's Works, vol. viii. p. 153.
[2] Jan. 10, 1785, Ibid., p. 221.

CHAPTER XVIII.

LOAN-OFFICE CERTIFICATES.

BEFORE sketching the financial administration of Robert Morris, a brief history of the loan-office experiment is needed to complete our survey of what may be considered the initial period in the financial history of the General Government.

When the question of issuing paper money was first discussed in Congress, as we have elsewhere related, Franklin, and perhaps other members, strongly favored a loan by the government: nevertheless several months elapsed before this step was taken. The plan was modelled upon a scheme invented in Virginia in 1765, when the House passed a bill for borrowing two hundred and forty thousand pounds sterling from British merchants, at five per cent interest.[1] A fund for paying the interest, and sinking the principal, was to be raised by an impost duty on tobacco; bills of exchange were to be drawn for a hundred thousand pounds, the avails of which were to be employed in redeeming the paper money in circulation; while the remainder of the loan was to be lent on permanent security. The council refused to sanction the scheme. Congress now revived it, confidently believing, that, if the people would liberally sub-

[1] Campbell's Hist. of Virginia, p. 539.

scribe, the necessity for issuing more paper money would cease, and its value be preserved. This was indeed a rational hope: if the people subscribed liberally enough, the government would certainly get all the funds needed; while this new use of paper money would sustain in no slight degree its value.

These loan-office certificates were of two kinds, — one kind bearing interest payable in specie; the other, in paper money. The former kind was the more popular. When the American commissioners in Europe gave assurance of their ability to borrow specie enough to pay interest upon all the sums which the government could probably borrow at home, and sustained their word by promptly paying all bills of exchange drawn on them for the discharge of interest, the more patriotic citizens of the country especially purchased certificates in considerable quantities. In numerous instances property was sold, and the sum received was invested in this manner.

When Congress authorized the certificates, it was not supposed they would be immediately thrown into circulation. The interest they bore, it was thought, would be a sufficient inducement to the holders to keep them, just as persons in the Eastern States had done, not long before, in respect to some bills of credit which had been issued bearing interest. Unhappily they were not hoarded: their circulation became general, effecting essentially the same consequences as would have attended the issue of an equal quantity of paper money. Instead of withdrawing paper money from circulation, the effect of this experiment was really to increase the quantity, and consequently diminish its value. The very fact that the loan-office certificates bore interest led persons to take them in preference to Continental paper money, thus depreciating the value of the latter. Such a consequence of issuing them the wisest men of the day had failed to foresee. Gouverneur Morris, writing in 1780, says[1] that when they were first issued, "it was truly ludicrous to see the solicitude of many well-meaning men, to pay the public debts with these certificates instead of the common paper, and even to give an advance in purchases to those who would accept of them. Nay, it was no uncommon argument in favor of a large grant, that some considerable part of it was a warrant which was to be liquidated by loan-office certificates."

In effect, therefore, the government circulated three kinds of paper money,—one, bearing no interest; the second, bearing interest payable in paper money ; and a third kind, the interest of which was payable in specie. But the interest paid by the government answered no valuable purpose. "A measure laudable, perhaps," says Gouverneur Morris, "for the generosity, if with the exuberance of public revenue, the treasury were running over, but favoring much of prodigality in some other circumstances."

When the evils caused by the certificates did appear, either the loan-offices ought to have been closed,[2] or some

---

[1] Penn. Packet, April 11.

[2] "I only contend for the immediate dissolution of the loan office; for why should the community be burthened with an addition of taxes, merely to pay an interest to moneyed men, for lending paper to government; when that very paper could be as well made without any other expense than striking it; and the larger these bills the better: if a thou-

other measure taken to check the unexpected consequences we have described. If, however, the negotiability of the certificates were destroyed or lessened by action of Congress, it was feared that the people would lend no more money to the government. Hence, while the mischief was seen, no one was wise enough to devise a remedy; and so the original plan was continued, the commissioners paying the bills of exchange given for interest until the 1st of March, 1782, when it was impossible for the government to pay interest any longer.[1]

When the government ceased to pay interest upon these obligations, the event was a very unwelcome one to many people. Meetings were held, and Congress was petitioned to continue the payment of interest.[2] The following letter, addressed to the printer of " The Pennsylvania Packet,"[3] expresses, doubtless, the sentiments of many others who were in a similar situation to the writer: " I am, sir, one of those unfortunate widows, who, at the commencement of this contest, was in possession of a comfortable income. My feelings dictated it as a duty to me, that I ought to lend every assistance in my power, tho' a weak woman: upon which I put what money I could spare into the public funds, and although but a

sand dollars each, it might help to retard the circulation and lessen the charge of printing and signing. It is to be observed, that the whole of my reasoning on this subject, turns upon the assertion, that loan-office certificates are money to all intents and purposes, and operate in proportion to their quantity, equal to a like sum of Continental bills — if I am wrong my conclusions fall to the ground." — *Penn. Packet*, Jan. 20, 1780.

[1] Am. State Papers by Lowrie and Clarke, Finance, vol. i. p. 147.

[2] Penn. Packet, July 6, 1782.   [3] Jan. 19, 1782.

trifle, received my interest in bills upon France very punctually. Encouraged and pleased at the attention paid to the public credit, I sold off my houses and lands, and immediately put my money into the loan office; but alas! how great have been my sufferings since that time, having never received for this last sum one shilling interest. 'Tis true, when I called upon the loan officer, he offered me certificates, but said he had no money and to my sorrow I found, that if I parted with these certificates it must be at the discount of twenty to thirty-three and a third per cent, therefore concluded it best rather to be satisfied with the whole than submit to such an imposition; and had not the heavy taxes we labor under, recalled to my mind my former happy circumstances, I should rather have been a silent sufferer than made known my wants, but when I look around me and find that the little furniture I have, is the only resource left to pay those taxes and support an aged woman I cannot help complaining tho' but imperfectly. Would to heaven some abler pen would take up the talk, and endeavor by representing the matter in its proper light, to awaken the feelings of Congress, and give them a proper idea of the extreme misery and distress which great numbers of the most virtuous of our fellow-citizens are involved in thro' the same neglect."

A resolution was passed at the same time as the Forty-for-one Act redeeming the loan-office certificates according to the value of money at the time they were respectively issued. "This is but justice," remarked Gerry[1] in a

[1] May 5, 1780, J. Adams's Works, vol. vii. p. 190.

letter to Adams, and such was the opinion prevailing at the time.   But a long anxious period was to pass before this class of creditors could receive their dues, even upon such a basis.

BOOK II.

FROM MORRIS'S FINANCIAL ADMINISTRATION TO THE CLOSE
OF THE CONFEDERATION.

CHAPTER I.

THE FINANCIAL ADMINISTRATION OF ROBERT MORRIS.

NOTWITHSTANDING Morris's acceptance,[1] which has been already described, the Board of Treasury, by his request, remained until he could disengage himself from private business, and devote his chief attention to the duties of his office. Thus, for several months, there was a mixed administration of the finances, Morris increasing his attention to them, until he was able to dispense wholly with the services of the Board of Treasury.

The news of his appointment was received with gladness by all the friends of the newly-created government. Several times he had been elected delegate to Congress, always serving with distinguished ability; and more than once, when Washington was sorely pressed for funds and other means to supply his army, Morris furnished the much-needed relief. At the time of accepting office, Morris was somewhat less than fifty years of age, and in the fulness of physical strength and financial experience. He possessed great energy and integrity, and his patriotism shone conspicuously throughout the Revolution.[2] Unquestionably, a fitter person for the office could not have been selected; and Hamilton's letter, — addressed to

[1] Morris accepted office May 7, 1781.

[2] Watson's Annals of Philadelphia, vol. ii. p. 329.

him after his election, but previous to his acceptance, while Congress was deliberating upon the conditions which Morris had imposed, — not only expressed the writer's opinion, but the opinion of all who were the most competent to judge concerning the man and the office. Hamilton assures Morris [1] that he had heard with the greatest satisfaction of his nomination to the department of finance, and that long ago he had informed his friend Duane how desirous he was for Congress to make the appointment. He then continues, "I know of no other in America who unites so many advantages; and, of course, every impediment to your acceptance is to me a subject of chagrin. I flatter myself, Congress will not preclude the public from your services, by an obstinate refusal of reasonable conditions; and as one deeply interested in the event, I am happy in believing you will not easily be discouraged from undertaking an office, by which you render America and the world no less a service than the establishment of American independence. 'Tis by introducing order into our finances, by restoring public credit, not by gaining battles, that we are finally to gain our object. 'Tis by putting ourselves in a condition to continue the war, not by temporary, violent, and unnatural efforts to bring it to a decisive issue, that we shall in reality bring it to a speedy and successful one. In the frankness of truth, I believe, sir, you are the man best capable of performing this great work." To Franklin the appointment was equally welcome; and he expresses his "great pleasure" to Morris,[2] "as from your intelligence, integrity and abili-

---

[1] Hist. of Repub., vol. ii. p. 212.

[2] July 26, 1781, Dip. Cor., vol. xi. p. 405.

ties, there is reason to hope every advantage, that the public can possibly receive from such an office."[1]

While Morris's acceptance remained in suspense,[2] the Board of Treasury were directed[3] to lay before Congress returns from the loan offices, specifying the amount of old emissions received, and of new emissions retained by order of Congress, also the amount of taxes paid by the respective States, and to make a monthly report thereof in the future.

Three days in the week were now set apart for the discussion of financial measures.[4]   On the 16th of March,

---

[1] Washington wrote to Morris, June 4, 1781: "I felt a most sensible pleasure when I heard of your acceptance of the late appointment of Congress to regulate the finances of this country" (SPARKS's *Wash.*, vol. viii. p 66).   "The public sentiment everywhere pointed to Robert Morris. whose great experience and success as a merchant, his ardor in the cause of American liberty, his firmness of character, fertility of mental resources, and profound knowledge of pecuniary operations, qualified him in a degree far beyond any other person for this arduous and responsible station" (SPARKS's *Life of G. Morris*, vol. i. p. 231).

[2] Varnum, a Rhode-Island delegate, wrote to Gov. Greene from Philadelphia, April 2, 1781: "We have experienced a recent instance of political diffidence. Mr. Robert Morris, of this city, has been chosen financier.   Previous to his final acceptance, he insisted upon the power of removing from office all persons intrusted with the expenditure of the public money, for abuse, fraud, &c., without being answerable, except to the party injured, in the courts of law.   Without this authority, he despaired of introducing economy, so essentially important at this critical situation.   A majority decided against the proposition. The consequence is, we are re-plunged into our old situation, so agreeable to some gentlemen, and I fear shall not be able to effect a reformation in point of revenue and expenditure, which some time since many of us hoped and firmly expected." —STAPLES's *Hist. of R. I. in the Cont. Cong.*, p. 335.

[3] Feb. 9, 1781.   [4] March 6, 1781.

1781, an important measure was adopted, providing that all debts then due from the United States, which had been liquidated in specie, "or other money equivalent," should be actually paid either in gold or silver, or other money equal thereto, according to the current exchange between such money and specie. At the same time, the States were recommended to repeal all prior legislation declaring Continental bills of credit a legal tender, thus making their legal, correspond with their real, value. For the purpose of continuing the war, the States were asked in November,[1] 1780, to furnish six million dollars, partly in specific articles at fixed prices, and the balance in gold and silver, in four quarterly payments. To discharge this requisition more easily, as well as prior ones issued by Congress, bills of credit of the new emission were to be received at the Federal treasury as equal to, and in lieu of, specie, and which were to draw interest from the time of payment until the quotas of the States were finally ascertained.[2] If in the end it should appear that any State had been assessed for more than its just quota, payment of interest was to be continued upon the surplus;[3] if for less, interest was to be charged upon the deficiency, until, by a future tax, the surplus or deficiency was adjusted. The States were also directed to make returns to the Board of War, to the first day of June following, of every thing which they had supplied to Congress or its officials; and all deficiencies then existing were to be paid within three months thereafter.[4]

Congress was earnest in rescuing the country from the

---

[1] Nov. 4.   [2] March 16, 1781.   [3] March 23, 1781.
[4] March 16, 1781.

grave financial perils which threatened its existence.[1] As an opinion prevailed that the bills of credit of the new emission were interest-bearing obligations, Congress, in order to settle the point, declared that they did not draw interest, when issued from loan-offices, or paid for supplies, or when given in discharge of public debts.[2] By this enactment, a controversy which had risen to considerable height was speedily ended. As Adams and Franklin were without funds, Congress directed[3] that no more bills should be drawn on them; more specific regulations were devised concerning the settlement of accounts;[4] and to Morris was confided,[5] by renewed authority, the control of all funds loaned by foreign countries.

The first investigation into the affairs of the treasury department occurred in 1781. For the more perfect transaction of the public business, the Board of Treasury allotted certain hours for receiving applications of persons having business with the department, besides directing the treasurer of loans to transmit to them all applications for loan-office certificates and bills of exchange. These orders gave rise to "the imputation of undue pride and insolence of office," and led to a serious investigation by Congress. The incident illustrates very forcibly the ever-present fear in the public mind towards office-holders, especially in men like Samuel Adams, who lived in constant danger of the office-holder snatching away the liberties of the people. The committee of investigation

---

[1] April 6, 1781.

[2] April 4, 1781, but see action of Congress of June 2 of the same year.

[3] April 10, 1781.   [4] June 4, 1781.   [5] Sept. 14, 23, 1782.

was composed of sensible men, who discovered the true motive of the Treasury Board in issuing these orders, which was to serve the public more effectively: consequently, the charges were considered groundless.[1]

On the 18th of April, 1781, a committee reported concerning the debt, the manner of its growth, and the needs of the year. The public debt in specie amounted to $24,057,577, and the estimate for the coming year was $19,507,457. The debts owed abroad, as nearly as the committee could ascertain, were six million dollars, and the annual interest thereon was three hundred and sixty thousand dollars. The record of the domestic debt was so badly tangled, that no one could give the correct amount, nor was it ever ascertained. The obligations of the government existed in several forms, and bore different rates of interest. Congress now resolved[2] to liquidate the entire public indebtedness in specie as soon as possible, and fund the same in interest-bearing obligations, if the creditors consented. The States were informed that the estimates of Congress were made in "solid coin," and that a literal compliance with the requisitions was expected. Congress could no longer wait for the balance of the quotas of three million dollars, which had been assigned nearly eight months before: so the Continental treasurer was directed to draw orders on the States, payable within thirty days, for the sum remaining unpaid.[3] He was further directed to draw for sums asked at a later date. Congress supposed the States would direct their treasurers to accept these orders when presented, and pay them when they fell due.

---

[1] May 16, 1781.   [2] May 22, 1781.   [3] Ibid.

The next financial discussion of much importance related to the establishment of a national bank, which was
suggested by Morris soon after his active assumption
of office. Hamilton had previously favored the trial of
this experiment, and, in a subsequent letter addressed
to Morris, all the details of a plan were laid before him.
Morris's plan was speedily approved by Congress,[1] and,
as soon as the subscriptions were filled, the bank was
incorporated under the name of " the president, directors
and company of the Bank of North America," and the
States were recommended to pass laws forbidding the
establishment of any rival institution during the war,
and that its notes,[2] which were payable on demand in
gold and silver, should be receivable in payment of taxes,
duties, and debts due to the United States. The capital
was four hundred thousand dollars, which could be increased, and the right of inspection was given to the
superintendent of finance. Morris relied for a supply
of coin upon the governor-general of Havana, who was
to be repaid by annual shipments of flour guaranteed by
France; but the first condition of the engagement was
never fulfilled. When the bank began operations, the
amount of specie in its vaults did not exceed forty thousand dollars, and the fear of an early exhaustion of this
sum was so great, that persons were employed, during the

[1] May 26, 1781. Jefferson, in a letter to one of his correspondents, says
that the incorporation of the bank by Congress " is, perhaps, the only
instance of their having done that which they had no power to do."
— *Works,* vol. ii. p. 24.

[2] Dec. 31, 1781. This was the first bank in America that redeemed
its bills in specie on presentation. — ARNOLD's *Hist. of R. I.,* vol. ii.
p. 481.

earlier and more critical days of its existence, to follow those who demanded specie, and urge them to return it, in order to preserve the precious foundation. Notwithstanding every effort to make the issues of the bank safe, they circulated in the beginning from ten to fifteen per cent below par in the Eastern States; and if Morris had not taken immediate measures to create a demand for them, and prevented further issues from going thither, their value would have been totally lost for a time. Their value once gone, it could not have been easily restored after the recent costly experience of the people in circulating paper money. Morris's efforts, however, quickly checked the depreciation. The issues of the bank soon rose to par, which was sustained without further difficulty.

As soon as the bank was opened,[1] Morris wrote to the governors of the States, declaring his confidence, that, with proper management, the institution would answer the most sanguine expectations of those who had befriended the undertaking.[2] Besides, it would facilitate the management of the finances of the United States. " The several States may, when their respective necessities require, and the abilities of the bank will permit, derive occasional advantages and accommodations from it. It will afford to the individuals of all the States a medium for their intercourse with each other, and for the payment of taxes more convenient than the precious metals, and

---

[1] Jan. 7, 1782. Morris's Diary, Dip. Cor., vol. xii. p. 76, note.

[2] Morris sought to interest the people everywhere in the bank, and they were solicited to subscribe to the stock; but in the South especially none were found willing to invest in the enterprise. — GREENE's *Letter to Morris*, Aug. 18, 1781, GREENE's *Life of Greene*, vol. iii. p. 370.

equally safe. It will have a tendency to increase both the internal and external commerce of North America, and undoubtedly will be infinitely useful to all the traders of every State in the Union, provided it is conducted on principles of equity, justice, prudence, and economy." Such were some of the advantages which Morris believed would spring from this institution.

Notwithstanding its early trials,[1] the concern surmounted them, ministered effectively to the government, and furnished the States with a safer and more convenient medium of exchange than specie. Pennsylvania, however, which had previously granted a charter, fearing the power of the corporation, repealed the Act: happily the State recovered from its fright, and renewed the charter at the next session of the Legislature. Such action was characteristic of the times: there was a terrible dread of the exercise of power. Having escaped from the tyranny of Great Britain, every fresh exercise of authority by any new body was equally dreaded, even if having a purely native growth.

Had it not been for a few hardy spirits like Morris, the enterprise of establishing public freedom in this land would have surely failed, for several times was the country reduced to an almost dying condition. Public credit was now gone,[2] requisitions upon the States for money

---

[1] Hamilton wrote to Morris, Sept. 21, 1782, that the contractors who received the bills carried them immediately to the collectors, and drew specie for them, in consequence of which they did not get into circulation at all. — *Works*, vol. i. p. 308.

[2] "The Congress is finally bankrupt. Last Saturday a large body of the inhabitants with paper dollars in their hats by way of cockades, paraded the streets of Philadelphia, carrying colors flying, with a dog

were little heeded, and the only aid furnished beside troops was specific supplies. There were a vast number of unfunded debts, "a cumbrous load of useless paper," and of certificates given by loan-officers and other officials for specific supplies; war had stripped many portions of the country; commerce was shattered; and no where did system, the indispensable handmaid of economy, prevail. Yet Morris despaired not. In a letter to Franklin, after depicting faithfully the condition of things, Morris[1] asks, "But what else could be expected from us? A revolution, a war; the dissolution of government, the creating of it anew; cruelty, rapine and devastation in the very midst of our very bowels. These, sir, are circumstances by no means favorable to finance. The wonder, then is, that we have done so much, that we have borne so much, and, the candid world will add, that we have dared so much."

The eye was turned at this juncture in several ways

tarred, and instead of the usual appendage and ornament of feathers, his back was covered with the Congress' paper dollars. This example of disaffection, immediately under the eyes of the rulers of the revolted Provinces, in solemn session at the state-house assembled, was directly followed by the jailer, who refused accepting the bills in purchase of a glass of rum, and afterwards by the traders of the city, who shut up their shops, declining to sell any more goods but for gold or silver. It was declared also by the popular voice, that if the opposition to Great Britain was not in future carried on by solid money instead of paper bills, all future resistance to the mother-country were vain, and must be given up." (RIVINGTON'S *Gazette*, May 12, 1781, cited in MOORE'S *Diary of the Am. Rev.*, vol. ii. p. 425.) Hamilton wrote to Greene, Jan. 10, 1781, "Public credit is so totally lost, that private people will not give their aid, though they see themselves involved in one common ruin." — *Works*, vol. i. p. 204.

[1] Nov. 27, 1781, Dip. Cor., vol. xii. p. 27.

for support. Many looked towards other nations for assistance. The slight aid furnished by them, instead of showing the futility of expecting much, only encouraged the people to expect a great deal more. Again and again did Franklin, Adams, and Jay recount the difficulties in the way of procuring loans from abroad. While Morris and Livingston urged the American ministers to renew their exertions, they never ceased to tell their own countrymen the truth, — to found their reliance upon themselves, and not upon foreign powers, for the means necessary to carry, on the war. Morris was continually writing to the governors of the States, and putting this obvious truth before them in the plainest light: nevertheless, many of them lived on the hope, that, as some aid had been contributed by foreign nations, they would grant still more abundant relief.

While counting upon some aid from France, and perhaps Holland, Morris's chief reliance was upon America herself. In most countries, the materials for waging war are obtained from within: the spectacle is rare to see a country lean so heavily as did America upon foreign nations for the means necessary to conduct a military enterprise. The American people, though bold in defying the authority of Great Britain, were extremely weak in exercising power over themselves and in displaying their latent energies. The States were rich enough in almost all things needed to wage successful campaigns, if these could be called forth. Therein lay the chief difficulty. How could the resources of the people be fully drawn out? Let us review some of the chief obstacles lying in the way.

In the first place, the necessity of taxing the people was seen clearly enough, and laws were enacted by all the States relating to the subject; besides, their governors were animated with a high degree of patriotism, and were enthusiastic in supporting the General Government: yet only small sums flowed into the public treasury. The people were not accustomed to taxes, nor had the various Legislatures adopted " proper modes of laying and levying them with convenience to the people." As Morris remarked in a letter to Luzerne, " Taxation requires time in all governments, and is to be perfected only by long experience in any country."[1]   America, divided as it was into numerous free States possessing sovereign power for all domestic purposes, could not be suddenly made to pay all which might have been spared from the wealth of her citizens. Moreover, the enemy always occupied a portion of the country, and prevented the collection of some taxes. At one time, nearly the whole of New Jersey was overrun; at another, Georgia and South Carolina seemed almost restored to British rule. All the States, in turn, felt the foreign oppressor taking possession of the country, despoiling the inhabitants, and rendering the collection of taxes uncertain and very unequal.

Again: a portion of the people were unwilling to pay them, except in paper. They had received paper money from the government: why should it not be repaid? If, however, Morris renewed the circulation of it, the mischief which he was trying to cure would be prolonged.[2] The paper issues were enormously inflated, and prudence

---

[1] Nov. 3, 1781, Dip. Cor., vol. xii. p. 4.   [2] Ibid., pp. 4, 5.

dictated the contraction of them as rapidly as possible: on that point, public opinion was undivided. Morris, at first, resolved to receive all that were offered, and to re-issue a portion, thus making contraction more gradual, while deriving some aid, though very slight, from the use of paper money. In no instance did he refuse it; for the people would lose less, he thought, by paying their taxes with it, than they would if the government refused to receive it, for, in that case, its value would totally disappear. So Morris, for several months, received all the paper tendered in payment of taxes; but he soon stopped re-issuing any of it, thus contracting the volume of money: though the redundancy was so great, and its value so slight, probably no one ever feared a disturbance of prices as a consequence of adopting such a policy.[1]

Although the people were free to return the money in payment of taxes, and a faithful execution of the recommendations of Congress and laws of the States in this respect would have proved most salutary in reducing the quantity, and preventing a part of the loss, at least, in the hands of holders, the people were very slow in paying either paper or specie to the collectors in discharge of their tax dues. After Morris had been in office more than a year, he wrote to Daniel Clarke,[2] in reply to the charge that he had robbed the Eastern States of their specie, "I have not received from the Eastern States, any more than from the Southern States, one shilling of specie, since I was appointed to my present office." In

[1] See Letter to Gov. of New York, Dec. 11, 1781, Dip. Cor., vol. xii. p. 65.

[2] May 30, 1782, Dip. Cor., vol. xii. p. 169.

November, 1781, he writes to Franklin,[1] that the past requisitions of Congress, notwithstanding his pressing entreaties, had yielded "not more than one hundred thousand dollars" during his administration. He informs the president of the State of Pennsylvania, that Congress, on the second day of November, 1781, assessed that State $1,127,794, payable in quarterly sums, commencing the 1st of April, 1782; yet, during the whole of that year, there had been received towards the payment of this quota only $107,925, — less than one-tenth of the sum required.[2] In July, 1783,[3] he addresses a circular letter to the governors of the States, telling them the unwelcome fact, that all the taxes brought into the treasury since 1781 did not amount to seven hundred and fifty thousand dollars. Shortly afterward he addressed the following communication to Congress, which shows how tardily the States had complied with the demands of Congress. South Carolina had furnished supplies to the troops serving there in sufficient quantity to pay her quota. The proportion of payment to assessment in the other States was as follows: —

Rhode Island	nearly	$\frac{1}{4}$
Pennsylvania	above	$\frac{1}{5}$
Connecticut and New Jersey	each about	$\frac{1}{7}$
Massachusetts	about	$\frac{1}{8}$
Virginia	about	$\frac{1}{12}$
New York and Maryland	each about	$\frac{1}{20}$
New Hampshire	about	$\frac{1}{121}$
North Carolina, Delaware, and Georgia	nothing at all.[4]	

[1] Nov. 27, 1781, Dip. Cor., vol. xii. p. 31.

[2] Jan. 20, 1783, Ibid., p. 323.   [3] July 28, 1783, Ibid., p. 389.

[4] Letter to Pres. of Cong., Aug. 1, 1783, Ibid., p. 395.

In the early part of 1784[1] he sent an account to Jefferson of the taxes which had been paid during his administration to the close of the year 1783, and also the arrearages on the requisitions for the years 1782 and 1783, which exceeded eight million dollars. Surely, this was a very large deficit. Well might Morris have been appalled with the magnitude of his task, when loans were obtained with so much difficulty abroad, and collections were so meagre at home.

Another source of aid was specific supplies, either furnished by the States, or taken by officers appointed for that purpose, who gave certificates therefor. A great portion of the supplies were irregularly obtained in this way. Morris was strongly opposed to the system,[2] because it was so "extremely wasteful and expensive," and led to widespread corruption.[3] He sought to furnish supplies by contract, because it was more economical:[4]

[1] Feb. 25, Dip. Cor., vol. xii. p. 468.

[2] Letter to Pres. of Cong., Nov. 5, 1781, Ibid., pp. 11, 66.

[3] Washington wrote in August, 1780, "Every day's experience proves more and more, that the present mode of obtaining supplies is the most uncertain, expensive, and injurious that could be devised" (SPARKS's *Washington*, vol. vii. p. 158). In October, the same year, he wrote, "The army, if it is to depend upon state supplies, must disband or starve" (*Ibid.*, p. 230; see also GREENE's *Life of Greene*, vol. ii. p. 247 and note).

[4] The plan of specific supplies was also defective, because there was no penalty for neglect to furnish them; yet the system continued to find advocates even as late as 1783. Dr. Stiles, in his Connecticut election sermon of that year, said, "'Two or three millions can more easily be raised in produce than one million in money. This collected and deposited in stores and magazines, would, by bills drawn upon these stores, answer all the expenditures of war and peace. The little imperfect experiment lately made here should not discourage us." — *Pulpit of Am. Rev. Sermons*, ed. by JOHN WINGATE THORNTON, p. 425.

several months elapsed, however, before he was permitted
to inaugurate this reform.[1] The quartermasters and commissaries issued the certificates, which were accepted by
the States in return for supplies, and were then sent to
the superintendent of finance to be credited on their
quotas, just as though they had furnished money. Morris complained because he could not use them as money
after accepting them. This complaint, however, was
based on no solid foundation. If the States furnished
supplies, surely it was the duty of the government to
acknowledge the fact; but why should the receipts, or
certificates of indebtedness, of the General Government
to the States, be retained by it, and used as money? This
was one step farther in the way of creating paper money
than Congress, even in its boldest and most adventurous
days, had dared to go. It was impossible to ascertain the
amount of certificates issued, and how many had been
returned in payment of taxes: moreover, they choked
every plan that was devised for restoring the public
credit, and supporting the war. In respect to the ras-
cality attending the policy, probably the certificates given
to individuals were more fraudulent than those received
by the governors of the States. Doubtless, State officials
were moved with greater patriotism in furnishing supplies
voluntarily, and taking receipts therefor, than were individuals whose property had been taken involuntarily from
them. Morris, therefore, had reason for saying that daily
observation confirmed his fears that frauds had been practised in giving such certificates; and he maintained the
opinion that a general permission to receive them in pay-

---

[1] July 10, 1781.

ment of taxes would be very injurious, not only to the public revenue, but to the success of other measures. "I am apprehensive," he adds, "that many honest men through the United States, who know the frauds committed in their neighborhoods, will imagine that sufficient attention is not paid to the detection of villany, and that idea will disincline them very much from the payment of taxes, because nothing induces men to part with their money so cheerfully, as the belief that it will be applied to the purposes for which it was granted, with economy and integrity." [1]

Morris's plan, therefore, was to destroy this system, to compel the States to pay their taxes, and to supply the army by contract, which he declared to be the universal and much more economical method. He writes to the governors of the three States [2] farthest south, saying it would give him a great deal of pleasure if he could be put in such a situation as to be able to contract at once for the supplies of the Southern army; but he had not enough specie at that time to do [3] this. Morris perse-

---

[1] Letter to Pres. of Cong., Nov. 5, 1781, Dip. Cor., vol. xii. p. 11.

[2] Dec. 19, 1781, Ibid., p. 66.

[3] When Morris had obtained means to send South, he intrusted it to George Abbot Hall, who followed the Southern army, and made advances to Greene when he became unable to get supplies from any other source (GREENE's *Life of Greene*, vol. iii. p. 412; MARSHALL's *Life of Wash.*, vol. ii. p. 25, Phil. 1832). Greene did not know that Hall was secretly employed by Morris for this purpose. See Life of Greene, Ibid.

The true explanation of Morris's mode of dealing with Greene was afterward made by Morris to Greene himself. Both were very warm friends, as the correspondence between them clearly shows; and Greene's latest biographer would have solved Morris's puzzling conduct in a very

vered. Writing to Phelps,[1] he affirms that the experience of other countries in regard to the best mode of furnishing supplies could not satisfy America: she must learn by dear experience of her own. He adds, however, that it had finally been bought; but the purchase had nearly been the ruin of the country. In the same communication he also states, "I have succeeded in obtaining

satisfactory way, had he vouchsafed the explanation to the reader which Morris gave to Greene during a subsequent interview at Philadelphia. When discussing the events of the campaign, Greene told Morris of the several critical junctures when money was furnished him by the secret agent, and which acts he regarded as interpositions of Providence. When Greene had finished his story, Morris smiled; and Greene asked him, "Why do you smile, Mr. Morris?" To which the latter replied, "Did you never suspect who sent this person to you, and employed him to watch your motions?" — "No," replied Greene. "Did it never occur to you that he was employed by me?" said Morris. "By you, sir," said Greene angrily, and, seizing the hilt of his sword, exclaimed, "And did you distrust me?" — "My confidence in you," replied Morris, "was greater than in almost any human being. I knew that your mental resources were such that you could surmount difficulties and extricate yourself from embarrassments under which any other man would have sunk — but I knew at the same time, that if this money were left at your disposal, you would use it before the time of your greatest and most indispensable necessity arrived — therefore, being limited in the sum of money appropriated to your army, and sorely pressed myself on every hand, I found it incumbent on me to provide for its being advanced to you, only when it became impossible for you to do without it." After reflecting a few minutes, Greene said, "You were right, sir; I should, without restriction, have made use of it too early, and your precaution has been the means of saving my army." — *Extract from an Essay entitled Revolutionary Reminiscences connected with the Life of Robert Morris, American Review, vol. vi. p. 72; see also* WALN's *Life of Morris, Biog. Signers to Dec. of Indep.,* vol. v. p. 203, *et seq.,* especially p. 281.

[1] March 30, 1782, Dip. Cor., vol. xii. p. 126.

many contracts on very reasonable terms. The saving to the United States thereby is immense." Nor could he leave the subject without observing that taxing in specifics is expensive to the people, cumbersome to the government, and generally inadequate to the object. If every individual were left to dispose of his property as he pleased, and compelled to pay his taxes in money or bank-notes, he would satisfy the tax by the sale of much less property than would be taken by a specific tax of commodities. Conclusive as was this reasoning, Massachusetts adhered to the former system, and opposed the plan of procuring supplies by contract; but it received the warm approval of Washington.[1] It was a great triumph for Morris, when, after long and severe opposition, he was permitted to try the experiment, and to see the end of a system which was extremely loose, and admirably adapted to the perpetration of enormous frauds.[2]

Another mode of getting supplies was the employment of Morris's own splendid credit, which he often stretched to the utmost, but never abused.[3] At one time, he requested Gen. Schuyler[4] to furnish the army with flour, agreeing to be personally responsible; at another, he

---

[1] April 23, 1782, Dip. Cor., vol. xii. p. 135.

[2] Inspectors for the Southern army, to watch contractors there, were not authorized until May 7, 1782.

[3] The amount of these notes voluntarily issued for the benefit of the government, and circulating as cash among merchants and shopkeepers, without depreciation, except very slightly, toward the close of the war, was $581,000. — WALN's *Life of Morris, Biog. Signers to Dec. of Indep.*, vol. v. p. 303.

[4] May 29, 1781, Dip. Cor., vol. ii. p. 367.

obtained funds from the commander of the French fleet, to pay the American army, upon his individual promise to return the same within a specified period; and many other transactions like these might be related. In no instance did he fail to fulfil his promise, though on several occasions he seemed to be near the brink of failure. At first, the people of the Eastern States distrusted Morris's ability to redeem his obligations, which, consequently, depreciated from ten to fifteen per cent: ere long they rose in value to par, and were taken without hesitation.

Such were the resources of Morris to maintain the government, and carry on the war. Foreign loans were small and precarious; taxation at home yielded still less; while specific supplies from the States, and by seizure, gave rise to much dissatisfaction and corruption. When every other means failed, he used his private credit, which was always higher than that of the government.[1]

Morris determined to change the American account in

[1] Hamilton wrote to Viscount de Noailles in 1782: "In one respect we are in a mending way. Our financier has hitherto conducted himself with great ability, has acquired an entire personal confidence; revived, in some measure, the public credit; and is conciliating fast the support of the moneyed men. His operations have hitherto hinged chiefly on the seasonable aids from your country; but he is urging the establishment of permanent funds among ourselves: and though, from the nature and temper of our governments, his applications will meet with a dilatory compliance, it is to be hoped they will by degrees succeed.

"The institution of a bank has been very serviceable to him: the commercial interest, finding great advantages in it, and anticipating much greater, is disposed to promote the plan; and nothing but moderate funds, permanently pledged for the security of lenders, is wanting to make it an engine of the most extensive and solid utility." — *Works*, vol. i. p. 316.

Paris from the banking-house of Grand to that of Le Couteulx, & Co.: his chief reason for the transfer was to keep his own accounts separate from those of the Board of Treasury.[1] This was a sufficient reason; for the American accounts abroad were confused, though not so badly as the accounts at home. M. Grand, however, had been exceedingly liberal in his dealings with the United States, and more than once had made heavy advances, which were not repaid for a long period. Franklin was so sensible of the great favors received by the country from this house, that he wrote warmly to Morris on the subject, and was doubtless pleased to learn of the effect of the appeal, as Morris concluded to follow Franklin's wishes in the matter.[2]

In various ways Congress sought to retire and destroy the old paper emissions. It was clearly seen how they deranged the finances by remaining in circulation. Accordingly, while efforts were made to destroy the issues of May, 1777, and April, 1778, which had been extensively counterfeited, other issues were received for taxes; the treasurers of the States exchanged them for bills of exchange; and they were borrowed, and payment was made in bills of the new emission. The commissioners who were appointed to settle the accounts of the States were also directed to destroy all the old issues found in the State treasuries, not exceeding the quota due to the General Government:[3] thus, by these various expedients, was paper money withdrawn from circulation.

---

[1] Letter to Franklin, June 8, 1781, Dip. Cor., vol. xi. p. 370.

[2] July 26, 1781, Ibid., p. 407.

[3] Feb. 20, 27, and Sept. 18, 1782.

Morris was opposed to issuing any more loan-office certificates, and directed the commissioners of those offices to settle their accounts.[1] Not only were certificates given for money borrowed, but, when interest due thereon was not paid, other certificates were issued therefor. Morris would not consent to giving certificates for this purpose, and declared that he would never consent to it. "Such accumulation of debt," he said to the governors of the States, " while it distresses the public, and destroys its credit, by no means relieves the unfortunate individual who is a public creditor; for, if revenue is not provided, increasing the certificates would only lessen their value. This would be such a fraud as would stamp our national character with indelible marks of infamy, and render us the reproach and contempt of mankind. It is high time to relieve ourselves from the ignominy we have already sustained, and to rescue and restore our national credit. This can only be done by solid revenue. Disdaining, therefore, those little timid artifices, which, while they postpone the moment of difficulty, only increase the danger and confirm the ruin, I prefer the open declaration to all of what is to be expected, and whence it is to be drawn. To the public creditors, therefore, I say that until the States provide revenues for liquidating the principal and interest of the public debt, they cannot be paid; and to the States, I say, that we are bound by every principle held sacred among men to make that provision." The real reason for giving such certificates,

<hr>

[1] See Letters Oct. 13, 1781, Dip. Cor., vol. xi. p. 488; Oct. 19, 1781, Ibid., p. 500; March 30, 1784, Ibid., vol. xii. p. 483; April 29, 1784, Ibid., p. 488.

so Morris believed, was to elude actual payments by making nominal ones. This practice he unhesitatingly condemned. Moreover, he wished to close the loan-offices to escape the expense of maintaining them. Nine-tenths of the expense incurred by them he thought could be saved by committing the business to the banks. Besides, very few loan-offices had conformed to their instructions; and their accounts, like all other public ones, were inextricably confused.

At the beginning of his financial administration, Morris found the amount of interest due on loan-office certificates to be seven thousand two hundred dollars, which was payable in France. Notwithstanding the interest was so well secured, the certificates had depreciated, and were daily offered for sale, producing an injurious effect upon public credit. As the interest was guaranteed by the Court of France, and amounted to the respectable figure of two million one hundred and sixty thousand livres annually, which would be equal to fifteen million dollars in ten years, Morris believed, that, with this sum, he could buy all the certificates, and urged Franklin to lay the plan of buying them before M. Neckar, and solicit his co-operation, as it was obviously for the advantage of both counries to effect, if possible, such an arrangement. The plan failed, as the French minister declined to grant the funds necessary for the purpose.[1]

The loan-office commissioners were not the only persons singled out to settle their accounts.[2] From the

---

[1] Letter to Franklin, July 13, 1781, Dip. Cor., vol. xi. p. 380.

[2] See action of Congress respecting the settling of the accounts of the army, July 4, 11, 1783.

beginning of his administration, Morris always kept two things before him, — the settlement of the State accounts and the funding of the public debt. The ascertainment and liquidation of these accounts, he believed, would produce a better feeling among the States, and bring more willing contributions from them into the public treasury. Some States went so far as to say, that, having contributed beyond their proportion, they would not furnish any thing more until there was a final settlement. Acts were passed by Congress for that purpose early in 1782,[1] in compliance with the wishes of Morris. In a circular letter to the governors, enclosing copies of them, Morris observes that "it is to the want of a decision on this point, that the languor and want of exertion of the several States are to be attributed. That fatal assertion, that each has done most, which each has made and repeated, until it has gained but too much credit, would never have obtained a place in the minds of men, who really love their country and cause, had the requisitions of Congress been made annually for money, and the quotas fixed finally at the date of the demand. The compliances of each would in that case have determined their respective merits or demerits ; we should then have seen a competition the very reverse of that which has for some time past prevailed ; and it is not yet too late." He then urges the governors to settle all accounts of past expenditures, adjust the shares of each State ; "but," he adds, " let the settlement be final, or we do nothing." [2]

[1] Jan. 9, 11, Feb. 20, 27, 1782; Feb. 27, March 4, July 16, Aug. 11, 1783.

[2] April 15, 1782, Dip. Cor., vol. xii. p. 130; see able letters, July 25,

He sent such accounts as he was able to extract from the treasury books to the governors of the States, and, in addition, requested them to furnish information respecting the revenue laws in force in their several jurisdictions, the mode of collecting taxes, the funds in the treasuries, the appropriation of them, and the date and amount of the various paper issues which had been authorized. To these inquiries and efforts hardly a response was heard: consequently no progress worth mentioning was made in adjusting the accounts between the States and the General Government. At a later period during his administration, Morris declared to the president of Congress his most serious apprehensions from the existence of unsettled accounts among the States. He likewise submitted to Congress the following plan for extricating the General Government and the States from the embarrassment caused by the confusion of accounts, — to place the whole sum expended for the public service, from the commencement of the war, by each State, to its credit, and allow interest thereon. "By these means," he assures Congress,[1] "the whole account would be equitably settled in the first instance. The States which are indebted on their own private account, would be able to wipe off such debts by an assignment of national stock. And on the first requisitions made by Congress for current expenditures, each might make payment, either in part, or perhaps in the whole, by a discharge of so much of the debt." The execution of such a plan, he thought, would

1781, Dip. Cor., vol. xi. p. 400; Aug. 28, 1781, Ibid., p. 442: Nov. 5, 1781, Ibid., vol. xii. p. 9.

[1] March 8, 1783, Ibid., p. 335.

introduce simplicity into the affairs of the government, and avoid many evils: but it was never adopted by Congress; indeed, the record of Congress does not show that any action was ever taken thereon.

Congress long and patiently strove to obtain the assent of the States to the imposition of a tax of five per cent upon importations, but in vain. At first it was proposed to vest the United States [1] with the right of superintending the commercial regulations of every State, in order to prevent the enactment of any laws partial, or contrary to the common interest; and also with the exclusive right to lay duties upon imports, though no restriction was to be valid, or duty laid, without the consent of nine States. The duties were to be uniform throughout the Union; the income therefrom was not to be used in paying "perpetual annuities," and the power of laying them was to continue only for a fixed period. Congress regarded this as a dangerous extension of power, which the States would not grant. Accordingly, the resolution was modified; and it was "recommended to the several States, as indispensably necessary, that they vest a power in Congress, to levy a tax for the use of the United States, a duty of five per cent *ad valorem*, at the time and place of importation, upon all goods, wares and merchandise of foreign growth and manufactures, which may be imported into any of the said States from any foreign port, island or plantation, after the first day of May, 1781, except arms, ammunition, clothing, and other articles imported on account of the United States, or any of them, and except wool-cards and cotton-cards and wire for making them; and

[1] Feb. 3, 1781.

also except salt during the war; also, a like duty of five per cent on all prizes and prize goods, condemned in the court of admiralty of any of these States as lawful prize; that the moneys arising from the said duties, be appropriated to the discharge of the principal and interest of the debts already contracted, or which may be contracted, on the faith of the United States, for supporting the present war; that the said duties be continued until the said debts shall be fully and finally discharged." As Congress supposed the States would assent to this arrangement, it was determined, that, as soon as any States consented to vest the power of laying duties in Congress, that body would proceed to collect them, giving each State credit for the duties collected within its territory. Morris declared this recommendation to be " of the utmost importance," and that every day gave it "an additional weight and magnitude." He answered various criticisms of the measure, among others the objection that commerce could not bear a five per cent duty. " Those who make such assertions," he affirmed, " must be very little acquainted with the subject. The articles of commerce are either such as people want, or such as they do not want. If they be such as people want, they must be purchased at the price for which they could be had, and the duty being on all, gives to no seller any advantage over another. If, on the contrary, the article be such as people do not want, they must either increase their industry, so as to afford the use of it with the duty, or else they must dispense with that use. In the former case, the commerce is just where it was, and in the latter case, the people consume less of foreign superfluities, which certainly is a public benefit."

Connecticut sought to appropriate the revenues flowing from this source for the payment of her own obligations, which gave rise to further discussion of the measure by Congress.[1] The State was recommended to revise her legislation, and conform to the resolves of Congress, which she afterwards did. All the States complied with the recommendation without long delay, except Rhode Island,[2] whose defence was essentially the following: The impost would draw a disproportionate supply from either merchant or consumer; she imported and consumed more

[1] March 22, 1781.

[2] However strongly the action of the governor and of others at home was to be condemned, the views of the delegates who represented Rhode Island, when this subject first arose for discussion in Congress, were eminently sound, as will appear from the following letter, which Varnum and Mowry wrote to the governor, Aug. 14, 1781: "We are at loss to conjecture the rumors which have induced the State of Rhode Island to delay complying with the requisitions of Congress, respecting the five per cent duty. This requisition was so essential to the adoption of a regular, frugal, and productive system of finance, that we cannot enter into the necessary details of a permanent revenue without realizing it. It must be obvious that, unless we call forth the resources of the respective States equally, it will be impossible to execute any great objects while the States who do most will be the greatest sufferers. It is as obvious that, without a permanent revenue in the disposal of the United States, we can neither fulfil past engagements, nor obtain future credit. The resources of the country are not sufficient to carry on the war, without anticipating the revenues. This cannot be done without credit, nor this exist without funds. We have not a doubt but what matters will soon be put into such a train as to settle the public accounts on equitable principles. Measures are undertaken by Congress to enable the financier to adopt such modes as will do justice to all the States, and remove those unhappy consequences which result from a mutual jealousy. We must therefore beg liberty to urge the propriety of the measures, and a compliance with them."—STAPLES's *Hist of R. I. in the Cont. Cong.*, p. 349.

foreign commodities in proportion than any other State; her maritime situation would expose her to great losses; the exclusive benefit of the impost should be carried to the account of the State; the impost would raise prices, and therefore manufactures bought from the neighboring States would draw a revenue from Rhode Island; the duties imposed by the neighboring States might compel her to subsist by foreign articles; many would be employed in their collection; smuggling would become prevalent; and, lastly, the collection might be objectionable. Morris was requested by a committee of Congress to answer these objections. To the first objection he replied,[1] that all must admit the necessity of a revenue from some source. "Is it then wise," he asks, "to raise a part of it from the consumption of foreign articles? I say the consumption, because the tax undoubtedly falls on the consumer and not on the importer. If this be not a wise tax, what shall we substitute? Articles of primary and immediate necessity are made in the State of Rhode Island. Both food and raiment can be had without crossing the Atlantic in search of them. Every man, therefore, is at liberty to use foreign articles or not. If he does use them the tax is voluntary, and therefore cannot be considered disproportionate, any more than for one to wear silk while another wears wool." The truth of the second objection was denied, and, in respect to the third, he thought New York had suffered as much and as long as Rhode Island, and that her advantageous maritime position could not be adduced as a plea for exempting her from bearing public burdens. That an import duty

---

[1] Aug. 2, 1782, Dip. Cor., vol. xii. p. 242.

should be carried to the account of the State collecting it, Morris declared was a "position unjust in itself," and "would forever prevent any duties." "Rhode Island, Pennsylvania and some other States carry on the commerce of their neighbors as well as their own, from which they derive great riches. . . . If then a considerable duty were laid by the commercial State, it would fall on its uncommercial neighbor." What, then, would happen? Morris answers, "The neighbor would immediately take measures to carry on its own commerce, and prohibit the bringing of articles from the commercial State." Such measures, he affirms, would cause a repeal of the duty. Concerning the fifth objection, he could hardly suppose the neighboring States would ever think of laying duties on produce, and, if they should lay them, their own citizens would be the worst sufferers. Concerning the next objection, if the article of produce were left uncontrolled by the government, every individual would be a check on the avidity of his neighbors, and if, by this means, a piece of American goods could be vended cheaper in Rhode Island than a piece of foreign goods, the consumer there by the purchase of it would save money to himself and therefore to the country. Morris thought the objection concerning the number employed to collect duties would apply more strongly to almost any other kind of tax; nor did he believe that smuggling would become a practice, because, if any person were so inclined, detection would be easy: moreover, there was no reason for supposing that Congress would devise means for oppressing their fellow-citizens. Such, in brief, was Morris's answer, which seemed conclusive; but Rhode Island refused to yield, and so this well-devised and practicable scheme came to nought.

Morris clearly perceived the weakness of the Articles of Confederation, from their lack of obligatory and coercive power over the States. Writing to Greene[1] soon after Rhode Island's refusal to consent to a Federal collection of taxes on imports, he says, with reference to the States, "At present they content themselves with the assertion, that each has done most, and that the people are not able to pay taxes. Languor and inexertion are the offspring of the doctrine, and finally the people who are said to be incapable of bearing taxation, actually pay double the sum that would be necessary in the first instance. Nothing on my part has been omitted that I could think of, to stimulate them to exertions, and I have given them every encouragement to support my arrangements, that could be derived from regularity, system and economy; but all this does not produce the effect it ought; there are in every Legislature, characters too full of local attachments and views to permit sufficient attention to the general interest."

In no way did the genius of Morris shine more brilliantly than in reducing the expenses of the government.[2] This step seemed more necessary than ever since the failure of the plan to obtain a revenue from imports. The economies introduced by him were very numerous: he totally destroyed the old system of granting specific

---

[1] April 24, 1782, Dip. Cor., vol. xii. p. 136.

[2] Reform in hospital department, see action of Cong., July 23, 1782; and in the army, April 8, 10, 22, 23, Aug. 1, 7, Sept. 3, Oct. 23, 29, Nov. 12, Dec. 3, 1782.

supplies, and giving certificates therefor; he vainly but persistently tried to close the loan-offices, and settle the accounts of the States, besides abolishing numerous offices, and executing other sweeping reforms, which provoked to wrath many who impugned his motives, and condemned his policy. His dealings with Pickering show how keenly Morris watched the business of his department. Pickering was quartermaster-general of the army, and Morris supplied him by weight with gold coins from the bank at Philadelphia. As they were severally heavier than required by law for their current value, and in paying them by tale the public would lose the excess of weight, to prevent this, the financier, as Morris was often called, required Pickering to reduce the coins to the standard weight by clipping them, which was to be done by himself, or at his expense. Of course, no wrong to the public was designed; yet Pickering regarded it as "harmful business," from which he would have gladly escaped. Mr. Hogdon, an officer in the ordnance department, wrote to him, "The financier will not permit the Continent to be a loser by the gold," continuing with instructions on the mode of clipping, to which he added the significant fact, "The matter should be kept a secret, as the army, not acquainted with circumstances, might suspect fraudulent intentions." To which Pickering replied, "'Tis a shameful business, and an unreasonable hardship on a public officer." Notwithstanding the exercise of considerable care, Pickering was obliged to send gold to Philadelphia on his own account, to reimburse the bank for the losses incurred through his imperfect clipping of the coins.[1]

---

[1] Life of Pickering, vol. i. p. 387.

It would require considerable space to enumerate all the abuses which Morris discovered and corrected. In a single day were brushed off one hundred and forty-six supernumerary officers, who for a long period had been sucking their nourishment from the nation. Expenses were greatly reduced in the quartermaster's, commissaries' of provisions and military stores, in the hospital, and in every department. It is related that an annual estimate of one hundred and forty tons of hay for a certain point was presented to him for examination. He reduced the estimate to twelve tons, and even this quantity proved an abundant supply, although the post was fully and as usefully occupied as it had been during any preceding period.[1]

It was too much for human nature to leave Morris wholly free from accusation and censure. Strongly intrenched as he was in the confidence of Congress, his assailants outside were numerous and malignant. Some of the charges against him were, on one occasion,[2] briefly noticed, and it may be worth while to lay them before the reader. He was charged with robbing the Eastern States of their specie; with showing partiality towards the disaffected, and towards Pennsylvania also, because of his numerous commercial relations with the merchants of Philadelphia; with establishing a bank from sinister motives; with forming a league with Pennsylvania to keep Virginia poor; and, lastly, in company with the secretary of Congress and another person, with engaging in speculation. The first charge was very easily answered, since

---

[1] Boudinot's speech in Congress, Ann. of Cong., vol. i. p. 394.

[2] Letter to Daniel Clarke, May 30, 1782, Dip. Cor., vol. xii. p. 168.

he had received, at the time these charges were made, not a shilling from any State. The charge of partiality towards Pennsylvania was very assiduously circulated; and Morris himself says it had gained "an extensive currency." He supposed the charge sprung from the fact of his residence in that State, as there was no other basis for it; while his partiality towards the disaffected "was among those threadbare topics of defamation, which have been so generally applied, that they have lost their effect." He confessed to establishing the bank, defended the act as wise, and declared the institution would "exist in spite of calumny, operate in spite of opposition, and do good in spite of malevolence." That Pennsylvania should desire to keep Virginia poor, he thought was "a strange assertion." He believed that Pennsylvania would be rich, as the soil and climate were good, and the people quiet and industrious. Their rulers, also, were sensible of their true interests. "They encourage commerce, have laid aside all the idle systems of specific supplies, and content themselves with laying money taxes. . . . On the other hand, if Virginia, or any other State be poor, it must be their own fault. Prudence, diligence, and economy, promote national prosperity; and vice, indolence, and prodigality, involve national ruin. I am so far from wishing to impoverish Virginia, that I have constantly labored, both in my public and private applications, to bring about those measures which are calculated to make her wealthy and powerful." In respect to the charge of speculating, it was "one of those foolish things which are not worth answer." In such a spirit and manner did Morris answer these charges. Had not the design in making them been to involve the national interests committed to him, rather than to injure himself merely, he assures one of his correspondents that he would not have answered them. It is highly probable that the public interests were not injured in consequence of them, for surely they were too unsubstantial to shake any one's confidence in Morris's ability or integrity.

One of the most interesting incidents in Morris's administration related to the coinage.[1] Having been instructed to report a table of rates at which foreign coins should circulate in the United States, he improved the opportunity to set forth reasons for establishing a uniform coinage throughout the country. He said the ideas annexed to a pound, a shilling, and a penny, which were the several kinds of money then current, were almost as various as the States themselves. Calculations were as necessary for inland as for foreign commerce. The commonest transactions grew intricate when money entered into them. "A farmer in New Hampshire, for instance, can readily form an idea of a bushel of wheat in South Carolina, weighing sixty pounds, and placed at one hundred miles from Charleston; but, if he were told, that in such situation it is worth twenty-one shillings and eightpence, he would be obliged to make many inquiries, and form some calculations before he could know that this sum meant in general what he would call four shillings; and even then he would have to inquire what kind of coin that four shillings was paid in, before he could estimate it in his own mind, according to the ideas of money, which he had imbibed." Surely there

---

[1] Letter to Pres. of Cong., Jan. 15, 1782, Dip. Cor., vol. xii. p. 81.

was need for establishing a uniform currency, when such money was in use. The need was not less pressing for providing money which could be employed as a just legal tender.

The reasons for using both gold and silver were next considered. Morris favored the adoption of a single silver standard. The expense of coining, he maintained, ought to be defrayed by the people. In order to coin money which should be perfectly intelligible to the whole people, it was necessary to preserve an affinity to their former currency. "The purposes of commerce require, that the lowest divisible point of money, or what is more properly called the money unit, should be very small, because by that means, price can be brought in the smallest things to bear a proportion to the value. And although it is not absolutely necessary, yet it is very desirable, that money should be increased in decimal ratio, because by that means all calculations of interest, exchange, insurance, and the like, are rendered much more simple and accurate, and of course, more within the power of the great mass of the people;" to which he added the very truthful observation, "Whenever such things require much labor, time, and reflection, the greater number who do not know, are made the dupes of the smaller number who do."

The values of all coins circulating in America, from time to time, had changed; and now, when Morris was considering the subject of coinage, there was no general standard, unless it was the Spanish dollar. It passed in Georgia at five shillings, in North Carolina and New York at eight shillings, in Virginia and the four Eastern

States at six shillings, and in all the other States, except South Carolina, at seven shillings and sixpence, and in South Carolina at thirty-two shillings and sixpence. The money unit of a new coin which should agree, without a fraction, with all these different values of a dollar, except the last, would be the fourteen hundred and fortieth part of a dollar. Of these units, twenty-four would be equal to a penny of Georgia, fifteen a penny of North Carolina and New York, twenty a penny of Virginia and the four Eastern States, sixteen a penny of all the other States except South Carolina, where thirteen pence would be equal to forty-eight of the proposed coinage.

Morris observed that it was not necessary to represent the money unit by a coin: it would be sufficient to ascertain its precise value. "On the present occasion, two copper coins will be proper, the one of eight units and the other of five. These may be called an Eight, and a Five. Two of the former will make a penny Proclamation, or Pennsylvania money, and three a penny Georgia money. Of the latter, three will make a penny New York money, and four a penny lawful, or Virginia money. The money unit will be equal to a quarter of a grain of fine silver in coined money. Proceeding thence in a decimal ratio, one hundred would be the lowest silver coin, and might be called a *Cent*. It would contain twenty-five grains of fine silver, to which may be added two grains of copper, and the whole would weigh one pennyweight and three grains. Five of these would make a Quint, or five hundred units, and ten would make a Mark, or one thousand units." Having established such a coin, the value of all others could be easily ascertained by assaying them at the mint.

His plan evinced a mastery of the subject. He digged to the bottom, and built on the true principle, — a decimal coinage. He was profoundly clear in devising a money unit which should disturb but slightly if possible former modes of valuation. Congress took no action until the next year, when the subject was discussed, and referred to a committee, of which Jefferson was a member. He declared that "the general views of the financier were sound, and the principle was ingenious on which he proposed to found his unit, but it was too minute for ordinary use, too laborious for computation, either by the head or in figures." Jefferson proposed, therefore, to adopt the dollar as a unit of account and payment, and that its divisions and subdivisions should be in the decimal ratio. He prepared some observations on the subject for the consideration of Morris. The financier replied, still adhering to his scheme, "only agreeing to take for his unit one hundred of those he first proposed." To Morris's communication, Jefferson wrote an answer, which he printed, together with his notes which were first sent to Morris, and gave copies thereof to members of Congress.[1] The committee were persuaded to support Jefferson's views; and the next year his system, as he called it, was adopted by Congress. It is essentially the same system as the one now in use. Jefferson claimed too much credit in devising the plan; for, though it differed in some respects from that proposed by Morris, the main outlines

[1] Jefferson's Works, vol. i., Appendix, Note F, p. 162.

were the same, and these the financier had sketched.[1] Morris's system was improved by Jefferson; but it cannot truthfully be said of him that he originated one.[2]

As Morris's ability to provide means for carrying on the government became more manifest, new burdens were imposed upon him. He was directed, not only to procure supplies for the army and navy, to provide for the transportation of the former, and to launch and equip ships for the latter, but also to act as agent of marine, to employ a packet which should serve between America and Europe, and to do many other difficult things outside the sphere of his office.[3]

The reduction of all indebtedness to a specie valuation was inaugurated as one of the features of the financial policy of the government in 1780. Once a month the depreciation of the currency was ascertained by the Board of Treasury, and payment was made by the scale of depreciation thus established.[4]   Morris was unceasing

---

[1] "We both agree," says Jefferson in his Supplementary Explanations, "that the ease of adoption with the people, is the thing to be aimed at" in establishing a monetary unit. — *Works*, vol. i., Appendix, p. 172.

[2] To Morris's system of coinage, Gouverneur Morris contributed no inconsiderable part. Randall, in his Life of Jefferson (vol. i. p. 396), says that Jefferson and Morris "share in the honor of founding a far simpler and more easily computed money system than before existed. The latter, or rather his assistant, the able Gouverneur Morris, is entitled to the credit of proposing the decimal system of computation, and Jefferson of proposing the unit and present coinage of the United States." For an able examination and criticism of the systems proposed by Morris and Jefferson, see Sparks's Life of G. Morris, vol. i. pp. 273–281. An excellent sketch of the coinage of the Colonies may be found in Hist. Mag., vol. i. p. 225, and Ibid., p. 297.

[3] June 21, 23, 28, Sept. 7, Nov. 27, Dec. 3, 1781.   [4] Aug. 2, 1781.

in his efforts to settle the multitudinous obligations of the government; and Congress was constantly passing resolves concerning them. To many obviously just claims a great variety of irregularities attached, which could be remedied only by congressional intervention.

The Board of Treasury continued to share in the administration of the finances until Morris was able to dispense with the body altogether, — an event which occurred on the 20th of September, 1781.[1] Notwithstanding the incompetency of the members, due, in part, to lack of ability, and partly to the want of time necessary to discharge their duties properly, the organization had been continued five years during a very critical period of the country's life. Their mode of conducting business was exceedingly slow and crude, and must have been often vexatious in the extreme to those having business with the board. An officer, while acting as quartermaster-general of the army, has left an account of the way the board served him in his official capacity: "I am obliged for every demand upon me, however trifling, to frame an estimate and make a special application; and sometimes, though not commonly, I get some kind of answer in the course of two or three weeks after applying. The 21st of June I sent an application on the estimate of Colonel Cox for drawing from the tradesmen and equipping the new wagons he had ordered in this State; about ten days afterwards I got a warrant for the sum; yesterday I got a letter of advice from the board to the treasurer, and to-day I have got near one-fifth of the money. This movement, slow as it may seem . . . has been pushed

----

[1] Action of Congress Sept. 11, 1781.

with uncommon assiduity and with more than common success; it is therefore one of the most favorable specimens I can give . . . of the course of business."[1] Considering this as a fair illustration of the slowness with which the Treasury Board conducted business, who will question the need existing at that time of putting a vast deal more energy into the financial department of the government? In place of the board, besides Morris, were a comptroller, treasurer, register, auditors, and clerks. The comptroller inspected and superintended the settlement of accounts; and it was his duty to see that they were expeditiously and properly adjusted, and safely kept. He was also vested with authority to hear the appeals of persons aggrieved by the judgment of the auditor. The treasurer rendered quarterly accounts to the comptroller; and every warrant " on the treasury or others " was entered and countersigned before making payment.

Again were the States asked for eight million dollars, payable in quarterly payments.[2] Notwithstanding the smallness of this requisition, compared with many former ones, Morris did not indulge the vain hope of receiving even so moderate a sum from the States. " The great arrearage of unfunded debt, the cumbrous load of useless paper, the multiplied mass of certificates, the distracted situation of the more southern States, the ravages which have been in them, the total loss of their commerce, the real want of coin in many States, and the

---

[1] Letter from Charles Pettit, acting quartermaster-general, July 13, 1780, Greene's Life of Greene, vol. ii. p. 313. See Ibid., pp. 269, 291, 293; also Hamilton's Hist. of Repub. vol. ii. pp. 92, 93.

[2] Oct. 30, Nov. 2, 1781.

equal want of system in all; — these, sir," he wrote in a letter to Franklin,[1] "are circumstances, which forbid the most sanguine temper to expect a full compliance." He assured Franklin that he should get what he could, making compositions whenever these were necessary, besides taking provisions in lieu of money, and resorting to other similar expedients. The States were recommended[2] to lay taxes for the collection of this sum, instead of mingling them with the taxes laid for State purposes, and to pass acts directing the collector to pay the same to the commissioners of the loan offices, or to any other persons appointed by the superintendent of finance. This requisition encountered opposition from New Hampshire.[3] This State claimed to have only eighty-two thousand inhabitants; but the apportionment was based on a higher estimate. By the Articles of Confederation, the value of the lands in each State was to form the basis for apportioning the public burdens, — a far more equitable basis than that of population. Congress, however, had been unable to ascertain the value of these: so recourse was had to the old expedient in apportioning this new assessment, and it was based on population. The claim of New Hampshire was heard by Congress; but the apportionment was not altered, because, while the census of population taken by the State was regarded as probably correct, the estimates of population in other States were, perhaps, as inaccurate, and therefore it was not clear that New Hampshire would suffer any wrong if the apportionment remained as originally fixed.

[1] Nov. 27, 1781, Dip. Cor., vol. xii. p. 34.   [2] Nov. 2, 1781.
[3] April 1, 1782.

All assessments, however, were to be adjusted at a future date upon a fair basis, and consequently New Hampshire would certainly not be a loser in the end. Other States reiterated the complaint, and justified themselves in not contributing, on similar grounds. What a pity that an Aristides did not live, whose fairness and probity should have caused his selection to superintend the difficult process of determining the forms, and assessing the amounts of contribution! — an expedient to which the members of the Hellenic Confederation resorted in fixing the mode and amount of payment towards the general fund for resisting Persian invasion.

Morris was requested to furnish a statement of the public indebtedness to the close of the year 1781, and also to prepare one semi-annually of "all moneys borrowed and bills emitted during such periods," for the purpose, more especially, of transmitting copies thereof to the States, as required by the Articles of Confederation.[1] Requiring prompt statements and settlements of persons intrusted with the public funds, he was not less exact and punctual in rendering his own account to the government. How different, indeed, was his conduct from that of the Treasury Board, who never rendered only partial accounts to Congress! It was in obedience to this request, probably, that Morris sent a statement, accompanied with a letter addressed to the president of Congress, on the 23d of May, in which he remarked that it would be perceived that every sou which the government could command during the year 1782 had been already anticipated.

[1] April 30, 1782.

The condition of the treasury was extremely critical. "The habitual inattention of the States," writes Morris to the president of Congress,[1] "has reduced us to the brink of ruin, and I cannot see a probability of relief from any of them. I rather perceive a disposition to take money from the public treasury, than to place any in it. A variety of causes prevents the collection of taxes, and delays the payment of them, even after they are collected. In many States they are not laid." Morris had prepared a circular letter to send to the governors of the States; but the condition of the finances was so plainly set forth, and revealed such nakedness and poverty, that he dared not transmit it without the advice and consent of Congress. He feared, that if the communication were sent, and it fell into improper hands, "the most dangerous consequences" would follow. The situation was truly startling, as disclosed in the foregoing letter to the president; for he says, "the public departments are now absolutely at a stand, for the want of money, and many things already commenced I must desist from. This cannot be wondered at, when it is considered, that near five months of the present year have elapsed without my having received any thing on account of its expenditures, except the trifling sum of five thousand five hundred dollars, and that sum, calculating on expenses at eight millions annually, is about one-fourth of what is necessary to support us for a single day."

Notwithstanding the emptiness of the treasury, the States contributed very feebly towards replenishing it. Taxes, it is true, were laid, and considerable sums were

---

[1] May 17, 1782, Dip. Cor., vol. xii. p. 154.

paid to the States. Pickering, writing to his brother from Verplanck's Point, says, " I was astonished at the enormous amount of our taxes, which you paid the last year. If all States paid in the like proportion, instead of eight millions of dollars, the taxes would reach to as many pounds, besides the internal taxes of each State. Everybody, go where I will, is complaining of the heavy taxes; yet those paid the United States are to the last degree insignificant." Not infrequently their collection was postponed;[1] and, whatever happened, the treasury did not get much from the chief source whence aid should have come.[2] Some believed that taxes could not be raised, from lack of specie; yet, as Morris wrote to the governor of Maryland,[3] nothing could be more unfounded. " If the people be put in the necessity of procuring specie they will procure it. They can if they will. Tobacco may not sell at one moment, grain at another, or cattle at a third; but there are some articles such as horses, which will sell at all times. The mischief is, that when a purchaser offers, the party not being under a necessity of selling, insists on a higher price than the other can afford to give. Thus the commerce is turned

---

[1] Letter to James Lowell, July 10, 1782, Dip. Cor., vol. xii. p. 209.

[2] Gen. Sullivan wrote to Lincoln from Boston, Jan. 16, 1782: " I am very sorry that a loan in Europe has failed, because I can see no way to comply with the requisitions of Congress for the million of dollars. A tax of three hundred thousand pounds has been out some time, and very little collected. There is another, lately assessed, of a like sum, and these I am confident cannot be collected till midsummer; and really, sir, the farms where I live would by no means rent for as much as they have been taxed the year past, if taxes were as moderate as they were in 1774." — AMORY's *Life of Sullivan*, vol. ii. p. 384.

[3] July 29, 1782, Dip. Cor., vol. xii. p. 210.

away to another quarter. Nothing but the necessity of getting money will bring men in general to lower their prices. When this is done purchasers will offer in abundance, and thus it will be found, that the tax instead of lessening will increase the quantity of specie. But so long as the want of it can be pleaded successfully against taxes, so long that want will continue."

While taxes were thus very tardily collected, and loans were small and infrequent, there were those who did not countenance the policy of sustaining the government by means of loans.[1] It was a new financial expedient, comparatively, in the history of nations. One of Gerry's correspondents did not believe in issuing bills of credit, and condemned the negotiation of loan-office certificates, because they produced the same effect upon the currency as the creation of additional issues. A petition of remonstrance was sent to Congress against contracting more loans, which was referred to Morris, who subsequently made an elaborate answer to it. It may be superfluous to add that his views concerning the policy of negotiating loans were very unlike the ideas entertained by the petitioners.

As the income of the government diminished, Morris was obliged to reduce expenditures, and withdraw support from many persons and objects justly requiring it. Inspectors of the army were appointed,[2] and in every branch of the service large reductions in expenditures were made. A commission was authorized to settle the accounts pending in Europe;[3] while Morris never wearied

---

[1] See elaborate Letter of Morris to Pres. of Congress on the subject, Dip. Cor., vol. xii. p. 211.

[2] May 6, 1782.   [3] May 28, 29, Nov. 18, 20, 1872.

in unravelling those at home.[1] No public officer, not even Ephialtes, ever sought more eagerly to settle the accounts of a government than did Morris to discharge the pecuniary obligations of the United States. Several letters passed between the French minister and the financier, during the earlier days of his administration, respecting the accounts between America and France; at which time Morris claimed the debt due to France to be 10,686,109 livres, while a balance almost as large remained subject to his order.[2] An agreement fixing the amount was happily concluded, with the assistance of Franklin, in whose honesty and soundness of judgment Morris confidently relied in all foreign affairs.[3]

In September,[4] Congress resolved that "1,200,000 be quotaed on the States as absolutely and immediately necessary for payment of the interest of the public debt," which was to be applied in each State in payment of loan-office certificates and other obligations of the United States held there before any portion fell into the Federal treasury. It was recommended to raise this sum in the old-fashioned, perpetually-failing way of taxes.

The income of the government shrank so heavily, that Congress endeavored to throw a part of the burden of fulfilling its obligations on the States.[5] Towards the close

---

[1] Ante, p. 289, Feb. 20, 27, 1782, Feb. 10, 17, 1783.

[2] Nov. 22, 1781, Dip. Cor., vol. xii. p. 22. See Letter to Franklin on same subject, Nov. 27, 1781, Ibid., p. 27.

[3] Ante, p. 244. [4] Sept. 4, 10, 1782.

[5] Nov. 20, Dec. 10, 1781; see action of Congress, Sept. 9, 1782. So low was the treasury, that in October, 1782, Morris was obliged to sell a portion of the clothing recently arrived from Europe for the use of the army to pay debts for needlework, amounting to twelve thousand dollars. —WALN's *Life of Morris, Biog. Signers to Dec. of Indep.*, vol. v. p. 334.

of 1781,[1] the secretary of war was directed to supply North Carolina with arms and other things, and charge them to that State; and, not long after that event, the States were recommended "to settle and discharge on account of the United States" the depreciation of pay of certain officers who had been confined to the general hospital.[2] Before the year closed, the States were recommended[3] to settle with other officers and men, and to "charge the same to the United States;" and this recommendation was renewed the following year. Subsequently a resolution was introduced, asking the States to assist in paying the heavy arrears to the army; but it was not adopted.

The estimates for the year 1783 were presented early to Congress by Morris, and with some modification were adopted.[4] He estimated the expense of the government for the year at nine million dollars, and counted on obtaining four million dollars from abroad, leaving five million dollars to be raised at home. Congress added another million to the amount for the States to raise, and then made a requisition for two millions as a part of the sum required for the year. This was apportioned among them in the following manner: —

New Hampshire .	. $80,000	Delaware .	.	. 28,000
Massachusetts .	. 320,000	Maryland .	.	. 220,000
Rhode Island	. 48,000	Virginia .		. 290,000
Connecticut .	. 222,000	North Carolina		. 148,000
New York . .	90,000	South Carolina .		. 120,000
New Jersey . .	. 110,000	Georgia .		. 24,000
Pennsylvania	. 300,000			

[1] Dec. 3.   [2] Feb. 20, 1782.   [3] Dec. 31, 1781.   [4] Oct. 16, 18, 1782.

It was also "impressed on the several States as absolutely necessary to lay taxes for raising their quotas of money for the United States, separately from those laid for their own particular use." Thus recommending gave way to impressing by Congress.

The financial prospect was not promising. Although a loan had been negotiated in Holland the previous year, only six hundred thousand dollars of it remained for paying the expenses of the ensuing year, nor was there any hope of procuring further pecuniary aid from Europe.[1] There was no other source of revenue, except taxation: only very small sums, however, were obtainable in this way.[2] Many thought that new loans could be negotiated with foreign countries; but Morris declared the conduct of the French court on the subject to be decisive: "Some persons have, indeed, flattered themselves, that her positive declarations were merely calculated to restrain our rashness, and moderate our excess, but these ideas can no longer have a place in any sound and discerning mind. Her conduct has been consistent with her declarations, and if she had ever so much inclination to assist us with money, it is not in her power." Thus writes Morris to the president of Congress, informing him, at the same time, there " can no longer be a doubt to Congress that our public credit is gone."

Morris, seeing the disinclination of the States to pay taxes, and that foreign support was well-nigh exhausted,

---

[1] Letter of Morris to Pres. of Cong., March 7, 1783, Dip. Cor., vol. xii. p. 341.

[2] Morris in a letter to Hamilton says, with reference to the inclination of the farmers to pay taxes, " that is an object they are not very violently devoted to." — Oct. 5, 1782, *Dip. Cor.*, vol. xii. p. 277.

continued to pare down the expenses of the government to the lowest possible limit. As soon as peace was declared, he favored the immediate disbanding of the army; but there was considerable opposition to the measure until the troops were paid.[1] The arrears were heavy, notwithstanding the strenuous efforts put forth on their behalf by Morris, who, more than once, had employed his own private credit to relieve them. Congress proposed that the States should pay the deficiency to the 1st of August, 1780, and directed the financier to take the necessary steps for effecting a settlement from that period. But the treasury was extremely low, and he assured Congress that it was impracticable to make any payment to the army unless the expenditures were " immediately and considerably reduced." He succeeded in paying them in specie for one month's service, and gave them his own note for three months' pay, payable six months from date. In six days Morris signed six thousand notes, besides transacting other business pertaining to his office. The amount of notes was seven hundred and fifty thousand dollars, which he expected to redeem principally from the receipts of sales of public property, and from taxes. From time to time, numerous furloughs were granted, and the organization melted away, and was

---

[1] Letter to Com. of Cong., May 15, 1783, Dip. Cor., vol. xii. p. 362. It is said that when Morris first paid the soldiers with hard money at the head of the Elk River, just before embarking for Yorktown, the heads of the kegs containing the half-crowns were knocked out for effect, and the specie rolled out, to the great joy and astonishment of the soldiers. So excited were they, that one of them shouted to the top of his voice, " Look! look! Jonathan! by jingo! it is hard money." — *American Review*, vol. vi. p. 76.

absorbed, without any evil consequences. Poorly paid as the troops had been, they separated not without reluctance; for they had grown old in the service, and many knew not where to go to earn a livelihood.[1] Congress seconded the efforts of Morris to reduce expenditures in all departments, and radical retrenchment was vigorously enforced.

The public debt to the 1st of January, 1783, was $42,000,375, of which sum, $7,885,088 were foreign debt; while the balance, $34,115,290, was owed at home. The amount of domestic debt as given by Morris to the president of Congress was $35,327,769. Of this sum, $11,463,802 were loan certificates with two years' interest due thereon, which amounted to $877,828; the army debt was $635,618; while other unliquidated debts, deficiencies, &c., composed the balance, a large part of which was interest, the foreign debt drawing four and five per cent, and the domestic debt one per cent more.[2]

The opening of the year 1784 was signalized by Morris with overdrawing his account in France, in consequence of a miscalculation of the amount which he supposed was due to the government. His explanation was satisfactory, and in a short time the error was properly adjusted.

The most important financial measure which now tasked the wisdom of Congress related to the funding of the public debt. Morris[3] had long before directed their atten-

---

[1] See Morris's Cor., Dip. Cor., vol. xii. pp. 362 386, especially Letter directed to Pres. of Congress, July 18, 1783, reviewing the whole subject. Action of Cong. Jan. 25, March 18, 22, May 12, June 19, July 4, 11, Sept. 18, 1783.

[2] April 24, 29, 1783.

[3] See elaborate Letter to Pres. of Congress on the subject July 29, 1782, Dip. Cor., vol. xii. p. 211.

tion to the matter; but 1782 was closing when Congress resolved,[1] that "whenever the net produce of any funds recommended by Congress and granted by the States, for funding the debt already contracted, or for procuring future loans for the support of the war, shall exceed the sum requisite for paying the interest of the whole amount of the national debt, which these States may owe at the termination of the present war, the surplus of such grants shall form a sinking fund, to be inviolably appropriated to the payment of the principal of the said debt, and shall on no account be directed to any other purpose."[2] This measure, however, did not go far enough.   Accordingly, another bill was debated at considerable length; and on the 18th of April the following year, Congress resolved to levy a specific tax upon spirituous liquors, tea, sugar, coffee, cocoa, and molasses, and an *ad valorem* duty of five per cent on the value of all other importations.   The collectors were to be appointed by the States; and the duties, which were not collectible for a longer period than twenty-five years, were to be applied towards the discharge of the principal and interest of the public debt.   One million and a half dollars were to be raised annually for this purpose; the proportions were assessed to the several States; and it was provided, that, if the duties collected in any State exceeded its assessment, the excess was to be refunded; and, if a deficiency oc-

---

[1] Dec. 16.

[2] Congress had indeed resolved, on the 22d of May, 1781, that "the whole debts already due by the United States, be liquidated as soon as may be to their specie value, and funded, if agreeable to the creditors, as a loan upon interest;" but no measures were taken for putting the Act in operation.

curred, the balance was to be paid in cash. The revenues collected in each State were to form a separate account, and Congress hoped that this resolve would be satisfactory to Rhode Island, as it was formed with the view of meeting the principal objections urged by that State against the former resolution relating to the taxation of imports. All the delegates voted in the affirmative, except the representatives of New York, who were divided, and the delegates from Rhode Island, both of whom voted no. The Act, however, met the same fate as its predecessor, for Rhode Island refused to accept it; and so it never took effect. Several of the States—Connecticut, New York, Virginia, and Massachusetts — ceded their claims to Western territory, the income from the sale of which was set apart as a fund to pay the public debts.[1]

Although steps had been taken to settle the accounts of the States, progress in this direction was exceedingly slow. Congress urged the States to press forward this business,[2] and so did Morris, who was equally desirous of having the claims of persons residing in Canada, who had furnished assistance to the United States during the war, ascertained; and he recommended the appointment of a commissioner to visit that country, with power to liquidate these obligations, and give certificates for the amount payable at some future time.[3]

So slowly, indeed, did Congress move in this important

---

[1] See action of Congress, Feb. 18, 20, 21, March 20, 21, 28, April 1, 18, 24, 1783.

[2] Feb. 27, Aug. 9, 11, 1783.

[3] Letter to Pres. of Cong., Jan. 24, 1784, Dip. Cor., vol. xii. p. 449.

business, that in August, 1782, a memorial was addressed to that body, signed by many citizens of Pennsylvania, complaining of their inability to " obtain payment of the debts due to them by the public," of their failure to receive interest on loan-office certificates, " and that the suspension of debts complained of, was a material impediment to the collection of taxes."   The action of Congress upon this memorial was characteristic of that body.   Not until the last of January [1] the following year was a reply made, though an answer equally explicit could have been given at an earlier period.   Congress declared that provision had been made for settling the accounts of the States with the General Government, and that " the plan adopted will speedily be in an effectual train of execution throughout the United States;" but how could payment of them be made, it was urged, unless the States contributed funds necessary for the purpose?   Congress, the last of October the previous year, had demanded of the States eight million dollars; yet of this sum only $420,031 had been received.   The attempt to raise a revenue on importations had signally failed, although every effort had been put forth to obtain the consent of the States to the collection of it.   Surely, how could the people, so long as they withheld the funds needed to discharge the obligations of the government, expect it could fulfil them?

Towards the close of October, Morris reported the amount of public indebtedness.[2]   Congress was very tardy in replying to his letter asking for advice concerning the answer he should make to the farmers-general of France,

---

[1] Jan. 30.   [2] Oct. 22, 1783.

who had failed to receive the interest due on their loans
to the United States. Morris's communication was sent
to Congress in September; but two months elapsed before
a reply was received.[1] The answer which Morris was
advised to send could not have been very satisfactory to
the farmers-general. But perhaps it was not unexpected;
for, besides setting forth the fact that Congress fully
appreciated the favors received, that body promised to
discharge all obligations of the government as soon as
circumstances would admit.

The estimates for 1784 were not issued until the first
quarter of the year had passed away;[2] yet there was not
much reason for issuing them at all, since the States were
so feeble in responding to the requisitions of Congress.
The entire sum wanted was less than six million dollars;
while the amount required for maintaining the government, excluding the payment of former claims, and of
the interest and principal of the public debt, fell below
half a million dollars. The figures are full of interest,
especially in contrast with those for maintaining the
government at the present day. Thus there was wanted
for, —

Civil Department	$107,525 33
Military Department	200,000 00
Marine Department.	30,000 00
Incidental expenses	60,000 00
Contingencies	60,000 00
	$457,525 33

Instead of making new requisitions on the States, Congress demanded the payment of taxes due on former calls,

[1] Nov. 1, 1783.   [2] April 5

especially on the eight-million assessment of 1781. Less than one-quarter thereof had been paid; and Congress asked the States to furnish one-half the amount, or four million dollars, during the year. The following table shows how the original assessment had been apportioned, and what sums the States had paid to the end of 1783:—

	ASSESSMENT.	AM'T PAID.
New Hampshire	$373,598	$3,000 00
Massachusetts	1,307,596	247,676 66
Rhode Island	216,684	67,847 95
Connecticut	747,196	131,577 83
New York	373,598	39,064 01
New Jersey	485,679	102,004 95
Pennsylvania	1,120,794	346,632 98
Delaware	112,085	
Maryland	993,996	89,302 11
Virginia	1,307,594	116,103 53
North Carolina	622,677	
South Carolina	373,598	344,301 57
Georgia	24,905	
	$8,000,000	$1,486,154 71

A new feature was now introduced in the payment of taxes, worthy of notice. We have already adverted to the fact, that, when the government ceased to pay interest on the loan-office certificates, the practice was initiated, by the loan-officers themselves, of giving certificates for interest due on the loan-office certificates, which were called indents. Although Morris was opposed to issuing them, the practice was continued, until they became so numerous that Congress, in April,[1] 1784, determined that one-fourth of the sum required of the States might be

---

[1] April 28.

paid in indents. The committee who reported this measure to Congress observed that three-fourths of the sum wanted by the government could "be answered by nothing but money itself;" but the other fourth, consisting of interest due on the domestic debt, might be effected "by procuring a discount of the demand in the hands of the holders; an operation which will be shorter, and less impoverishing to the State." In times of greater plenty, it was admitted, "the accuracy of fiscal administration might require all transactions to be in actual money, at the treasury itself," yet, till the people had had some respite from their late difficulties, it behooved Congress "to prefer their easements." The committee, therefore, were of the opinion that the several Legislatures might be allowed "so to model the collection of the sums now called for," that three-fourths of any sum might be paid in money, and the other fourth discharged by procuring "discounts of interest" with domestic creditors, "always taking care that the collection of money shall proceed at least in threefold proportion with the operations of discount." To ascertain the evidences of discount receivable in lieu of money, the holders of loan-office certificates were at liberty to carry them to the office where they were issued, as well as the holders of certificates of other liquidated debts of the United States, and have the interest due thereon settled and certified to the last day of the year 1782, and receive certificates therefor. Such a certificate or indent, when "parted with by the holder of the principal," was regarded as evidence that he had received satisfaction for the same, and therefore was "receivable from the bearer, within the same State, and from the State where obtained from the bearer, in lieu of money;" while payment of indents by a State into the public treasury was regarded as a discharge of an equal amount of the interest of the domestic debt. More briefly stated, the operation consisted: first, in giving certificates for interest due on public obligations; secondly, allowing the people to return them, in lieu of money, in payment of taxes to a limited extent; while new certificates were issued for the interest constantly accruing.

Victory was won, and peace had been declared, still the people continued not less remiss in paying taxes.[1] All willingly admitted the necessity of taxation to a certain extent; yet, as Morris writes to Franklin, each was desirous of shifting the burden from his own shoulders to those of his neighbors.

A very fair picture of the conditions of the finances at the opening of 1784 is presented in Morris's letter to Franklin,[2] written in February. The accounts on the first of that month were thus stated: —

Balance due for past services	$100,000
Dues for bills of exchange drawn	200,000
Due to the National Bank	340,000
Add for contingencies	10,000
	$650,000

What were his expectations about paying this sum? The taxes for the last four months had slightly exceeded two hundred thousand dollars. Delaware, North Caro-

---

[1] Letter to Franklin, Sept. 30, 1783, Dip. Cor., vol. xii. p. 417.

[2] Feb. 13, 1784, Dip. Cor., vol. xii. p. 464.

lina, and Georgia had paid nothing. New Hampshire, Connecticut, New York, Maryland, and Virginia had paid very little in proportion to their ability. Morris expected to derive some income from the sale of confiscated lands, perhaps two hundred and fifty thousand dollars, by the last of September, leaving four hundred thousand dollars which he hoped to obtain in the following manner: " I shall borrow immediately one hundred thousand dollars of the bank, and direct purchases of tobacco and rice, partly with cash, partly on credit, and partly by bills drawn on me. By this means, I can with that one hundred thousand dollars, have the purchases all made in March and April, so that the shipments to the required amount of two thousand dollars will take place, some in March, some in April, and all of them I hope by the end of May. The taxes during April and May will pay the purchases on credit, and the bills drawn on me; and the taxes in June and July will pay the hundred thousand dollars due to the bank. By the end of September, therefore, I may calculate upon a full discharge of all these debts." To what expedients was Morris obliged to resort for the purpose of getting so small a sum with which to pay the public indebtedness! With what great difficulty was even a slight portion of the taxes collected! and how precarious were all the sources of revenue! Only by exercising the utmost watchfulness and vigilance were any funds obtained. A financier less fertile in expedients than Morris would have collected nothing.

Jefferson imagined the assistance needed by the government could be procured from the banks: like most of his ideas on finance, his plan was impracticable. Morris [1]

---

[1] April 8, 1784, Dip. Cor., vol. xii. p. 486.

declared they would not grant any loans unless they could clearly see " a prospect of speedy re-imbursement from the taxes," and, if they were collectible, surely there was no need of asking the banks for any aid whatever.

Notwithstanding the poverty of the treasury, specie was abundant among the people:[1] the foreign armies had brought large quantities into the country, while foreign loans and trade had largely added to the stock of gold and silver.[2] Bills on Europe were currently sold at twenty to forty per cent below par, — a rate so favorable to the merchants, that they purchased bills, and remitted them

[1] Lord Sheffield, in his Additional Notes to his work on Observations on American Commerce, discusses in a very intelligent manner the question, What had become of the money sent to America during the war? The question is not without interest to the present reader: so we venture to give the noble author's observations on the subject. "Some is come back — a considerable part is the circulating cash within our lines — Many British subjects in New York have very large sums in their possession. The Dutch and Germans, whose number is not inconsiderable, have hoarded up — and it is believed considerable sums are concealed. Part went into the country for provisions, much provisions could not be brought in clandestinely, and the greatest part of the money came back to New York, to purchase British goods, or to purchase bills of exchange, which were sent in payment to Europe and the West Indies. Money to a considerable amount came also to New York for the same purposes from Philadelphia, got by a very advantageous trade to the Havanna, which is now at an end. And much money went from Philadelphia, and other parts of the American States to St. Eustatia before it was taken, to purchase our manufactures from the Dutch; so that it is not probable, much specie will remain in America in consequence of the war." — P. 68.

[2] Thomas Paine wrote in April, 1782, " The progress and revolution of our domestic circumstances are as extraordinary as the Revolution itself. We began with paper, and we end with gold and silver." — *Penn. Packet*, April 4, 1782.

to Europe in payment of imports, which flowed into the country in great quantities.[1] War-freight and insurance added very considerably to the expense of importation; yet, owing to the scarcity of foreign goods, the abundance of cash, and the luxury and pride of the people, they sold rapidly, and large profits were acquired.

In June,[2] 1784, Congress passed a noteworthy Act relating to the settlement of the accounts of the States. Money and supplies furnished by the United States to any State were to be charged at their just value in specie, with six per cent interest from the date of furnishing the same, until a final adjustment and payment of the account; while the same rule was to be applied in all transactions between the State and the government in which the latter was the debtor. A rule was established for charging the depreciation of bills of credit advanced by any State or person for the benefit of the government. The kind of evidence required to establish claims against the government was prescribed, and when compensation should be allowed for the ravages of war, beside other very important regulations. Certificates bearing six per cent interest were given to all creditors in payment of their claims; while those issued by any commissary or quartermaster-general were exchangeable for new ones, the same as were given to other creditors. They were worth about two shillings and sixpence per pound, at

[1] "Thirty per cent is made on the purchase of French bills, when money at lawful interest cannot be hired by public or private bodies." — *Gen. Sullivan to Lincoln*, Jan. 16, 1782; AMORY'S *Life of Sullivan*, vol. ii. p. 384.

[2] June 3.

which price, says Webster, their circulation "became very general."

The end of Morris's career as superintendent of finance was drawing near. Several months before, he did resign, but, yielding to the earnest solicitations of Congress, remained in office. His strict integrity, devotion to business, and constant urging of all delinquents to settle their accounts, yielded fruit both sweet and bitter; for while he enjoyed, on the one hand, the serene satisfaction which always comes from a faithful performance of duty and from the thousand good opinions of those who love their country, on the other hand, he could not escape the condemnation of those who felt the pressure of his vigorous administration. His desire to reduce expenses was inspired by the mean wish, so it was asserted, of impairing the strength, and lessening the respectability, of the country. His enemies accused him of speculating in the funds of the government; but he stoutly denied the charge. He was accused of ruining the public credit; but this accusation was groundless. During his administration the public finances had been much improved, and the credit of the government had been considerably strengthened.

The belief of Congress in his integrity and ability was never shaken by any reports circulated about him. A year previous to his resignation, a committee were appointed to examine all matters concerning the administration of his office, who made a report which was entered on the journal of Congress.[1] They declared that the

<hr>

[1] June 17, 1783. The committee reported that the sum expended under his administration from the fourteenth day of May, 1781, to the 1st of January, 1783, amounted to $3,131,046; amount brought into the

business of the office had been conducted with great ability and assiduity, in a manner highly advantageous to the United States, and in conformity with the system established by Congress. The public accounts of receipts and expenditures had been regularly and punctually kept, which had never been done previous to his administration. Morris had settled many accounts that were several years old when he accepted office, and most all others were in course of adjustment. Many reforms also had been introduced, effecting large reductions in expense, preventing corruption, and lessening the liabilities of the government. Surely this was commendation enough, especially from a body possessing such an exalted character.[1]

Morris's own notes, given to a large amount for the benefit of the government, were in due time redeemed, and every obligation which he had assumed was fulfilled. No person was ever more punctual or scrupulous in executing his promises than Morris, or entertained loftier ideas concerning the sacredness of public obligations. In one of his last official letters, addressed to the president of Congress,[2] he says, "I have invariably in my official correspondence (as indeed upon every other occasion,

public treasury during the same period was $2,726,334; and that the expenditures in 1782 exceeded the receipts to the extent of $404,713, which sum "was supplied by a circulation in the notes of the financier."

[1] H. G. Otis, in a letter written in 1857, containing reminiscences of John Lowell, says, that when Lowell visited Philadelphia, after the Revolution was over, "among others, he was waited upon by Robert Morris, who was still in his glory, and regarded in public estimation, next to Washington, as the man on whose financial exertions had depended the success of the Revolution." — *Hist. Mag.*, vol. i. p. 262.

[2] Sept. 30, 1784, Dip. Cor., vol. xii. p. 497.

both public and private), expressed the conviction which I feel, that however the several States may, from a difference in local circumstances, differ in their opinions about the mode of providing for public debts, all of them will concur in the just sentiment, that these debts ought to be most punctually discharged."

The breadth and soundness of Morris's financial views were remarkable; and only one other person during this period displayed an insight in these things equally clear and deep, namely, Alexander Hamilton. In the same letter from which we have just quoted, Morris declares himself to be "grounded in the assertion" that when proper provision is made for the payment of the public debt, "the public credit of America will be the best of any in the world, that it will cost less to maintain it by us, than by any other nation, and that considering the infant state of our cultivation in general, and the frontiers in particular, it is of more importance to us than it can be to any other country. It is also a commercial problem, which admits of absolute demonstration, that the punctual payment of interest on all our debts will produce a clear annual gain of more than such interest can possibly amount to. So that the eternal and immutable principles of truth and justice, being for a moment out of the question, and stifling those sentiments of humanity, which arise from a view of what the public creditors must suffer, should their dues be withheld (if indeed it be possible to stifle such sentiments), still it will indisputably appear to be the interest of the merchant as well as of the husbandman and mechanic, to pay their just proportions towards discharging the public engagements. For this plain and simple system of common honesty, while it invigorates the springs of our credit, strengthens also the bands of our union, proceeding with equal motion towards the public weal and private prosperity." Thus did Morris, in his closing advice to Congress, show how harmonious were the teachings of policy and honesty in respect to one of the gravest questions of his time. Nor did he, on any other occasion during his financial career, display a less inflexible observance of the principle of honesty in all the pecuniary measures of the government.[1]

His correspondence exhibits a remarkable mastery of every question that engaged his attention. He was no empiric: he digged deeply, and based his policy on sound principles. A practical financier, he was also familiar with the true theories of finance; and his decisions were never accidental, but always the fruit of investigation and reflection. Of course he was the executor of the

[1] Morris formed and inflexibly maintained a rule in respect to not diverting public funds from the use to which they were originally and legally appropriated; the observance of which by some of his predecessors would have added much to their reputation for honesty, and regard for the public interests. In a letter to Nathan Appleton he says, " I will most inflexibly adhere to my determination, for I will not participate in the guilt of deceiving those who trust their property to the public. And surely it is a deception to accumulate promise upon promise, and debt upon debt, without the means of performance or payment. The States alone can give those means, and if they will give them I will cheerfully and honestly apply them to the purpose for which they shall be given. So I will the moneys which are given for other purposes. But I will neither pay the interest of our debts out of the moneys which are called for to carry on the war, nor pay the expenses of the war from the funds which are called for to pay the interest of our debts." — Jan. 22, 1782, *Hist. Mag.*, vol. vi. p. 169.

will of Congress; yet, from the beginning of his financial career, he constantly kept a few great principles in sight, whose source was the unfailing spring of moral rectitude. In one of his letters to the governors of the Southern States, he says, " I have no system of finance, except that which results from the plain, self-evident dictates of moral honesty." [1]   Taxation and economy were the two pillars supporting his financial structure, and they were as solid as the foundation on which they rested.   Morris was in truth the peerless financier of the Revolution.[2]

[1] Dec. 19, 1781, Dip. Cor., vol. xii. p. 71.

[2] Samuel Breck, writing, after the Revolution had closed, of the men who figured in that great event, says, " Among the very leading men in all respects at that time was Robert Morris.   History has not yet done justice to this great man's noble exertions during our revolutionary war.   His patriotism was superior to the fears which too often seize upon the wealthy in moments of evil commotion, and he freely risked every thing in the good cause." — *Recollections of Samuel Breck*, p. 203.

CHAPTER II.

ADMINISTRATION OF THE NEW BOARD OF TREASURY.

CONGRESS having been duly apprised by Morris of his intended retirement from office, it became necessary to elect a successor, or provide a new mode of administering the finances. As no other financier was known to whom Congress was willing to confide such powers as had been given to Morris, they were jointly conferred on three persons, who were designated "The Board of Treasury." This action was taken in May,[1] 1784; but, as the first appointees[2] would not serve,[3] nearly eight months passed away before John Lewis Gervais, Samuel Osgood, and Walter Livingston, were appointed.[4] Several weeks more elapsed previous to their embarking on the much dreaded sea of finance. In the mean time the comptroller performed the duties of financier, having been temporarily clothed with power to appoint persons to liquidate accounts between the States and the General Government.[5] It was the more fitting to intrust to him the financial administration of the government, since he had been especially employed in adjusting its accounts for a long time prior to Morris's resignation.

The period covered by this chapter is extremely barren

---

[1] May 27, 28.   [2] June 3, 1784.   [3] Nov. 30, Dec. 10, 1784.
[4] Jan. 25, 1785.   [5] March 23, 1784.

in financial measures of any kind. The more important
events relate to the adjustment of accounts, which were
exceedingly numerous and complicated; all the States
having numerous badly tangled transactions with the
government, while an army of individuals, officials, and
private persons, were debtors or creditors to the United
States. By the constitution of Solon all officials, at the
close of their public career, were required to render their
account, and apply for a certificate, undergoing at the
same time the closest scrutiny. This excellent political
regulation was unknown in the early history of the
American Union; and consequently, beside the enormous
mass of accounts awaiting settlement, many of them
were full of irregularities.

Commissioners had been appointed in February,[1] 1782,
for adjusting accounts with the States; and three years
later the number was increased.[2] A special measure was
enacted[3] for ascertaining the specific supplies furnished
by Pennsylvania; and the time for presenting claims to
the commissioners was limited to one year from the date
of the enactment, March 17, 1785. Just as this period
was closing, an unsuccessful attempt was made to extend
the time. In October,[4] 1786, however, a new ordinance
was passed on the subject: the duties of the commissioners were to cease on the 1st of April the following year;[5]
and a board, consisting of three members, was created,
possessing all the powers exercised by the previous commissioners. Additional regulations were framed concern-

---

[1] Feb. 20.   [2] Feb. 23, 1785.   [3] Sept. 5, 1786.   [4] Oct. 13.

[5] Except in the States of North Carolina and Georgia, where they
were to continue in office six months longer.

ing the testimony requisite to establish claims; the time for presenting them was extended; and a period of three years was allotted to the board for doing the work. Within seven months, the ordinance was repealed.[1] The States were divided into five districts; in each of which a commissioner, appointed by the Board of Treasury, was to go, and receive from the States embraced therein "all their accounts and vouchers for payments made on account of bounties, pay and depreciation of pay" to the army and militia, and send the same to the commissioner of army accounts, who was required to examine and pass such as were authorized by the resolves of Congress, and "to state such" as did not fall under the above description, "together with such remarks" as tended to elucidate their nature. The commissioners were also to receive in like manner the accounts and vouchers for moneys paid, and supplies furnished, on the requisitions of Congress made previously to October, 1781; and these were to be forwarded to the comptroller of the treasury. There was a third class of claims held by the States against the government, which it was the duty of the commissioners to receive and examine. These related chiefly to advances or disbursements for the use of the commissary, quartermaster, clothing, marine, and hospital departments. The commissioners were to pass on all that were authorized by the resolves of Congress "and supported by proper vouchers," and "to state such" as were not "thus warranted or supported," accompanying them with remarks explanatory of their nature, "and the reasons offered for the deficiency of vouchers." Six per cent

---

[1] May 7, 1787.

interest per annum was allowed on all accounts; and the States were given six months for presenting them to the commissioners, who were required within a year to repair to the place where Congress was in session, and deliver the accounts and vouchers received by them to the comptroller of the treasury, whereupon their commission was to terminate.

At the same time Congress appointed three commissioners to receive from the comptroller of the treasury and from the commissioner of army accounts every account of the States in the possession of those officers, and to examine such as the district commissioners had passed, " in order that the same might be finally adjusted on uniform and equitable principles." Additional instructions were given them to light their intricate pathway; yet with a large number of accounts Congress could do no more than vest the commissioners " with full power and authority to make such allowance for the same as they shall think consistent with the general principles of equity." A very dangerous power, surely, to confide to commissioners, — an authority which no Congress of the present day would dare confer; yet accounts between the States and the government were so confused, that it was necessary to grant a very wide latitude of discretion to some body in order to effect a settlement.

Notwithstanding the several extensions of time already granted for presenting claims, in July,[1] 1787, Congress carved out another period of eight months for presenting accounts of the commissary, quartermaster, hospital, clothing, and marine departments, and one year to per-

---

[1] July 23.

sons having claims against any other department of the government. When this time expired, no renewal was granted under the old Confederation, although the expediency of granting one was considered.[1]

The government, while trying to adjust accounts with the States, did not forget the claims of individuals, especially of those who had served in the recent war. In 1782,[2] for the purpose of liquidating the numerous claims held by individuals, the country was divided into five departments, — quartermasters, commissary, hospital, clothing, and marine; and for each a commissioner was appointed, with authority to adjust the claims of persons residing within his jurisdiction. Four years later a single commissioner was appointed[3] to perform the same duties; but after serving diligently for two years, and with imperfect success, an additional commissioner was assigned[4] to the same unpromising task.

Many of the loan-office commissioners and other officials had been extremely negligent in keeping their accounts, and not a few had proven recreant to their trusts. Their duties at first were not very strictly defined: consequently it was quite easy for them to do many things condemned alike by honesty and public policy. It was not until September,[5] 1785, that Congress prescribed with any accuracy the duties of this class of officials. They were required to receive and keep the money arising from Continental taxes in the different States, to pay the interest due from the General Government, and to "hold all moneys collected within the several States, on account of

[1] Aug. 28, 1788.   [2] Feb. 27.   [3] March 24, 1786.   [4] May 8, 1788.
[5] Sept. 30.

the requisitions of Congress," subject only to the orders of that body, or the Board of Treasury. They were also required to form estimates of the "interest falling due monthly within their respective States," to keep an accurate account of their transactions, and make a return thereof to the Board of Treasury and comptroller, and should not "directly or indirectly be concerned in trade," and in all their official transactions were to govern themselves by the acts and resolves of Congress or the orders of the Board of Treasury.

So loose was the financial system of the government, that negligence and fraud rankly grew out of it. Numerous as were the frauds exposed, probably many fraudulent transactions entirely escaped the attention of Congress. A committee who investigated the unsettled accounts of the government in May,[1] 1788, reported that "many millions of dollars were advanced by the United States to sundry persons" during the late war, concerning the expenditure of which "proper accounts have not been rendered," though they had been frequently requested to render them. The committee believed the United States had suffered "very great inconveniencies by inexcusable negligence and unauthorized delays in persons intrusted with public moneys, in not rendering and settling their accounts," and recommended the Board of Treasury to begin suits against all who were "charged with public moneys or other property," within a short period from the date of making their report, allowing them a sufficient number of days of grace to settle their accounts, if they were so inclined. This recommendation was subsequently

---

[1] May 22.

negatived by a committee of the third Congress held under the present Constitution, " except in cases where a balance appeared to be clearly due to the public, or where special circumstances seemed to render this course expedient." [1]

Progress in settling the accounts of both States and individuals was exceedingly slow. Loan-officers who held commissions in 1788, except those of South Carolina and Georgia, accounted to the end of March, 1788; but the accounts of loan-officers appointed during the administration of the finances by the former Treasury Board, with only two or three exceptions, remained unsettled during the old Confederation. " With respect to the commissioners appointed for settling accounts in the several States," say a committee who reported to Congress on the subject,[2] " no return of books and papers has been made by them, except the States of New York, New Jersey, Maryland, Georgia, and Pennsylvania. The certificates liquidated and taken up, included in those returns, were lodged in the comptroller's office, but they were not cancelled or otherwise defaced; in this situation they lay neglected, until a number of those taken up in the State of New York, which were negotiable, were feloniously taken away by one of the clerks in the register's office," where the papers were put after closing the comptroller's office. Happily most of the certificates were recovered; but the incidents surrounding the theft show how carelessly the financial business of the day was conducted. Not only did great negligence prevail in presenting ac-

---

[1] Am. State Papers by Lowrie and Clarke, Finance, vol. i. p. 347.
[2] Sept. 30, 1788.

counts to the commissioners, but also in making their returns to the government, and in keeping them afterwards. Not until the new government, under the inspiring genius of Hamilton, sought to collect and adjust the obligations of the old Confederation, were its financial transactions finally reduced to order.

In respect to the settlement of foreign accounts, Thomas Barclay was sent on a special mission to Europe in 1782, for the purpose of adjusting them.[1] Jefferson described him as honest, but slow and indecisive.[2] Pursuing his difficult way for several years with fidelity and considerable success, misfortunes at home compelled him to return before he had completely fulfilled his mission.

The loan-offices were still employed as a part of the financial machinery of the government; but on the 1st of July, 1785, all other receivers of money from the States were discontinued.[3] The certificates which they had issued, like most of the obligations of the government, remained unpaid, and also the interest due on them: finally Congress resolved [4] that the holders might present them to the loan-officers of the State where they were issued, for the purpose of having their specie value ascertained, and to receive a new one for this amount in place of the original, which was to be surrendered.[5] Congress also issued new ones [6] in several cases where the originals had been destroyed.

Congress could not escape seeing the evils which flowed from the absence of a system of money: so it was re-

---

[1] Ante, p. 312.   [2] Works, vol. ii. p. 155; Ibid., pp. 183, 211.
[3] April 15, 1785.   [4] Feb. 1, 1786.   [5] Oct. 11, 1787.
[6] Aug. 19, 1785; Sept. 12, 1781.

solved[1] to establish one dollar as the money unit of the United States; the smallest coin consisting of copper, two hundred of which were to be equal to one dollar. The value of the several pieces was to increase in a decimal ratio. It was afterward declared[2] "that the standard of the United States of America, for gold and silver, shall be eleven parts fine and one part alloy.

"That the money unit of the United States, being by the resolve of Congress on the 6th July, 1785, a dollar, shall contain of fine silver $375\frac{64}{100}$ grains.[3]

"That the money of account, to correspond with the division of coins, agreeably to the above resolve, proceed in a decimal ratio, agreeably to the forms and manner following, viz.;

"Mills: The lowest money of account, of which 1,000
    shall be equal to the Federal dollar, or money unit   0.001
Cents: The highest copper piece of which 100 shall be
    equal to the dollar 0.010
Dimes: The lowest silver coin, 10 of which shall be
    equal to the dollar 0.100
Dollar: The highest silver coin 1.000

"That betwixt the dollar and the lowest copper coin, as fixed by the resolve of Congress of the 6th July, 1785, there shall be three silver coins and one copper coin.

"That the silver coins shall be as follows: One coin containing $187\frac{82}{100}$ grains of fine silver to be called A Half-Dollar; One coin containing $75\frac{128}{1000}$ grains of fine

---

[1] July 6, 1785.   [2] Aug. 8, 1786.

[3] The money unit, therefore, established at that time was the silver dollar. See Hamilton's Report on the Establishment of the Mint, January, 1791.

silver, to be called A Double Dime; and one coin containing $37\frac{560}{1000}$ grains of fine silver to be called A Dime.

"That the two copper coins shall be as follows: One equal to the 100th part of the Federal dollar, to be called A Cent; and one equal to the 200th part of the Federal dollar to be called A Half-Cent.

"That two pounds and a quarter avoirdupois weight of copper, shall constitute 100 cents.

"That there shall be two gold coins: One containing $246\frac{268}{1000}$ grains of fine gold, equal to ten dollars, to be stamped with the impression of the American eagle, and to be called An Eagle; One containing $123\frac{134}{1000}$ grains of fine gold, equal to five dollars, to be stamped in like manner and to be called A Half-Eagle."

Previous to the adoption of this measure, the Spanish dollar had been employed as the standard of value; and obligations had been incurred with the expectation of paying and receiving it, or its equivalent, in discharge of them. But the Spanish dollar exceeded in value the American by more than two per cent; and the question soon arose whether a debt could be honestly as well as legally discharged by paying only the same number of dollars of the new kind as specified in the contract. It was contended that the difference in value of the two kinds ought to be exactly ascertained, that debts already contracted to be paid in dollars, or for which dollars were a legal tender, should "not be paid in American dollars, without an allowance for the deficiency of their value, compared to that of the Spanish. Otherwise," a writer affirmed, "evident injustice must follow."[1] Notwithstanding the truth of his conclusion, Congress took no note of the matter; and debtors were at liberty to pay debts contracted during the Spanish-dollar reign in American dollars, if they chose, without recognizing any difference between the two kinds in value. The Coinage Act, however, was never put in operation; and this is the reason, doubtless, why Congress made no further regulation on the subject. Of course, so long as no American dollar existed with which to make payments, creditors could not complain of injustice on the part of the government growing out of the new coinage system.

A mint was subsequently established;[2] and the copper coin of the government was declared "receivable in all" taxes or payments due to the United States, in the proportion of five dollars for every hundred dollars so paid. Foreign copper coins were declared to be not current after the first day of September, 1787: at the same time the value of the copper coinage of the States was established.

During the year 1785[3] the merchants of New York sent a petition to Congress, setting forth the losses which

---

[1] American Museum, August, 1787, vol. ii. p. 184. The same writer was opposed to a double standard. He observed, that, while silver was made the standard, "gold might still be coined, to ascertain its quantity and fineness; but should not, like money, have a value annexed to it by public authority, but be left, like any other commodity, to find it at market."

[2] Oct. 16, 1786. Three or four dies were made for striking copper coins, a number of pieces were struck; but no regular issue of coin took place. — LINDERMAN, *Money and Legal Tender*, p. 21.

[3] March 28.

they had sustained from the depreciation of paper money, loan-office certificates, and other obligations of the government, and desiring that some compensation might be made to them. The reader will doubtless admire the adroit answer of Congress. Not denying the justness of the petitioners to receive compensation from some source, they were referred to the Legislature of New York as the proper body to repair their losses. Surely Congress could not have assented to their request without increasing the public burdens, which were now very poorly borne. Had Congress consented to make reparation for these losses, that body could not have done otherwise than make a similar adjustment with every other creditor of the United States having a claim of the same nature. The way in which Congress solved the problem was certainly free from imputation of partiality towards any creditor, or class of creditors.

The government continued to receive paper money long after individuals had declined to take it; but, in 1785, the government itself refused to accept it, even in payment of postage-stamps.[1] The States, too, were required to pay specie on the requisitions of Congress:[2] truly the day of paper money had finally come to an inglorious end. Discredited by its authors, the virtue of paper money went out of it, never to return.

The issues of the Bank of North America continued to circulate at their full value. The difficulties which environed the institution in its earlier days disappeared: all fears respecting its ability to redeem its promises subsided, and in the third year of its existence its cash

---

[1] Sept. 20, 1786.   [2] Sept. 18, Oct. 21, 1786; May 3, 1787.

account arose to 5,957,000 Mexican dollars. Notwithstanding the attacks made on the bank during the succeeding year, "such was its great internal strength and the energy of its very nature," that its transactions amounted nearly to thirty-seven million dollars: indeed, its success now endangered its life. Others wished to share the fat dividends; and, when the directors refused to increase the capital of the bank, the erection of a rival institution was proposed. This was in 1784. The directors of the old concern were stoutly opposed to the scheme, and urged the fatal consequences which were likely to spring from the existence of two banks operating in Philadelphia in opposition to each other. "Two shops to go to," was the phrase of the day. The excitement ran high. The Assembly of Pennsylvania was "plagued with long arguments on both sides;" but "all at once the thing was hushed up, and accommodated." The directors of the bank consented to increase the capital from four hundred thousand dollars to two millions, and allow the projectors of the new enterprise to become stockholders in the other.

No sooner, however, was this contest settled, than another and still fiercer was forced on the bank. A numerous party arose in Pennsylvania, who demanded the issue of more paper money; but "unless the bank would give it currency, which everybody saw plain enough the directors could not do," a new paper issue could not be created, as the State was powerless to put forth one having the confidence of anybody. The bank, therefore, was regarded as the opponent of the paper-money scheme, the friends of which, unfortunately, were powerful enough to procure, by way of revenge, a repeal of the charter in September,[1] 1785. The bank, however, possessed another charter from the United States, under which it continued to transact business and thrive, till March, 1787, when Pennsylvania re-incorporated the concern. The new charter, however, was unlike the former one, so different, indeed, that the bank was no longer regarded as a national institution.[2]

During the period we are now considering, fresh attempts were made to raise a revenue from imports, and the States were urged to adopt the recommendations of Congress passed in 1783 relating to the subject. The States slowly adopted the system then proposed,[3] but with various qualifications; Pennsylvania insisting upon the consent of all the States before the measure became operative anywhere. The conditions imposed by New York were still worse, as they essentially changed the nature of the measure, and effectually killed it. Not until the adoption of the present Constitution was the government able to lay a tax on imports.

Failing to get any funds from this source to maintain the government, it was obliged to depend almost wholly on the States; as the sales of government property, including the public lands, yielded only a very trifling sum.[4] The issuing of "indents," or certificates for interest accruing on loan-office certificates and liquidated debts, was

---

[1] Sept. 13.

[2] See Hamilton's report on establishing a national bank, Works, vol. iii. p. 126; also Webster's Essay on Credit, giving a history of the bank, Political Essays, p. 427.

[3] Feb. 15, July 27, Aug. 11, 22, 1786.

[4] See Act, May 28, 1784.

authorized;[1] but these neither paid debts, nor satisfied creditors. Requisitions on the States were poorly heeded. All authority over them seemed to be dying out, while their interest in the government was rapidly waning.

Yet the sale of the public lands, even at that early day, was confidently regarded by many as a source whence considerable sums could be obtained for the government. The States, after a long dispute, ceded their interest in the Western lands, thus essentially fixing their own boundaries, and determining what portion remained for public disposal. It was in 1787 that the celebrated ordinance was passed regulating the government of the territory north-west of the Ohio; and every needed requisite was soon adopted to make the title of lands secure to those who were desirous of purchasing any part of the public domain. As certificates of the public debt could be received in payment, Jefferson was so confident in 1785, as to express the opinion that this arrangement would very soon absorb all the certificates given by the government for debts, "and thus rid us of our domestic debt,"[2] which at that time comprised four-fifths of the total indebtedness of the government.

The estimates for the year 1785 were not fixed until the close of September[3] of that year, and the resolutions accompanying them reveal the poverty and weakness of the government. Only $404,553 were required for the civil and military departments and contingencies; the in-

---

[1] Aug. 23, Oct. 30, 1786.

[2] Works, Letter to David Hartley, Sept. 5, 1785, vol. i. p. 424: see Ibid., vol. ii. pp. 325, 333, 358.

[3] Sept. 27.

terest on the foreign debt was $440,252; and $743,054 were required to pay the interest on the domestic debt.[1] Beside these expenditures, the interest on soldiers' certificates was estimated at $289,423; while the expenses of the previous year had exceeded the estimate by $1,141,-551. Congress asked for three million dollars; and, as more than two-thirds of this sum was to be applied in payment of interest on the domestic debt, it was believed that the Legislatures of the States might "so model the collection of the sums called for that one-third of any sum being paid in actual money, the other two-thirds may be discharged by the interest due upon loan-office certificates, and upon other certificates of liquidated debts of the United States." As the States had not fully paid the eight-million requisition of 1781, and no portion of the two-million one of 1782, it was decided to apply the sums received on these two requisitions. In October the States were urgently asked to fulfil the recommendations of Congress; but the months rolled away, the stones of the tax-mill turned slowly, and only very small sums fell into the treasury. Four requisitions had been ordered since Oct. 30, 1781, for $15,670,987; yet towards this sum all the States had contributed, by the 1st of February, 1786, in the aggregate, only $2,450,803.[2] Were States ever so able to bear burdens more disinclined to do their

---

[1] Madison writes to Monroe, May 29, 1785, "The use of certificates as a medium for discharging the interest of the home debt is a great evil, though I suppose a necessary one. The advantage it gives to sharpers and collectors can scarcely be described, and what is more noxious, it provokes violations of public faith more than the weight of the burden itself." — *Writings*, vol. i. p. 153.

[2] Report of Com. to Cong., Feb. 3, 1786.

duty in this regard? Everywhere did individuals seek to evade the payment of taxes; not because they were too poor to pay, for the sums asked were small compared with the resources of the people, but rather from habit, and because evasion of the duty was so general.

It was during this period that a new mania broke out for paper money. Pennsylvania and North Carolina led in the movement. In the former State the sum emitted was not large, nor was it made a legal tender; but ere long its value was totally gone. North Carolina issued a larger sum, which was endowed with a legal tender quality. It was issued partly in payments to military creditors, and partly for purchases of tobacco on public account. Madison, in describing the method employed of introducing it in that State, says, "The agent was authorized to give nearly the double of the current price; and as the paper was a tender, debtors ran to him with their tobacco, and the creditors paid the expense of the farce." South Carolina followed next: her emissions consisted of loans to individuals, but were not a legal tender. New Jersey issued more than a hundred thousand pounds as loans to her citizens, to which were attached the legal tender attribute. New York followed in the same way, though the money was declared to be a legal tender in suits only. In Rhode Island one hundred thousand pounds were issued to individuals in the way of loans, which were not only made a legal tender, but severe penalties were visited upon the head of any person who directly or indirectly should give a preference to specie. Nearly all the States imitated the example. Prices rapidly rose, or, in other words, the money depreciated, and, after causing a great variety of serious mischiefs, disappeared, like too many former issues, leaving nothing but misery and dishonesty to mark its course.[1]

August of 1786[2] had come before Congress fixed the estimates for the year, amounting to $3,777,062. As the policy was established of receiving indents from the States in payment of their quotas, the sum asked for the ensuing year was apportioned in the following manner: —

	INDENTS.	SPECIE.
New Hampshire	$56,452	$76,268
Massachusetts	240,370	324,746
Rhode Island	34,613	446,764
Connecticut	141,474	191,135
New York	137,434	185,567
New Jersey	89,279	120,619
Pennsylvania	219,765	296,908
Delaware	24,037	32,475
Maryland	151,570	204,775
Virginia	274,707	371,136
North Carolina	116,349	157,732
South Carolina	103,015	139,017
Georgia	17,167	23,388
	$1,606,632	$2,170,430

Total $3,777,062.

As the annual interest due on the domestic debt amounted to $1,606,560, Congress proposed to raise this sum by allowing the people to pay indents therefor in lieu of money. The policy had now become settled, of allowing payments of indents, to a limited extent, in place of money for taxes, and continued as long as the government existed under the Articles of Confederation.

[1] Writings of Madison, vol. i. p. 244.
[2] Aug. 2; see also Act, Oct. 17, 1786.

Notwithstanding the failure of the government to pay its domestic obligations, and also what was due to France in the way of interest, the wages of foreign officers, and other claims abroad, the credit of the government in Holland especially was so well maintained, that Jefferson wrote to Madison, in May,[1] 1788, that the Dutch "consider us as the most certain nation on earth for the principal; but they see that we borrow of themselves to pay the interest, so that this is only a conversion of their interest into principal. Our paper, for this reason, sells for from four to eight per cent below par, on the exchange, and our loans are negotiated with the patriots only. But the whole body of money-dealers, patriot and stadtholderian, look forward to our new government with a great degree of partiality and interest. They are disposed to have much confidence in it, and it was the prospect of its establishment, which enabled us to set the loan of last year into motion again." The contract respecting the payment of interest on the loans in Holland had been honestly fulfilled, which accounted for the strength of American credit there; but the government had repeatedly failed to keep its engagements with France. The time had now come, however, when a failure to fulfil the obligations made with this latter power would inevitably affect the credit of the United States. The previous non-payment of French interest had caused but little injury, because nothing had been said about the matter: evidently France was willing to give America a little breathing-space before insisting upon payment. "It is now seen," writes Jefferson from Paris, in May, 1788,[2]

---

[1] Works, vol. ii. p. 376.   [2] Ibid., p. 377.

"that they call for it, and they will publish annually the effect of that call. A failure here, therefore, will have the same effect on our credit hereafter, as a failure at Amsterdam." France had treated the United States with the utmost consideration and leniency; but it was impolitic, at least, to lean on her forbearance any longer. Honesty and wisdom alike demanded that America should arouse herself, and fulfil her obligations.

During the same period the account of the government with its banker in Paris, M. Grand, was overdrawn to the amount of thirty-two thousand livres. About fifteen thousand livres also had been advanced from a fund belonging to Virginia, that had been placed in his posession for the purchase of arms, a statue to Washington, and other things.[1] Jefferson had previously borrowed on two different occasions from the United States for the benefit of Virginia,— first ten thousand livres, and afterward 2,724 livres more, the funds being in the possession of M. Grand: Jefferson now put his hand into the Virginia pocket, and borrowed a still larger sum for the use of the government he represented, expecting the amount would be speedily repaid, but which was not returned until another loan had been obtained in Holland.[2]

Nearly half of October,[3] 1787, was gone when the estimates for that year were presented, which were essentially the same as those of the previous year. The Board of Treasury had been successful in paying interest on its obligations to Holland by making remittances from America, and by applying in this way the balance of the last Holland loan; but the government very narrowly escaped

---

[1] Jefferson's Works, vol. ii. p. 223.   [2] Ibid., p. 385.   [3] Oct. 11.

defaulting the interest due in June, 1787. The impending default was averted by Adams, who negotiated a new loan for one million guilders, which cost the United States eight per cent, including premium, commission of brokers, brokerage, and other charges, — a very high rate truly; but it was impossible to procure money on more favorable conditions.[1] Among other consequences following this event, Congress the next year did not ask the States to contribute towards paying interest or principal on the foreign debt: the quotas included merely the estimated expense of running the machinery of government, and interest on the domestic debt, amounting in the aggregate to $1,686,541.[2]

It was practicable, so thought Adams and Jefferson, to transfer the domestic as well as the French debt of the United States to Holland; but it is difficult to discover what advantages would have accrued to the United States, had the transfer been made. It might, indeed, have proved an accommodation to France, as she was at this time in great need of money; but the Board of Treasury had sound reasons for believing the transfer would unfavorably affect the credit of their own country. Hitherto the credit of the United States in Holland had been preserved; but the prospect of maintaining it was by no means flattering. In the opinion of the board, it would be unjust, as well as impolitic, to sanction the proposed transaction, — unjust, because the United States would contract an engagement without any well grounded expectation of discharging it with punctuality; impolitic,

---

[1] J. Adams's Works, vol. viii. p. 440.

[2] Estimates for 1788, see Act of Aug. 20 of that year.

because a failure to pay interest to the Dutch creditors would justly blast all hopes of credit with the citizens of the United Netherlands when the exigencies of the Union might render new loans indispensably necessary.[1] Meanwhile the Holland bankers of the United States were purchasing "immense quantities of American paper,"[2] and were desirous of obtaining an agreement from the government to pay it in Europe. Adams deemed this a very impolitic measure; and in a letter to Jefferson, after alluding to the fact that the Continental certificates and interest thereon were payable in America, he says, "If a precedent is set of paying them in Europe I pretend not to sufficient foresight to predict the consequences; they appear, however, to me to be horrid. If the interest of one million of dollars is paid this year in Europe, you will find the interest of ten millions demanded next year." Happily, these consequences were averted by sticking fast to the practice of paying interest on all foreign obligations in the United States, except in those cases where another place had been specified in the original agreement.

[1] Secret Journal of Foreign Affairs, Oct. 2, 1787.

[2] Yet Jefferson had written to N. and J. Van Staphorst, July 30, 1785: "Some people in America have seriously contended, that the certificates, and other evidences of our domestic debt, ought to be redeemed only at what they have cost the holder; for I must observe to you, that these certificates of domestic debt, having as yet no provision for the payment of principal and interest, and the original holders being mostly needy, have been sold at a very great discount. When I left America (July, 1784) they sold, in different States, at from fifteen shillings to two shillings and sixpence in the pound; and any amount of them might then have been purchased." — JEFFERSON's *Works*, vol, i. p. 369.

The payment of interest on the Holland loans for the following year caused new financial difficulties. Moreover, the Fiseaux loan, amounting to fifty-one thousand florins, became due the 1st of January, 1788,[1] and the holders demanded payment. A very considerable portion of the domestic debt had been purchased by Dutch bankers at a heavy discount; and one of them, M. Stanetski, who had acted as a broker for the United States, held $4,340,000 of it. He offered to complete the subscriptions to the new loan, which at that time was making no progress, provided the government would pay him a year's interest upon that portion of the government debt owned by himself. The amount remaining to be subscribed was 622,840 florins, about two-thirds of the whole; while the sum he wished to retain for interest due to himself was 180,000 florins, — a deduction of ten per cent from the entire amount, which he was willing to allow for receiving payment in Europe instead of America.[2] This offer was not favorably received; although Messrs. Willinck and Van Staphorsts, who were trying to negotiate the loan for the United States, favored its acceptance.[3] They, too, were owners of a portion of the domestic debt, and consequently were to gain more if the plan could be forced upon the government.[4] Whatever might have been the real motives for seconding this scheme, when they found it would not be entertained, they quickly succeeded in completing the loan, as well as an additional one for one million florins, which the government, upon the suggestion of Jefferson and Adams,[5] authorized for the purpose of

---

[1] Jefferson's Works, vol. ii. p. 339.   [2] Ibid., p. 351.
[3] Ibid., pp. 352, 363.   [4] Ibid., p. 368.   [5] Ibid., p. 473.

obtaining funds sufficient to pay the interest for the year following, rather than depend upon remittances from home. This was the last loan of the kind raised; for the new government came into operation, and furnished money thereafter to pay its annually-recurring obligations. The loans thus obtained were more than sufficient to meet the interest on the Holland loans: so the balance was applied in paying the sum borrowed from Virginia and from M. Grand,[1] and the interest due to foreign officers,[2] now amounting to 60,393 livres[3] annually, many of whom were loudly clamoring for their pay,[4] and unceasing in their denunciations of the government because of its failure to pay them.

The sale of the public lands had been begun, and Jefferson says it had been "immensely successful." The statement is made, solely upon his authority, that five million acres had been sold at private sale for a dollar an acre, in certificates; and that at the public sales as much as two dollars and forty cents had been paid, in some cases. "By these means," he adds, "taxes, and our domestic debt, originally twenty-eight millions of dollars, was reduced, by the first day of last October, to twelve millions, and they were then in treaty for two millions of acres more, at a dollar, private sale. Our domestic debt will thus be soon paid off, and that done, the sales will go on for money at a cheaper rate, no doubt, for the payment of our foreign debt."[5] Jefferson, with his sanguine temperament, never looked at any thing in a more rosy-colored

---

[1] Jefferson's Works. vol. ii. p. 394.   [2] Ibid., vol. iii. pp. 28, 37.

[3] Ibid., p. 91.   [4] Ibid., vol. i. p. 479.

[5] Letter to William Carmichael, Dec. 11, 1787, Works, vol. ii. p. 325.

way than he did the finances. From first to last he never failed to blunder whenever he said much about them. Some sales of land were, indeed, made, but no such quantity as he stated. Upon what foundation he based such a reckless statement, it is impossible to conceive. How marked is the contrast between his bold coloring and the soberer tints of Madison, contained in a letter to Randolph![1] — "Our situation is becoming every day more and more critical. No money comes into the Federal treasury; no respect is paid to the Federal authority; and people of reflection unanimously agree that the existing Confederacy is tottering to its foundation."

On the last day of September, 1788, a committee made a report concerning the receipts and expenditures of the treasury from November, 1784, when Morris resigned, to April 21, 1788, — a period of three years and five months. The report contains some very striking figures; for example, the receivers of taxes had paid into the treasury only · $143,648 from the time of Morris's resignation to April 21, 1785, and for the next three years only $996,448 were received from the same source. The rest of the funds obtained by Congress during this period consisted chiefly of indents, or certificates of interest, which amounted to $1,881,139, beside a few small sums realized from the sale of war material and public lands. To the income thus derived must be added the balance of the first Holland loan, and also the loan of 1788. The committee, moreover, sought to ascertain the condition of the

---

[1] Feb. 25, 1787, Madison Papers, vol. ii. p. 620: same facts also stated in Letter to Jefferson, Dec. 20, 1787, Ibid., p. 658.

public accounts; but they were unable to glean any satisfactory information in regard to them. To the secret
committee of Congress had been advanced more than two
million dollars; "and a considerable part of this money,"
said the committee, "remains to be accounted for, otherwise than by contracts made with individuals of their own
body, while those individuals neglect to account." Other
sums had been paid by the Board of Treasury without
authority of Congress: in respect to large sums received
from France, the manner of their expenditure seemed "to
be involved in darkness." The remainder of the report is,
for the most part, a continuation of the dismal story. Extraordinary negligence, wastefulness, disorder, and corruption marked the early years of the government: even in
the darkest periods through which the country has since
passed, it may be questioned whether a greater lack of
system or moral rectitude has prevailed. Yet Adams,
writing to Jefferson, declares that "all the perplexities,
confusions, and distress in America arise, not from defects in their Constitution or Confederation, not from a
want of honor or virtue, so much as from downright
ignorance of the nature of coin, credit, and circulation."[1]
Ignorance in respect to those things was indeed very apparent; but still graver lacks were honesty, diligence, and
capacity among officials in the fulfilment of their duties.
A want greater still was a strong, well-cemented government. Adams's long absence from the country had
prevented him from seeing its worst defects, and he discovered only those flaws which appeared in the course of

[1] Aug. 25, 1787, J. Adams's Works, vol. viii. p. 447.

his business with the government. But the most cursory reader of the foregoing pages cannot have failed to see the extreme weakness of the government in other ways than a want of knowledge among its members concerning the nature of coin, credit, and circulation.

Electrotyped and printed by Rand, Avery, & Co., Boston.

www.ingramcontent.com/pod-product-compliance
Lightning Source LLC
Chambersburg PA
CBHW021709110726
47902CB00005B/1122